United States Mortgage and Financial Companies Directory

Just The facts101 Textbook Key Facts

by Cram101
Textbook NOT Included

Table of Contents

Title Page

Copyright

Foundations of Business

Management

Business law

Finance

Human resource management

Information systems

Marketing

Manufacturing

Commerce

Business ethics

Accounting

Index: Answers

Just The Facts101

Exam Prep for

United States Mortgage and Financial Companies Directory

Just The Facts101 Exam Prep is your link from
the textbook and lecture to your exams.

**Just The Facts101 Exam Preps are unauthorized and comprehensive reviews
of your textbooks.**

All material provided by CTI Publications (c) 2019

Textbook publishers and textbook authors do not participate in or contribute to these reviews.

Just The Facts101 Exam Prep

Copyright © 2019 by CTI Publications. All rights reserved.

eAIN 449364

Foundations of Business

A business, also known as an enterprise, agency or a firm, is an entity involved in the provision of goods and/or services to consumers. Businesses are prevalent in capitalist economies, where most of them are privately owned and provide goods and services to customers in exchange for other goods, services, or money.

:: Management accounting ::

_____ s are costs that change as the quantity of the good or service that a business produces changes. _____ s are the sum of marginal costs over all units produced. They can also be considered normal costs. Fixed costs and _____ s make up the two components of total cost. Direct costs are costs that can easily be associated with a particular cost object. However, not all _____ s are direct costs. For example, variable manufacturing overhead costs are _____ s that are indirect costs, not direct costs. _____ s are sometimes called unit-level costs as they vary with the number of units produced.

Exam Probability: **Medium**

1. *Answer choices:*

(see index for correct answer)

- a. Resource consumption accounting
- b. Variable cost
- c. Corporate travel management
- d. Target costing

Guidance: level 1

:: Industry ::

_____ describes various measures of the efficiency of production. Often, a _____ measure is expressed as the ratio of an aggregate output to a single input or an aggregate input used in a production process, i.e. output per unit of input. Most common example is the labour _____ measure, e.g., such as GDP per worker. There are many different definitions of _____ and the choice among them depends on the purpose of the _____ measurement and/or data availability. The key source of difference between various _____ measures is also usually related to how the outputs and the inputs are aggregated into scalars to obtain such a ratio-type measure of _____ .

Exam Probability: **Medium**

2. *Answer choices:*

(see index for correct answer)

- a. Tube and clamp scaffold
- b. Industry classification
- c. Standard Industrial Classification
- d. Industrial robot

Guidance: level 1

:: International trade ::

The law or principle of _____ holds that under free trade, an agent will produce more of and consume less of a good for which they have a _____. _____ is the economic reality describing the work gains from trade for individuals, firms, or nations, which arise from differences in their factor endowments or technological progress. In an economic model, agents have a _____ over others in producing a particular good if they can produce that good at a lower relative opportunity cost or autarky price, i.e. at a lower relative marginal cost prior to trade. One shouldn't compare the monetary costs of production or even the resource costs of production. Instead, one must compare the opportunity costs of producing goods across countries.

Exam Probability: **Medium**

3. *Answer choices:*
(see index for correct answer)

- a. Comparative advantage
- b. Silk Road
- c. Franz Oppenheimer
- d. International Association for Technology Trade

Guidance: level 1

:: Legal terms ::

An _____ is an action which is inaccurate or incorrect. In some usages, an _____ is synonymous with a mistake. In statistics, "_____" refers to the difference between the value which has been computed and the correct value. An _____ could result in failure or in a deviation from the intended performance or behaviour.

Exam Probability: **High**

4. *Answer choices:*

(see index for correct answer)

- a. Dumb laws
- b. Antedated
- c. Integration clause
- d. Error

Guidance: level 1

:: Business law ::

A _____ is a group of people who jointly supervise the activities of an organization, which can be either a for-profit business, nonprofit organization, or a government agency. Such a board's powers, duties, and responsibilities are determined by government regulations and the organization's own constitution and bylaws. These authorities may specify the number of members of the board, how they are to be chosen, and how often they are to meet.

Exam Probability: **Medium**

5. *Answer choices:*

(see index for correct answer)

- a. Inslaw
- b. Board of directors
- c. Arbitration award
- d. Statutory liability

Guidance: level 1

:: Occupations ::

An _____ is a person who has a position of authority in a hierarchical organization. The term derives from the late Latin from officiarius, meaning "official".

Exam Probability: **Low**

6. *Answer choices:*

(see index for correct answer)

- a. Signwriter
- b. Drawing-in frame
- c. Mountain guide
- d. Village head

Guidance: level 1

:: Debt ::

_____, in finance and economics, is payment from a borrower or deposit-taking financial institution to a lender or depositor of an amount above repayment of the principal sum, at a particular rate. It is distinct from a fee which the borrower may pay the lender or some third party. It is also distinct from dividend which is paid by a company to its shareholders from its profit or reserve, but not at a particular rate decided beforehand, rather on a pro rata basis as a share in the reward gained by risk taking entrepreneurs when the revenue earned exceeds the total costs.

Exam Probability: **Medium**

7. *Answer choices:*

(see index for correct answer)

- a. Recourse debt
- b. Interest
- c. Cohort default rate
- d. Bad debt

Guidance: level 1

:: Generally Accepted Accounting Principles ::

Expenditure is an outflow of money to another person or group to pay for an item or service, or for a category of costs. For a tenant, rent is an _____. For students or parents, tuition is an _____. Buying food, clothing, furniture or an automobile is often referred to as an _____. An _____ is a cost that is "paid" or "remitted", usually in exchange for something of value. Something that seems to cost a great deal is "expensive". Something that seems to cost little is "inexpensive". "_____ s of the table" are _____ s of dining, refreshments, a feast, etc.

Exam Probability: **Low**

8. *Answer choices:*

(see index for correct answer)

- a. Trial balance
- b. Deferred income
- c. Cost principle
- d. Statement of recommended practice

Guidance: level 1

:: Legal terms ::

_____, a form of alternative dispute resolution, is a way to resolve disputes outside the courts. The dispute will be decided by one or more persons, which renders the "_____ award". An _____ award is legally binding on both sides and enforceable in the courts.

Exam Probability: **Low**

9. *Answer choices:*

(see index for correct answer)

- a. Force
- b. Lineal descendant
- c. Arbitration
- d. Innominate jury

Guidance: level 1

:: Asset ::

In financial accounting, an _____ is any resource owned by the business. Anything tangible or intangible that can be owned or controlled to produce value and that is held by a company to produce positive economic value is an _____ . Simply stated, _____ s represent value of ownership that can be converted into cash . The balance sheet of a firm records the monetary value of the _____ s owned by that firm. It covers money and other valuables belonging to an individual or to a business.

Exam Probability: **Low**

10. *Answer choices:*

(see index for correct answer)

- a. Current asset

- b. Fixed asset

Guidance: level 1

:: ::

A _____ is any person who contracts to acquire an asset in return for some form of consideration.

Exam Probability: **Medium**

11. *Answer choices:*

(see index for correct answer)

- a. imperative
- b. process perspective
- c. levels of analysis
- d. surface-level diversity

Guidance: level 1

:: ::

_____ is an abstract concept of management of complex systems according to a set of rules and trends. In systems theory, these types of rules exist in various fields of biology and society, but the term has slightly different meanings according to context. For example,

Exam Probability: **Medium**

12. *Answer choices:*

(see index for correct answer)

- a. Regulation
- b. surface-level diversity
- c. Character
- d. empathy

Guidance: level 1

:: Financial regulatory authorities of the United States ::

The _____ is the revenue service of the United States federal government. The government agency is a bureau of the Department of the Treasury, and is under the immediate direction of the Commissioner of Internal Revenue, who is appointed to a five-year term by the President of the United States. The IRS is responsible for collecting taxes and administering the Internal Revenue Code, the main body of federal statutory tax law of the United States. The duties of the IRS include providing tax assistance to taxpayers and pursuing and resolving instances of erroneous or fraudulent tax filings. The IRS has also overseen various benefits programs, and enforces portions of the Affordable Care Act.

Exam Probability: **High**

13. *Answer choices:*

(see index for correct answer)

- a. Federal Deposit Insurance Corporation
- b. Municipal Securities Rulemaking Board
- c. Office of Thrift Supervision
- d. Internal Revenue Service

Guidance: level 1

:: Strategic alliances ::

A _____ is an agreement between two or more parties to pursue a set of agreed upon objectives needed while remaining independent organizations. A _____ will usually fall short of a legal partnership entity, agency, or corporate affiliate relationship. Typically, two companies form a _____ when each possesses one or more business assets or have expertise that will help the other by enhancing their businesses. _____ s can develop in outsourcing relationships where the parties desire to achieve long-term win-win benefits and innovation based on mutually desired outcomes.

Exam Probability: **Medium**

14. *Answer choices:*

(see index for correct answer)

- a. Bridge Alliance
- b. Defensive termination
- c. Strategic alliance
- d. International joint venture

Guidance: level 1

:: Poker strategy ::

> _____ is any measure taken to guard a thing against damage caused by outside forces. _____ can be provided to physical objects, including organisms, to systems, and to intangible things like civil and political rights. Although the mechanisms for providing _____ vary widely, the basic meaning of the term remains the same. This is illustrated by an explanation found in a manual on electrical wiring.

Exam Probability: **High**

15. *Answer choices:*

(see index for correct answer)

- a. Bluff
- b. Check-raise
- c. Steal
- d. Protection

Guidance: level 1

:: Financial markets ::

A _____ is a financial market in which long-term debt or equity-backed securities are bought and sold. _____ s channel the wealth of savers to those who can put it to long-term productive use, such as companies or governments making long-term investments. Financial regulators like the Bank of England and the U.S. Securities and Exchange Commission oversee _____ s to protect investors against fraud, among other duties.

Exam Probability: **High**

16. *Answer choices:*

(see index for correct answer)

- a. Capital market
- b. Shelf registration
- c. Crossing network
- d. Public offering

Guidance: level 1

:: Service industries ::

_____ are the economic services provided by the finance industry, which encompasses a broad range of businesses that manage money, including credit unions, banks, credit-card companies, insurance companies, accountancy companies, consumer-finance companies, stock brokerages, investment funds, individual managers and some government-sponsored enterprises. _____ companies are present in all economically developed geographic locations and tend to cluster in local, national, regional and international financial centers such as London, New York City, and Tokyo.

Exam Probability: **Low**

17. *Answer choices:*

(see index for correct answer)

- a. Allotment
- b. Financial services
- c. Excel Insurance Solutions
- d. Association of Special Fares Agents

Guidance: level 1

:: Management occupations ::

_____ ship is the process of designing, launching and running a new business, which is often initially a small business. The people who create these businesses are called _____ s.

Exam Probability: **High**

18. Answer choices:

(see index for correct answer)

- a. Entrepreneur
- b. City manager
- c. Store manager
- d. Faculty consulting

Guidance: level 1

:: Critical thinking ::

> In psychology, _____ is regarded as the cognitive process resulting in the selection of a belief or a course of action among several alternative possibilities. Every _____ process produces a final choice, which may or may not prompt action.

Exam Probability: **Low**

19. Answer choices:

(see index for correct answer)

- a. Project Reason
- b. Precision questioning
- c. Seven Types of Ambiguity
- d. Decision-making

Guidance: level 1

:: International trade ::

An _____ is a good brought into a jurisdiction, especially across a national border, from an external source. The party bringing in the good is called an _____ er. An _____ in the receiving country is an export from the sending country. _____ ation and exportation are the defining financial transactions of international trade.

Exam Probability: **High**

20. *Answer choices:*
(see index for correct answer)

- a. Export-led growth
- b. Import
- c. International monetary systems
- d. Trade diversion

Guidance: level 1

:: Business planning ::

_____ is an organization's process of defining its strategy, or direction, and making decisions on allocating its resources to pursue this strategy. It may also extend to control mechanisms for guiding the implementation of the strategy. _____ became prominent in corporations during the 1960s and remains an important aspect of strategic management. It is executed by strategic planners or strategists, who involve many parties and research sources in their analysis of the organization and its relationship to the environment in which it competes.

Exam Probability: **Medium**

21. *Answer choices:*
(see index for correct answer)

- a. Strategic planning
- b. Exit planning
- c. Gap analysis
- d. Community Futures

Guidance: level 1

:: Generally Accepted Accounting Principles ::

An _____ or profit and loss account is one of the financial statements of a company and shows the company's revenues and expenses during a particular period.

Exam Probability: **High**

22. Answer choices:

(see index for correct answer)

- a. Revenue
- b. Liability
- c. Paid in capital
- d. Income statement

Guidance: level 1

:: Real estate valuation ::

_____ or OMV is the price at which an asset would trade in a competitive auction setting. _____ is often used interchangeably with open _____, fair value or fair _____, although these terms have distinct definitions in different standards, and may or may not differ in some circumstances.

Exam Probability: **Medium**

23. Answer choices:

(see index for correct answer)

- a. Appraisal Standards Board
- b. Hedonic regression
- c. Zoopla
- d. Market value

Guidance: level 1

:: Statistical terminology ::

_____ is the ability to avoid wasting materials, energy, efforts, money, and time in doing something or in producing a desired result. In a more general sense, it is the ability to do things well, successfully, and without waste. In more mathematical or scientific terms, it is a measure of the extent to which input is well used for an intended task or function. It often specifically comprises the capability of a specific application of effort to produce a specific outcome with a minimum amount or quantity of waste, expense, or unnecessary effort. _____ refers to very different inputs and outputs in different fields and industries.

Exam Probability: **Medium**

24. *Answer choices:*
(see index for correct answer)

- a. Probability distribution function
- b. Noncentrality parameter
- c. Invariant estimator
- d. Efficiency

Guidance: level 1

:: Business process ::

A _____ or business method is a collection of related, structured activities or tasks by people or equipment which in a specific sequence produce a service or product for a particular customer or customers. _____ es occur at all organizational levels and may or may not be visible to the customers. A _____ may often be visualized as a flowchart of a sequence of activities with interleaving decision points or as a process matrix of a sequence of activities with relevance rules based on data in the process. The benefits of using _____ es include improved customer satisfaction and improved agility for reacting to rapid market change. Process-oriented organizations break down the barriers of structural departments and try to avoid functional silos.

Exam Probability: **Medium**

25. *Answer choices:*

(see index for correct answer)

- a. Steering committee
- b. Business process
- c. Captive service
- d. Process mining

Guidance: level 1

:: Financial statements ::

In financial accounting, a _____ or statement of financial position or statement of financial condition is a summary of the financial balances of an individual or organization, whether it be a sole proprietorship, a business partnership, a corporation, private limited company or other organization such as Government or not-for-profit entity. Assets, liabilities and ownership equity are listed as of a specific date, such as the end of its financial year. A _____ is often described as a "snapshot of a company's financial condition". Of the four basic financial statements, the _____ is the only statement which applies to a single point in time of a business' calendar year.

Exam Probability: **High**

26. *Answer choices:*

(see index for correct answer)

- a. Financial statement
- b. Emphasis of matter
- c. Statement on Auditing Standards No. 70: Service Organizations
- d. Balance sheet

Guidance: level 1

:: Marketing ::

_____ is based on a marketing concept which can be adopted by an organization as a strategy for business expansion. Where implemented, a franchisor licenses its know-how, procedures, intellectual property, use of its business model, brand, and rights to sell its branded products and services to a franchisee. In return the franchisee pays certain fees and agrees to comply with certain obligations, typically set out in a Franchise Agreement.

Exam Probability: **High**

27. *Answer choices:*

(see index for correct answer)

- a. Audience segmentation
- b. Bass diffusion model
- c. Postmodern branding
- d. Discounting

Guidance: level 1

:: Analysis ::

_____ is the process of breaking a complex topic or substance into smaller parts in order to gain a better understanding of it. The technique has been applied in the study of mathematics and logic since before Aristotle, though _____ as a formal concept is a relatively recent development.

Exam Probability: **Low**

28. *Answer choices:*

(see index for correct answer)

- a. DESTEP
- b. Analysis
- c. Pinch analysis
- d. Paradox of analysis

Guidance: level 1

:: Quality management ::

_____ ensures that an organization, product or service is consistent. It has four main components: quality planning, quality assurance, quality control and quality improvement. _____ is focused not only on product and service quality, but also on the means to achieve it. _____ , therefore, uses quality assurance and control of processes as well as products to achieve more consistent quality. What a customer wants and is willing to pay for it determines quality. It is written or unwritten commitment to a known or unknown consumer in the market . Thus, quality can be defined as fitness for intended use or, in other words, how well the product performs its intended function

Exam Probability: **Low**

29. *Answer choices:*

(see index for correct answer)

- a. Quality management
- b. Bureau Veritas

- c. Flemish Quality Management Center
- d. Regulatory translation

Guidance: level 1

:: Money ::

In economics, _____ is money in the physical form of currency, such as banknotes and coins. In bookkeeping and finance, _____ is current assets comprising currency or currency equivalents that can be accessed immediately or near-immediately. _____ is seen either as a reserve for payments, in case of a structural or incidental negative _____ flow or as a way to avoid a downturn on financial markets.

Exam Probability: **High**

30. *Answer choices:*

(see index for correct answer)

- a. Cash
- b. Cash in lieu of commodities
- c. Slang terms for money
- d. Real de alerce

Guidance: level 1

:: Goods ::

In most contexts, the concept of _____ denotes the conduct that should be preferred when posed with a choice between possible actions. _____ is generally considered to be the opposite of evil, and is of interest in the study of morality, ethics, religion and philosophy. The specific meaning and etymology of the term and its associated translations among ancient and contemporary languages show substantial variation in its inflection and meaning depending on circumstances of place, history, religious, or philosophical context.

Exam Probability: **Low**

31. *Answer choices:*

(see index for correct answer)

- a. Demerit good
- b. Ersatz good
- c. Yellow goods
- d. Complementary good

Guidance: level 1

:: Office administration ::

An _____ is generally a room or other area where an organization's employees perform administrative work in order to support and realize objects and goals of the organization. The word "_____" may also denote a position within an organization with specific duties attached to it ; the latter is in fact an earlier usage, _____ as place originally referring to the location of one's duty. When used as an adjective, the term "_____" may refer to business-related tasks. In law, a company or organization has _____ s in any place where it has an official presence, even if that presence consists of a storage silo rather than an establishment with desk-and-chair. An _____ is also an architectural and design phenomenon: ranging from a small _____ such as a bench in the corner of a small business of extremely small size , through entire floors of buildings, up to and including massive buildings dedicated entirely to one company. In modern terms an _____ is usually the location where white-collar workers carry out their functions. As per James Stephenson, "_____ is that part of business enterprise which is devoted to the direction and co-ordination of its various activities."

Exam Probability: **Low**

32. *Answer choices:*

(see index for correct answer)

- a. Activity management
- b. Office administration
- c. Office
- d. Inter departmental communication

Guidance: level 1

:: Energy and fuel journals ::

In physics, energy is the quantitative property that must be transferred to
an object in order to perform work on, or to heat, the object. Energy is a
conserved quantity; the law of conservation of energy states that energy can be
converted in form, but not created or destroyed. The SI unit of energy is the
joule, which is the energy transferred to an object by the work of moving it a
distance of 1 metre against a force of 1 newton.

Exam Probability: **Low**

33. *Answer choices:*

(see index for correct answer)

- a. Energy-Safety and Energy-Economy
- b. Renewable and Sustainable Energy Reviews
- c. Energies
- d. Advanced Energy Materials

Guidance: level 1

:: Project management ::

In political science, an _____ is a means by which a petition signed
by a certain minimum number of registered voters can force a government to
choose to either enact a law or hold a public vote in parliament in what is
called indirect _____ , or under direct _____ , the proposition is
immediately put to a plebiscite or referendum, in what is called a Popular
initiated Referendum or citizen-initiated referendum).

Exam Probability: **High**

34. *Answer choices:*

(see index for correct answer)

- a. Project accounting
- b. Initiative
- c. Lean project management
- d. Project portfolio management

Guidance: level 1

:: ::

_____ or accountancy is the measurement, processing, and communication of financial information about economic entities such as businesses and corporations. The modern field was established by the Italian mathematician Luca Pacioli in 1494. _____ , which has been called the "language of business", measures the results of an organization's economic activities and conveys this information to a variety of users, including investors, creditors, management, and regulators. Practitioners of _____ are known as accountants. The terms " _____ " and "financial reporting" are often used as synonyms.

Exam Probability: **Low**

35. *Answer choices:*

(see index for correct answer)

- a. imperative
- b. levels of analysis
- c. Accounting
- d. hierarchical

Guidance: level 1

:: Derivatives (finance) ::

_____ is any bodily activity that enhances or maintains physical fitness and overall health and wellness. It is performed for various reasons, to aid growth and improve strength, preventing aging, developing muscles and the cardiovascular system, honing athletic skills, weight loss or maintenance, improving health and also for enjoyment. Many individuals choose to _____ outdoors where they can congregate in groups, socialize, and enhance well-being.

Exam Probability: **Low**

36. *Answer choices:*
(see index for correct answer)

- a. Expiration
- b. Dividend swap
- c. Forward freight agreement
- d. Options spread

Guidance: level 1

:: Television commercials ::

_____ is a phenomenon whereby something new and somehow valuable is formed. The created item may be intangible or a physical object.

Exam Probability: **Low**

37. *Answer choices:*

(see index for correct answer)

- a. Pipes
- b. Second Generation
- c. Creativity
- d. Spongmonkeys

Guidance: level 1

:: ::

Some scenarios associate "this kind of planning" with learning "life skills". Schedules are necessary, or at least useful, in situations where individuals need to know what time they must be at a specific location to receive a specific service, and where people need to accomplish a set of goals within a set time period.

Exam Probability: **Low**

38. *Answer choices:*

(see index for correct answer)

- a. information systems assessment
- b. Scheduling
- c. Character
- d. personal values

Guidance: level 1

:: Loans ::

In finance, a _____ is the lending of money by one or more individuals, organizations, or other entities to other individuals, organizations etc. The recipient incurs a debt, and is usually liable to pay interest on that debt until it is repaid, and also to repay the principal amount borrowed.

Exam Probability: **Medium**

39. *Answer choices:*

(see index for correct answer)

- a. Loan servicing
- b. Mortgage Assumption Value
- c. Loan

- d. Home equity loan

Guidance: level 1

:: Stock market ::

A _____, securities exchange or bourse, is a facility where stock brokers and traders can buy and sell securities, such as shares of stock and bonds and other financial instruments. _____ s may also provide for facilities the issue and redemption of such securities and instruments and capital events including the payment of income and dividends. Securities traded on a _____ include stock issued by listed companies, unit trusts, derivatives, pooled investment products and bonds. _____ s often function as "continuous auction" markets with buyers and sellers consummating transactions via open outcry at a central location such as the floor of the exchange or by using an electronic trading platform.

Exam Probability: **Medium**

40. *Answer choices:*
(see index for correct answer)

- a. Tech Buzz
- b. Investor relations
- c. Shadow stock
- d. Trading turret

Guidance: level 1

:: Non-profit technology ::

> Instituto del Tercer Mundo is a Non-Governmental Organization that performs information, communication and education activities. _____ , which was established in 1989, shares the same secretariat and coordinating personnel as Social Watch and is based in Montevideo, Uruguay.

Exam Probability: **Low**

41. *Answer choices:*

(see index for correct answer)

- a. Charon
- b. Aplos Software
- c. Entertainment Consumers Association
- d. The Malian Foundation

Guidance: level 1

:: Health promotion ::

> _____ , as defined by the World _____ Organization , is "a state of complete physical, mental and social well-being and not merely the absence of disease or infirmity." This definition has been subject to controversy, as it may have limited value for implementation. _____ may be defined as the ability to adapt and manage physical, mental and social challenges throughout life.

Exam Probability: **Low**

42. *Answer choices:*

(see index for correct answer)

- a. Unwarranted variation
- b. National Care Standards
- c. Health
- d. Hopkins Center for Health Disparities Solutions

Guidance: level 1

:: Costs ::

In microeconomic theory, the _____ , or alternative cost, of making a particular choice is the value of the most valuable choice out of those that were not taken. In other words, opportunity that will require sacrifices.

Exam Probability: **Medium**

43. *Answer choices:*

(see index for correct answer)

- a. Repugnancy costs
- b. Social cost
- c. Opportunity cost
- d. Prospective costs

Guidance: level 1

:: Market research ::

_____ is "the process or set of processes that links the producers, customers, and end users to the marketer through information used to identify and define marketing opportunities and problems; generate, refine, and evaluate marketing actions; monitor marketing performance; and improve understanding of marketing as a process. _____ specifies the information required to address these issues, designs the method for collecting information, manages and implements the data collection process, analyzes the results, and communicates the findings and their implications."

Exam Probability: **Medium**

44. *Answer choices:*

(see index for correct answer)

- a. Industry analyst
- b. Marketing research
- c. Computer-assisted web interviewing
- d. Media Technology Monitor

Guidance: level 1

:: Generally Accepted Accounting Principles ::

In accounting, _____ is the income that a business have from its normal business activities, usually from the sale of goods and services to customers. _____ is also referred to as sales or turnover. Some companies receive _____ from interest, royalties, or other fees. _____ may refer to business income in general, or it may refer to the amount, in a monetary unit, earned during a period of time, as in "Last year, Company X had _____ of $42 million". Profits or net income generally imply total _____ minus total expenses in a given period. In accounting, in the balance statement it is a subsection of the Equity section and _____ increases equity, it is often referred to as the "top line" due to its position on the income statement at the very top. This is to be contrasted with the "bottom line" which denotes net income .

Exam Probability: **Low**

45. *Answer choices:*

(see index for correct answer)

- a. Revenue
- b. Net income
- c. Operating income before depreciation and amortization
- d. Earnings before interest, taxes, depreciation, and amortization

Guidance: level 1

:: Graphic design ::

An _____ is an artifact that depicts visual perception, such as a photograph or other two-dimensional picture, that resembles a subject—usually a physical object—and thus provides a depiction of it. In the context of signal processing, an _____ is a distributed amplitude of color.

Exam Probability: **High**

46. *Answer choices:*

(see index for correct answer)

- a. Graphic Exchange
- b. Image
- c. Best Art Vinyl
- d. American Graphics Institute

Guidance: level 1

:: Management ::

A _____ is a method or technique that has been generally accepted as superior to any alternatives because it produces results that are superior to those achieved by other means or because it has become a standard way of doing things, e.g., a standard way of complying with legal or ethical requirements.

Exam Probability: **Medium**

47. *Answer choices:*

(see index for correct answer)

- a. Best practice
- b. Scenario planning
- c. Organizational conflict
- d. Private defense agency

Guidance: level 1

:: Security compliance ::

A _____ is a communicated intent to inflict harm or loss on another person. A _____ is considered an act of coercion. _____ s are widely observed in animal behavior, particularly in a ritualized form, chiefly in order to avoid the unnecessary physical violence that can lead to physical damage or the death of both conflicting parties.

Exam Probability: **Medium**

48. *Answer choices:*

(see index for correct answer)

- a. Month of bugs
- b. Threat
- c. Security Content Automation Protocol
- d. Vulnerability management

Guidance: level 1

:: Supply chain management terms ::

In business and finance, _____ is a system of organizations, people, activities, information, and resources involved in moving a product or service from supplier to customer. _____ activities involve the transformation of natural resources, raw materials, and components into a finished product that is delivered to the end customer. In sophisticated _____ systems, used products may re-enter the _____ at any point where residual value is recyclable. _____ s link value chains.

Exam Probability: **High**

49. *Answer choices:*

(see index for correct answer)

- a. Supply-chain management
- b. Capital spare
- c. Supply chain
- d. Most valuable customers

Guidance: level 1

:: Debt ::

_____ is the trust which allows one party to provide money or resources to another party wherein the second party does not reimburse the first party immediately, but promises either to repay or return those resources at a later date. In other words, _____ is a method of making reciprocity formal, legally enforceable, and extensible to a large group of unrelated people.

Exam Probability: **Low**

50. *Answer choices:*

(see index for correct answer)

- a. Zombie company
- b. Internal debt
- c. Credit
- d. Extendible bond

Guidance: level 1

:: Regression analysis ::

A _____ often refers to a set of documented requirements to be satisfied by a material, design, product, or service. A _____ is often a type of technical standard.

Exam Probability: **Medium**

51. Answer choices:

(see index for correct answer)

- a. Multinomial probit
- b. Seemingly unrelated regressions
- c. Specification
- d. Local regression

Guidance: level 1

:: ::

_____ is the production of products for use or sale using labour and machines, tools, chemical and biological processing, or formulation. The term may refer to a range of human activity, from handicraft to high tech, but is most commonly applied to industrial design, in which raw materials are transformed into finished goods on a large scale. Such finished goods may be sold to other manufacturers for the production of other, more complex products, such as aircraft, household appliances, furniture, sports equipment or automobiles, or sold to wholesalers, who in turn sell them to retailers, who then sell them to end users and consumers.

Exam Probability: **Medium**

52. Answer choices:

(see index for correct answer)

- a. information systems assessment
- b. imperative

- c. empathy
- d. similarity-attraction theory

Guidance: level 1

:: Human resource management ::

> _____ encompasses values and behaviors that contribute to the unique social and psychological environment of a business. The _____ influences the way people interact, the context within which knowledge is created, the resistance they will have towards certain changes, and ultimately the way they share knowledge. _____ represents the collective values, beliefs and principles of organizational members and is a product of factors such as history, product, market, technology, strategy, type of employees, management style, and national culture; culture includes the organization's vision, values, norms, systems, symbols, language, assumptions, environment, location, beliefs and habits.

Exam Probability: **High**

53. *Answer choices:*
(see index for correct answer)

- a. Corporate Equality Index
- b. Personal development planning
- c. Organizational culture
- d. Herrmann Brain Dominance Instrument

Guidance: level 1

Culture is the social behavior and norms found in human societies. Culture is considered a central concept in anthropology, encompassing the range of phenomena that are transmitted through social learning in human societies. _____ universals are found in all human societies; these include expressive forms like art, music, dance, ritual, religion, and technologies like tool usage, cooking, shelter, and clothing. The concept of material culture covers the physical expressions of culture, such as technology, architecture and art, whereas the immaterial aspects of culture such as principles of social organization, mythology, philosophy, literature, and science comprise the intangible _____ heritage of a society.

Exam Probability: **High**

54. *Answer choices:*

(see index for correct answer)

- a. surface-level diversity
- b. hierarchical perspective
- c. Cultural
- d. empathy

Guidance: level 1

_____ is the collection of techniques, skills, methods, and processes used in the production of goods or services or in the accomplishment of objectives, such as scientific investigation. _____ can be the knowledge of techniques, processes, and the like, or it can be embedded in machines to allow for operation without detailed knowledge of their workings. Systems applying _____ by taking an input, changing it according to the system's use, and then producing an outcome are referred to as _____ systems or technological systems.

Exam Probability: **Medium**

55. *Answer choices:*

(see index for correct answer)

- a. hierarchical perspective
- b. process perspective
- c. cultural
- d. personal values

Guidance: level 1

:: Semiconductor companies ::

_____ Corporation is a Japanese multinational conglomerate corporation headquartered in Konan, Minato, Tokyo. Its diversified business includes consumer and professional electronics, gaming, entertainment and financial services. The company owns the largest music entertainment business in the world, the largest video game console business and one of the largest video game publishing businesses, and is one of the leading manufacturers of electronic products for the consumer and professional markets, and a leading player in the film and television entertainment industry. _____ was ranked 97th on the 2018 Fortune Global 500 list.

Exam Probability: **High**

56. *Answer choices:*

(see index for correct answer)

- a. Sony
- b. Ingenic Semiconductor
- c. GEO Semiconductor Inc
- d. Sharp Corporation

Guidance: level 1

:: Marketing ::

A _____ is something that is necessary for an organism to live a healthy life. _____ s are distinguished from wants in that, in the case of a _____ , a deficiency causes a clear adverse outcome: a dysfunction or death. In other words, a _____ is something required for a safe, stable and healthy life while a want is a desire, wish or aspiration. When _____ s or wants are backed by purchasing power, they have the potential to become economic demands.

Exam Probability: **Medium**

57. *Answer choices:*

(see index for correct answer)

- a. Market segmentation index
- b. Need
- c. Aspirational brand
- d. Premium pricing

Guidance: level 1

:: Stochastic processes ::

_____ is a system of rules that are created and enforced through social or governmental institutions to regulate behavior. It has been defined both as "the Science of Justice" and "the Art of Justice". _____ is a system that regulates and ensures that individuals or a community adhere to the will of the state. State-enforced _____ s can be made by a collective legislature or by a single legislator, resulting in statutes, by the executive through decrees and regulations, or established by judges through precedent, normally in common _____ jurisdictions. Private individuals can create legally binding contracts, including arbitration agreements that may elect to accept alternative arbitration to the normal court process. The formation of _____ s themselves may be influenced by a constitution, written or tacit, and the rights encoded therein. The _____ shapes politics, economics, history and society in various ways and serves as a mediator of relations between people.

Exam Probability: **Low**

58. *Answer choices:*

(see index for correct answer)

- a. Stationary process
- b. Quadratic variation
- c. Law
- d. Law of the iterated logarithm

Guidance: level 1

:: Critical thinking ::

An _____ is a set of statements usually constructed to describe a set of facts which clarifies the causes, context, and consequences of those facts. This description of the facts et cetera may establish rules or laws, and may clarify the existing rules or laws in relation to any objects, or phenomena examined. The components of an _____ can be implicit, and interwoven with one another.

Exam Probability: **Low**

59. *Answer choices:*

(see index for correct answer)

- a. Explanation
- b. Attacking Faulty Reasoning
- c. Center for Critical Thinking
- d. Argumentation theory

Guidance: level 1

Management

Management is the administration of an organization, whether it is a business, a not-for-profit organization, or government body. Management includes the activities of setting the strategy of an organization and coordinating the efforts of its employees (or of volunteers) to accomplish its objectives through the application of available resources, such as financial, natural, technological, and human resources.

:: Organizational behavior ::

In organizational behavior and industrial and organizational psychology, _____ is an individual's psychological attachment to the organization. The basis behind many of these studies was to find ways to improve how workers feel about their jobs so that these workers would become more committed to their organizations. _____ predicts work variables such as turnover, organizational citizenship behavior, and job performance. Some of the factors such as role stress, empowerment, job insecurity and employability, and distribution of leadership have been shown to be connected to a worker's sense of _____ .

Exam Probability: **Medium**

1. *Answer choices:*

(see index for correct answer)

- a. Organizational commitment
- b. Civic virtue
- c. Boreout
- d. Affective events theory

Guidance: level 1

:: Business law ::

A _____ is a group of people who jointly supervise the activities of an organization, which can be either a for-profit business, nonprofit organization, or a government agency. Such a board's powers, duties, and responsibilities are determined by government regulations and the organization's own constitution and bylaws. These authorities may specify the number of members of the board, how they are to be chosen, and how often they are to meet.

Exam Probability: **High**

2. *Answer choices:*

(see index for correct answer)

- a. Board of directors
- b. Complex structured finance transactions
- c. Examinership
- d. United States labor law

Guidance: level 1

:: Production economics ::

In microeconomics, _____ are the cost advantages that enterprises obtain due to their scale of operation, with cost per unit of output decreasing with increasing scale.

Exam Probability: **Low**

3. *Answer choices:*

(see index for correct answer)

- a. Economies of scale
- b. Division of work
- c. Synergy
- d. Total factor productivity

Guidance: level 1

:: Project management ::

In political science, an _____ is a means by which a petition signed by a certain minimum number of registered voters can force a government to choose to either enact a law or hold a public vote in parliament in what is called indirect _____ , or under direct _____ , the proposition is immediately put to a plebiscite or referendum, in what is called a Popular initiated Referendum or citizen-initiated referendum).

Exam Probability: **Low**

4. *Answer choices:*

(see index for correct answer)

- a. RationalPlan
- b. Participatory impact pathways analysis
- c. Point of total assumption
- d. Initiative

Guidance: level 1

:: Labor ::

The workforce or labour force is the labour pool in employment. It is generally used to describe those working for a single company or industry, but can also apply to a geographic region like a city, state, or country. Within a company, its value can be labelled as its "Workforce in Place". The workforce of a country includes both the employed and the unemployed. The labour force participation rate, LFPR, is the ratio between the labour force and the overall size of their cohort. The term generally excludes the employers or management, and can imply those involved in manual labour. It may also mean all those who are available for work.

Exam Probability: **High**

5. *Answer choices:*
(see index for correct answer)

- a. Designated Suppliers Program
- b. Credentialism
- c. New Unionism
- d. Labour economics

Guidance: level 1

:: Decision theory ::

A _____ is a deliberate system of principles to guide decisions and achieve rational outcomes. A _____ is a statement of intent, and is implemented as a procedure or protocol. Policies are generally adopted by a governance body within an organization. Policies can assist in both subjective and objective decision making. Policies to assist in subjective decision making usually assist senior management with decisions that must be based on the relative merits of a number of factors, and as a result are often hard to test objectively, e.g. work-life balance _____. In contrast policies to assist in objective decision making are usually operational in nature and can be objectively tested, e.g. password _____.

Exam Probability: **High**

6. *Answer choices:*

(see index for correct answer)

- a. Mean-preserving spread
- b. Strategic assumptions
- c. Evidential decision theory
- d. Subjective expected utility

Guidance: level 1

:: Human resource management ::

_____, executive management, upper management, or a management team is generally a team of individuals at the highest level of management of an organization who have the day-to-day tasks of managing that organization — sometimes a company or a corporation.

Exam Probability: **High**

7. *Answer choices:*

(see index for correct answer)

- a. Flextime
- b. Mergers and acquisitions
- c. Continuing professional development
- d. Senior management

Guidance: level 1

:: ::

An _____ is a process where candidates are examined to determine their suitability for specific types of employment, especially management or military command. The candidates' personality and aptitudes are determined by techniques including interviews, group exercises, presentations, examinations and psychometric testing.

Exam Probability: **Medium**

8. *Answer choices:*

(see index for correct answer)

- a. imperative
- b. Assessment center

- c. surface-level diversity
- d. information systems assessment

Guidance: level 1

:: Generally Accepted Accounting Principles ::

In accounting, _____ is the income that a business have from its normal business activities, usually from the sale of goods and services to customers. _____ is also referred to as sales or turnover. Some companies receive _____ from interest, royalties, or other fees. _____ may refer to business income in general, or it may refer to the amount, in a monetary unit, earned during a period of time, as in "Last year, Company X had _____ of $42 million". Profits or net income generally imply total _____ minus total expenses in a given period. In accounting, in the balance statement it is a subsection of the Equity section and _____ increases equity, it is often referred to as the "top line" due to its position on the income statement at the very top. This is to be contrasted with the "bottom line" which denotes net income.

Exam Probability: **Low**

9. *Answer choices:*

(see index for correct answer)

- a. Fin 48
- b. Earnings before interest, taxes and depreciation
- c. Revenue
- d. Operating statement

Guidance: level 1

:: Statistical terminology ::

> _____ is the magnitude or dimensions of a thing. _____ can be measured as length, width, height, diameter, perimeter, area, volume, or mass.

Exam Probability: **High**

10. *Answer choices:*

(see index for correct answer)

- a. Size
- b. Bias
- c. Statistical parameter
- d. Covariate

Guidance: level 1

:: ::

The business environment is a marketing term and refers to factors and forces that affect a firm's ability to build and maintain successful customer relationships. The business environment has been defined as "the totality of physical and social factors that are taken directly into consideration in the decision-making behaviour of individuals in the organisation."

Exam Probability: **Low**

11. *Answer choices:*

(see index for correct answer)

- a. Environmental scanning
- b. surface-level diversity
- c. hierarchical
- d. interpersonal communication

Guidance: level 1

:: Organizational theory ::

_____ is the process of creating, retaining, and transferring knowledge within an organization. An organization improves over time as it gains experience. From this experience, it is able to create knowledge. This knowledge is broad, covering any topic that could better an organization. Examples may include ways to increase production efficiency or to develop beneficial investor relations. Knowledge is created at four different units: individual, group, organizational, and inter organizational.

Exam Probability: **Low**

12. *Answer choices:*

(see index for correct answer)

- a. Organizational theory
- b. The three circles model
- c. Mutual aid
- d. Organizational learning

Guidance: level 1

:: Marketing ::

_____ or stock is the goods and materials that a business holds for the ultimate goal of resale.

Exam Probability: **Medium**

13. *Answer choices:*

(see index for correct answer)

- a. Lead generation
- b. Impulse purchase
- c. Inventory
- d. Bayesian inference in marketing

Guidance: level 1

:: Offshoring ::

A _____ is the temporary suspension or permanent termination of employment of an employee or, more commonly, a group of employees for business reasons, such as personnel management or downsizing an organization. Originally, _____ referred exclusively to a temporary interruption in work, or employment but this has evolved to a permanent elimination of a position in both British and US English, requiring the addition of "temporary" to specify the original meaning of the word. A _____ is not to be confused with wrongful termination. Laid off workers or displaced workers are workers who have lost or left their jobs because their employer has closed or moved, there was insufficient work for them to do, or their position or shift was abolished. Downsizing in a company is defined to involve the reduction of employees in a workforce. Downsizing in companies became a popular practice in the 1980s and early 1990s as it was seen as a way to deliver better shareholder value as it helps to reduce the costs of employers. Indeed, recent research on downsizing in the U.S., UK, and Japan suggests that downsizing is being regarded by management as one of the preferred routes to help declining organizations, cutting unnecessary costs, and improve organizational performance. Usually a _____ occurs as a cost cutting measure.

Exam Probability: **High**

14. *Answer choices:*

(see index for correct answer)

- a. Layoff
- b. Offshore custom software development
- c. Avasant

- d. American Jobs

Guidance: level 1

:: ::

_____ Corporation was an American energy, commodities, and services company based in Houston, Texas. It was founded in 1985 as a merger between Houston Natural Gas and InterNorth, both relatively small regional companies. Before its bankruptcy on December 3, 2001, _____ employed approximately 29,000 staff and was a major electricity, natural gas, communications and pulp and paper company, with claimed revenues of nearly $101 billion during 2000. Fortune named _____ "America's Most Innovative Company" for six consecutive years.

Exam Probability: **Low**

15. *Answer choices:*

(see index for correct answer)

- a. levels of analysis
- b. Enron
- c. Character
- d. functional perspective

Guidance: level 1

:: Security compliance ::

A _____ is a communicated intent to inflict harm or loss on another person. A _____ is considered an act of coercion. _____ s are widely observed in animal behavior, particularly in a ritualized form, chiefly in order to avoid the unnecessary physical violence that can lead to physical damage or the death of both conflicting parties.

Exam Probability: **Medium**

16. *Answer choices:*

(see index for correct answer)

- a. Nikto Web Scanner
- b. Security Content Automation Protocol
- c. Threat
- d. Vulnerability management

Guidance: level 1

:: Management ::

_____ is a technique used by some employers to rotate their employees' assigned jobs throughout their employment. Employers practice this technique for a number of reasons. It was designed to promote flexibility of employees and to keep employees interested into staying with the company/organization which employs them. There is also research that shows how _____ s help relieve the stress of employees who work in a job that requires manual labor.

Exam Probability: **Medium**

17. *Answer choices:*

(see index for correct answer)

- a. Job rotation
- b. Data Item Descriptions
- c. Inside job
- d. Decentralized decision-making

Guidance: level 1

:: ::

In production, research, retail, and accounting, a _____ is the value of money that has been used up to produce something or deliver a service, and hence is not available for use anymore. In business, the _____ may be one of acquisition, in which case the amount of money expended to acquire it is counted as _____ . In this case, money is the input that is gone in order to acquire the thing. This acquisition _____ may be the sum of the _____ of production as incurred by the original producer, and further _____ s of transaction as incurred by the acquirer over and above the price paid to the producer. Usually, the price also includes a mark-up for profit over the _____ of production.

Exam Probability: **High**

18. *Answer choices:*

(see index for correct answer)

- a. levels of analysis
- b. hierarchical
- c. interpersonal communication
- d. Cost

Guidance: level 1

:: Market research ::

_____ is an organized effort to gather information about target markets or customers. It is a very important component of business strategy. The term is commonly interchanged with marketing research; however, expert practitioners may wish to draw a distinction, in that marketing research is concerned specifically about marketing processes, while _____ is concerned specifically with markets.

Exam Probability: **Low**

19. *Answer choices:*

(see index for correct answer)

- a. IDDEA
- b. Indian Readership Survey
- c. Shanghai Metals Market
- d. Market research

Guidance: level 1

:: Legal terms ::

_____ is a type of meaning in which a phrase, statement or resolution is not explicitly defined, making several interpretations plausible. A common aspect of _____ is uncertainty. It is thus an attribute of any idea or statement whose intended meaning cannot be definitively resolved according to a rule or process with a finite number of steps.

Exam Probability: **Low**

20. *Answer choices:*

(see index for correct answer)

- a. Blunt instrument
- b. Ambiguity
- c. Colour of right
- d. respondent

Guidance: level 1

:: Evaluation ::

_____ solving consists of using generic or ad hoc methods in an orderly manner to find solutions to _____ s. Some of the _____ -solving techniques developed and used in philosophy, artificial intelligence, computer science, engineering, mathematics, or medicine are related to mental _____ -solving techniques studied in psychology.

Exam Probability: **Medium**

21. *Answer choices:*

(see index for correct answer)

- a. Immanent evaluation
- b. Problem
- c. Evaluation Assurance Level
- d. Princeton Application Repository for Shared-Memory Computers

Guidance: level 1

:: Human resource management ::

_____ means increasing the scope of a job through extending the range of its job duties and responsibilities generally within the same level and periphery. _____ involves combining various activities at the same level in the organization and adding them to the existing job. It is also called the horizontal expansion of job activities. This contradicts the principles of specialisation and the division of labour whereby work is divided into small units, each of which is performed repetitively by an individual worker and the responsibilities are always clear. Some motivational theories suggest that the boredom and alienation caused by the division of labour can actually cause efficiency to fall. Thus, _____ seeks to motivate workers through reversing the process of specialisation. A typical approach might be to replace assembly lines with modular work; instead of an employee repeating the same step on each product, they perform several tasks on a single item. In order for employees to be provided with _____ they will need to be retrained in new fields to understand how each field works.

Exam Probability: **Low**

22. *Answer choices:*

(see index for correct answer)

- a. Chief human resources officer
- b. Job enlargement
- c. Corporate Equality Index
- d. Emotional labor

Guidance: level 1

:: ::

The _____ or just chief executive , is the most senior corporate, executive, or administrative officer in charge of managing an organization especially an independent legal entity such as a company or nonprofit institution. CEOs lead a range of organizations, including public and private corporations, non-profit organizations and even some government organizations . The CEO of a corporation or company typically reports to the board of directors and is charged with maximizing the value of the entity, which may include maximizing the share price, market share, revenues or another element. In the non-profit and government sector, CEOs typically aim at achieving outcomes related to the organization's mission, such as reducing poverty, increasing literacy, etc.

Exam Probability: **Medium**

23. *Answer choices:*

(see index for correct answer)

- a. information systems assessment
- b. interpersonal communication
- c. Chief executive officer
- d. hierarchical

Guidance: level 1

:: Management ::

_____ is the practice of initiating, planning, executing, controlling, and closing the work of a team to achieve specific goals and meet specific success criteria at the specified time.

Exam Probability: **Low**

24. *Answer choices:*

(see index for correct answer)

- a. Project management
- b. Community-based management
- c. Intopia
- d. Best current practice

Guidance: level 1

_____ is a form of development in which a person called a coach supports a learner or client in achieving a specific personal or professional goal by providing training and guidance. The learner is sometimes called a coachee. Occasionally, _____ may mean an informal relationship between two people, of whom one has more experience and expertise than the other and offers advice and guidance as the latter learns; but _____ differs from mentoring in focusing on specific tasks or objectives, as opposed to more general goals or overall development.

Exam Probability: **High**

25. *Answer choices:*

(see index for correct answer)

- a. deep-level diversity
- b. process perspective
- c. empathy
- d. information systems assessment

Guidance: level 1

_____ is the assignment of any responsibility or authority to another person to carry out specific activities. It is one of the core concepts of management leadership. However, the person who delegated the work remains accountable for the outcome of the delegated work. _____ empowers a subordinate to make decisions, i.e. it is a shifting of decision-making authority from one organizational level to a lower one. _____ , if properly done, is not fabrication. The opposite of effective _____ is micromanagement, where a manager provides too much input, direction, and review of delegated work. In general, _____ is good and can save money and time, help in building skills, and motivate people. On the other hand, poor _____ might cause frustration and confusion to all the involved parties. Some agents, however, do not favour a _____ and consider the power of making a decision rather burdensome.

Exam Probability: **Low**

26. *Answer choices:*

(see index for correct answer)

- a. Delegation
- b. hierarchical perspective
- c. co-culture
- d. open system

Guidance: level 1

:: Management ::

A _____ is when two or more people come together to discuss one or more topics, often in a formal or business setting, but _____ s also occur in a variety of other environments. Many various types of _____ s exist.

Exam Probability: **High**

27. *Answer choices:*

(see index for correct answer)

- a. Meeting
- b. Tacit knowledge
- c. Earned value management
- d. Automated decision support

Guidance: level 1

:: Game theory ::

_____ is the idea that rationality is limited when individuals make decisions: by the tractability of the decision problem, the cognitive limitations of the mind, and the time available to make the decision. Decision-makers, in this view, act as satisficers, seeking a satisfactory solution rather than an optimal one.

Exam Probability: **High**

28. *Answer choices:*

(see index for correct answer)

- a. Proper equilibrium
- b. Airport problem
- c. Grand coalition
- d. Bounded rationality

Guidance: level 1

:: Strategic management ::

_____ is a strategic planning technique used to help a person or organization identify strengths, weaknesses, opportunities, and threats related to business competition or project planning. It is intended to specify the objectives of the business venture or project and identify the internal and external factors that are favorable and unfavorable to achieving those objectives. Users of a _____ often ask and answer questions to generate meaningful information for each category to make the tool useful and identify their competitive advantage. SWOT has been described as the tried-and-true tool of strategic analysis.

Exam Probability: **High**

29. *Answer choices:*

(see index for correct answer)

- a. Operating model
- b. BSC SWOT
- c. Business system planning

- d. SWOT analysis

Guidance: level 1

:: ::

_____ is the process of two or more people or organizations working together to complete a task or achieve a goal. _____ is similar to cooperation. Most _____ requires leadership, although the form of leadership can be social within a decentralized and egalitarian group. Teams that work collaboratively often access greater resources, recognition and rewards when facing competition for finite resources.

Exam Probability: **High**

30. *Answer choices:*

(see index for correct answer)

- a. similarity-attraction theory
- b. corporate values
- c. surface-level diversity
- d. Collaboration

Guidance: level 1

:: Evaluation ::

A _____ is an evaluation of a publication, service, or company such as a movie, video game, musical composition, book; a piece of hardware like a car, home appliance, or computer; or an event or performance, such as a live music concert, play, musical theater show, dance show, or art exhibition. In addition to a critical evaluation, the _____'s author may assign the work a rating to indicate its relative merit. More loosely, an author may _____ current events, trends, or items in the news. A compilation of _____s may itself be called a _____. The New York _____ of Books, for instance, is a collection of essays on literature, culture, and current affairs. National _____, founded by William F. Buckley, Jr., is an influential conservative magazine, and Monthly _____ is a long-running socialist periodical.

Exam Probability: **Medium**

31. *Answer choices:*

(see index for correct answer)

- a. Cryptographic Module Testing Laboratory
- b. Scale of one to ten
- c. Review
- d. Princeton Application Repository for Shared-Memory Computers

Guidance: level 1

:: Business ethics ::

_____ is a type of harassment technique that relates to a sexual nature and the unwelcome or inappropriate promise of rewards in exchange for sexual favors. _____ includes a range of actions from mild transgressions to sexual abuse or assault. Harassment can occur in many different social settings such as the workplace, the home, school, churches, etc. Harassers or victims may be of any gender.

Exam Probability: **Low**

32. *Answer choices:*

(see index for correct answer)

- a. Corporate behaviour
- b. Sexual harassment
- c. Destructionism
- d. Interfaith Center on Corporate Responsibility

Guidance: level 1

:: Planning ::

_____ is a high level plan to achieve one or more goals under conditions of uncertainty. In the sense of the "art of the general," which included several subsets of skills including tactics, siegecraft, logistics etc., the term came into use in the 6th century C.E. in East Roman terminology, and was translated into Western vernacular languages only in the 18th century. From then until the 20th century, the word "_____" came to denote "a comprehensive way to try to pursue political ends, including the threat or actual use of force, in a dialectic of wills" in a military conflict, in which both adversaries interact.

Exam Probability: **Medium**

33. *Answer choices:*

(see index for correct answer)

- a. Strategy
- b. Resource-Task Network
- c. Interactive planning
- d. Default effect

Guidance: level 1

:: Industrial relations ::

_____ or employee satisfaction is a measure of workers' contentedness with their job, whether or not they like the job or individual aspects or facets of jobs, such as nature of work or supervision. _____ can be measured in cognitive, affective, and behavioral components. Researchers have also noted that _____ measures vary in the extent to which they measure feelings about the job, or cognitions about the job.

Exam Probability: **High**

34. *Answer choices:*

(see index for correct answer)

- a. Industrial violence
- b. European Journal of Industrial Relations
- c. Injury prevention
- d. Job satisfaction

Guidance: level 1

:: Time management ::

_____ is the process of planning and exercising conscious control of time spent on specific activities, especially to increase effectiveness, efficiency, and productivity. It involves a juggling act of various demands upon a person relating to work, social life, family, hobbies, personal interests and commitments with the finiteness of time. Using time effectively gives the person "choice" on spending/managing activities at their own time and expediency.

Exam Probability: **High**

35. *Answer choices:*

(see index for correct answer)

- a. Time management
- b. Time allocation
- c. Getting Things Done
- d. HabitRPG

Guidance: level 1

:: Lean manufacturing ::

_____ is the Sino-Japanese word for "improvement". In business, _____ refers to activities that continuously improve all functions and involve all employees from the CEO to the assembly line workers. It also applies to processes, such as purchasing and logistics, that cross organizational boundaries into the supply chain. It has been applied in healthcare, psychotherapy, life-coaching, government, and banking.

Exam Probability: **Low**

36. *Answer choices:*

(see index for correct answer)

- a. Manufacturing supermarket
- b. Kaizen

- c. Genchi Genbutsu
- d. Lean Government

Guidance: level 1

:: Management ::

The term _____ refers to measures designed to increase the degree of autonomy and self-determination in people and in communities in order to enable them to represent their interests in a responsible and self-determined way, acting on their own authority. It is the process of becoming stronger and more confident, especially in controlling one's life and claiming one's rights. _____ as action refers both to the process of self-_____ and to professional support of people, which enables them to overcome their sense of powerlessness and lack of influence, and to recognize and use their resources. To do work with power.

Exam Probability: **High**

37. *Answer choices:*

(see index for correct answer)

- a. Empowerment
- b. Competitive heterogeneity
- c. Management buyout
- d. Intopia

Guidance: level 1

:: Human resource management ::

_____ , also known as management by results, was first popularized by Peter Drucker in his 1954 book The Practice of Management. _____ is the process of defining specific objectives within an organization that management can convey to organization members, then deciding on how to achieve each objective in sequence. This process allows managers to take work that needs to be done one step at a time to allow for a calm, yet productive work environment. This process also helps organization members to see their accomplishments as they achieve each objective, which reinforces a positive work environment and a sense of achievement. An important part of MBO is the measurement and comparison of an employee's actual performance with the standards set. Ideally, when employees themselves have been involved with the goal-setting and choosing the course of action to be followed by them, they are more likely to fulfill their responsibilities. According to George S. Odiorne, the system of _____ can be described as a process whereby the superior and subordinate jointly identify common goals, define each individual's major areas of responsibility in terms of the results expected of him or her, and use these measures as guides for operating the unit and assessing the contribution of each of its members.

Exam Probability: **Medium**

38. *Answer choices:*

(see index for correct answer)

- a. Salary
- b. Applicant tracking system
- c. Human resource consulting
- d. Management by objectives

Guidance: level 1

:: Management ::

A _____ describes the rationale of how an organization creates, delivers, and captures value, in economic, social, cultural or other contexts. The process of _____ construction and modification is also called _____ innovation and forms a part of business strategy.

Exam Probability: **Low**

39. *Answer choices:*
(see index for correct answer)

- a. Core competency
- b. Business model
- c. Relevance paradox
- d. Customer Benefit Package

Guidance: level 1

:: Marketing techniques ::

In industry, product lifecycle management is the process of managing the entire lifecycle of a product from inception, through engineering design and manufacture, to service and disposal of manufactured products. PLM integrates people, data, processes and business systems and provides a product information backbone for companies and their extended enterprise.

Exam Probability: **High**

40. *Answer choices:*

(see index for correct answer)

- a. Co-promotion
- b. AIDA
- c. unique selling point
- d. Product life cycle

Guidance: level 1

:: Personality tests ::

The Myers–Briggs Type Indicator is an introspective self-report questionnaire with the purpose of indicating differing psychological preferences in how people perceive the world around them and make decisions. . Though the test superficially resembles some psychological theories it is commonly classified as pseudoscience, especially as pertains to its supposed predictive abilities.

Exam Probability: **High**

41. *Answer choices:*

(see index for correct answer)

- a. personality quiz
- b. Keirsey Temperament Sorter
- c. Myers-Briggs Type Indicator
- d. Johari window

Guidance: level 1

:: ::

An _____ is the production of goods or related services within an economy. The major source of revenue of a group or company is the indicator of its relevant _____ . When a large group has multiple sources of revenue generation, it is considered to be working in different industries. Manufacturing _____ became a key sector of production and labour in European and North American countries during the Industrial Revolution, upsetting previous mercantile and feudal economies. This came through many successive rapid advances in technology, such as the production of steel and coal.

Exam Probability: **Medium**

42. *Answer choices:*

(see index for correct answer)

- a. surface-level diversity
- b. information systems assessment

- c. levels of analysis
- d. deep-level diversity

Guidance: level 1

:: Employment compensation ::

_____ refers to various incentive plans introduced by businesses that provide direct or indirect payments to employees that depend on company's profitability in addition to employees' regular salary and bonuses. In publicly traded companies these plans typically amount to allocation of shares to employees. One of the earliest pioneers of _____ was Englishman Theodore Cooke Taylor, who is known to have introduced the practice in his woollen mills during the late 1800s.

Exam Probability: **Low**

43. *Answer choices:*

(see index for correct answer)

- a. My Family Care
- b. Merit pay
- c. Law Enforcement Availability Pay
- d. Employees%27 Compensation Appeals Board

Guidance: level 1

:: Management accounting ::

_____ s are costs that change as the quantity of the good or service that a business produces changes. _____ s are the sum of marginal costs over all units produced. They can also be considered normal costs. Fixed costs and _____ s make up the two components of total cost. Direct costs are costs that can easily be associated with a particular cost object. However, not all _____ s are direct costs. For example, variable manufacturing overhead costs are _____ s that are indirect costs, not direct costs. _____ s are sometimes called unit-level costs as they vary with the number of units produced.

Exam Probability: **Low**

44. *Answer choices:*

(see index for correct answer)

- a. Direct material total variance
- b. Management control system
- c. Fixed cost
- d. Holding cost

Guidance: level 1

:: Types of marketing ::

In microeconomics and management, _____ is an arrangement in which the supply chain of a company is owned by that company. Usually each member of the supply chain produces a different product or service, and the products combine to satisfy a common need. It is contrasted with horizontal integration, wherein a company produces several items which are related to one another. _____ has also described management styles that bring large portions of the supply chain not only under a common ownership, but also into one corporation.

Exam Probability: **Medium**

45. *Answer choices:*

(see index for correct answer)

- a. Vertical integration
- b. Vertical disintegration
- c. Affinity marketing
- d. Proximity marketing

Guidance: level 1

:: Power (social and political) ::

_____ is a form of reverence gained by a leader who has strong interpersonal relationship skills. _____ , as an aspect of personal power, becomes particularly important as organizational leadership becomes increasingly about collaboration and influence, rather than command and control.

Exam Probability: **Low**

46. *Answer choices:*

(see index for correct answer)

- a. need for power
- b. Hard power
- c. Expert power

Guidance: level 1

:: Psychometrics ::

_____ is a dynamic, structured, interactive process where a neutral third party assists disputing parties in resolving conflict through the use of specialized communication and negotiation techniques. All participants in _____ are encouraged to actively participate in the process. _____ is a "party-centered" process in that it is focused primarily upon the needs, rights, and interests of the parties. The mediator uses a wide variety of techniques to guide the process in a constructive direction and to help the parties find their optimal solution. A mediator is facilitative in that she/he manages the interaction between parties and facilitates open communication. _____ is also evaluative in that the mediator analyzes issues and relevant norms , while refraining from providing prescriptive advice to the parties .

Exam Probability: **Medium**

47. *Answer choices:*

(see index for correct answer)

- a. NOMINATE
- b. Frederic M. Lord
- c. Activity vector analysis
- d. SESAMO

Guidance: level 1

:: Management ::

The _____ is a strategy performance management tool – a semi-standard structured report, that can be used by managers to keep track of the execution of activities by the staff within their control and to monitor the consequences arising from these actions.

Exam Probability: **Low**

48. *Answer choices:*

(see index for correct answer)

- a. Resource breakdown structure
- b. Balanced scorecard
- c. Control
- d. Local management board

Guidance: level 1

:: Project management ::

_____ is the right to exercise power, which can be formalized by a state and exercised by way of judges, appointed executives of government, or the ecclesiastical or priestly appointed representatives of a God or other deities.

Exam Probability: **Medium**

49. *Answer choices:*

(see index for correct answer)

- a. Hammock activity
- b. Authority
- c. Deliverable
- d. Arrow diagramming method

Guidance: level 1

:: Office administration ::

An _____ is generally a room or other area where an organization's employees perform administrative work in order to support and realize objects and goals of the organization. The word "_____" may also denote a position within an organization with specific duties attached to it ; the latter is in fact an earlier usage, _____ as place originally referring to the location of one's duty. When used as an adjective, the term "_____ " may refer to business-related tasks. In law, a company or organization has _____ s in any place where it has an official presence, even if that presence consists of a storage silo rather than an establishment with desk-and-chair. An _____ is also an architectural and design phenomenon: ranging from a small _____ such as a bench in the corner of a small business of extremely small size , through entire floors of buildings, up to and including massive buildings dedicated entirely to one company. In modern terms an _____ is usually the location where white-collar workers carry out their functions. As per James Stephenson, "_____ is that part of business enterprise which is devoted to the direction and co-ordination of its various activities."

Exam Probability: **High**

50. *Answer choices:*

(see index for correct answer)

- a. Fish! Philosophy
- b. Activity management
- c. Office
- d. Inter departmental communication

Guidance: level 1

A _____, or also known as foreman, overseer, facilitator, monitor, area coordinator, or sometimes gaffer, is the job title of a low level management position that is primarily based on authority over a worker or charge of a workplace. A _____ can also be one of the most senior in the staff at the place of work, such as a Professor who oversees a PhD dissertation. Supervision, on the other hand, can be performed by people without this formal title, for example by parents. The term _____ itself can be used to refer to any personnel who have this task as part of their job description.

Exam Probability: **High**

51. *Answer choices:*
(see index for correct answer)

- a. open system
- b. functional perspective
- c. information systems assessment
- d. Supervisor

Guidance: level 1

:: ::

_____ is the administration of an organization, whether it is a business, a not-for-profit organization, or government body. _____ includes the activities of setting the strategy of an organization and coordinating the efforts of its employees to accomplish its objectives through the application of available resources, such as financial, natural, technological, and human resources. The term "_____" may also refer to those people who manage an organization.

Exam Probability: **High**

52. *Answer choices:*

(see index for correct answer)

- a. process perspective
- b. co-culture
- c. cultural
- d. interpersonal communication

Guidance: level 1

:: Economic globalization ::

_____ is an agreement in which one company hires another company to be responsible for a planned or existing activity that is or could be done internally, and sometimes involves transferring employees and assets from one firm to another.

Exam Probability: **High**

53. *Answer choices:*

(see index for correct answer)

- a. reshoring
- b. Outsourcing

Guidance: level 1

:: Business planning ::

> _____ is an organization's process of defining its strategy, or direction, and making decisions on allocating its resources to pursue this strategy. It may also extend to control mechanisms for guiding the implementation of the strategy. _____ became prominent in corporations during the 1960s and remains an important aspect of strategic management. It is executed by strategic planners or strategists, who involve many parties and research sources in their analysis of the organization and its relationship to the environment in which it competes.

Exam Probability: **Medium**

54. *Answer choices:*

(see index for correct answer)

- a. Stakeholder management
- b. Joint decision trap
- c. Strategic planning
- d. Business war games

Guidance: level 1

:: ::

In business strategy, _____ is establishing a competitive advantage by having the lowest cost of operation in the industry. _____ is often driven by company efficiency, size, scale, scope and cumulative experience. A _____ strategy aims to exploit scale of production, well-defined scope and other economies, producing highly standardized products, using advanced technology. In recent years, more and more companies have chosen a strategic mix to achieve market leadership. These patterns consist of simultaneous _____, superior customer service and product leadership. Walmart has succeeded across the world due to its _____ strategy. The company has cut down on exesses at every point of production and thus are able to provide the consumers with quality products at low prices.

Exam Probability: **Medium**

55. *Answer choices:*

(see index for correct answer)

- a. Cost leadership
- b. empathy
- c. imperative
- d. corporate values

Guidance: level 1

:: E-commerce ::

_____ is the activity of buying or selling of products on online services or over the Internet. Electronic commerce draws on technologies such as mobile commerce, electronic funds transfer, supply chain management, Internet marketing, online transaction processing, electronic data interchange, inventory management systems, and automated data collection systems.

Exam Probability: **High**

56. *Answer choices:*

(see index for correct answer)

- a. E-commerce
- b. ITransact
- c. AS 2805
- d. Eagle Cash

Guidance: level 1

:: Data analysis ::

In statistics, the _____ is a measure that is used to quantify the amount of variation or dispersion of a set of data values. A low _____ indicates that the data points tend to be close to the mean of the set, while a high _____ indicates that the data points are spread out over a wider range of values.

Exam Probability: **Medium**

57. *Answer choices:*

(see index for correct answer)

- a. Exponential smoothing
- b. Standard deviation
- c. Limited dependent variable
- d. Aggregative Contingent Estimation

Guidance: level 1

:: Business models ::

_____ es are privately owned corporations, partnerships, or sole proprietorships that have fewer employees and/or less annual revenue than a regular-sized business or corporation. Businesses are defined as "small" in terms of being able to apply for government support and qualify for preferential tax policy varies depending on the country and industry. _____ es range from fifteen employees under the Australian Fair Work Act 2009, fifty employees according to the definition used by the European Union, and fewer than five hundred employees to qualify for many U.S. _____ Administration programs. While _____ es can also be classified according to other methods, such as annual revenues, shipments, sales, assets, or by annual gross or net revenue or net profits, the number of employees is one of the most widely used measures.

Exam Probability: **Medium**

58. *Answer choices:*

(see index for correct answer)

- a. Business model pattern
- b. Dependent growth business model
- c. Co-operative Wholesale Society
- d. Open Music Model

Guidance: level 1

:: ::

A _____ is monetary compensation paid by an employer to an employee in exchange for work done. Payment may be calculated as a fixed amount for each task completed, or at an hourly or daily rate, or based on an easily measured quantity of work done.

Exam Probability: **Low**

59. *Answer choices:*

(see index for correct answer)

- a. Character
- b. Wage
- c. imperative
- d. co-culture

Guidance: level 1

Business law

Corporate law (also known as business law) is the body of law governing the rights, relations, and conduct of persons, companies, organizations and businesses. It refers to the legal practice relating to, or the theory of corporations. Corporate law often describes the law relating to matters which derive directly from the life-cycle of a corporation. It thus encompasses the formation, funding, governance, and death of a corporation.

:: ::

A concept of English law, a _____ is an untrue or misleading statement of fact made during negotiations by one party to another, the statement then inducing that other party into the contract. The misled party may normally rescind the contract, and sometimes may be awarded damages as well .

Exam Probability: **Medium**

1. *Answer choices:*

(see index for correct answer)

- a. co-culture
- b. corporate values
- c. Misrepresentation
- d. personal values

Guidance: level 1

:: Insurance terms ::

> _____ is the assumption by a third party of another party's legal right to collect a debt or damages. It is a legal doctrine whereby one person is entitled to enforce the subsisting or revived rights of another for one's own benefit. A right of _____ typically arises by operation of law, but can also arise by statute or by agreement. _____ is an equitable remedy, having first developed in the English Court of Chancery. It is a familiar feature of common law systems. Analogous doctrines exist in civil law jurisdictions.

Exam Probability: **Medium**

2. *Answer choices:*

(see index for correct answer)

- a. Gross premiums written
- b. surrender value
- c. Subrogation

- d. replacement cost

Guidance: level 1

:: ::

> In law, a _____ is a coming together of parties to a dispute, to present information in a tribunal, a formal setting with the authority to adjudicate claims or disputes. One form of tribunal is a court. The tribunal, which may occur before a judge, jury, or other designated trier of fact, aims to achieve a resolution to their dispute.

Exam Probability: **Medium**

3. *Answer choices:*

(see index for correct answer)

- a. Trial
- b. co-culture
- c. hierarchical perspective
- d. levels of analysis

Guidance: level 1

:: ::

In logic and philosophy, an _____ is a series of statements, called the premises or premisses, intended to determine the degree of truth of another statement, the conclusion. The logical form of an _____ in a natural language can be represented in a symbolic formal language, and independently of natural language formally defined " _____ s" can be made in math and computer science.

Exam Probability: **Medium**

4. *Answer choices:*

(see index for correct answer)

- a. imperative
- b. functional perspective
- c. personal values
- d. deep-level diversity

Guidance: level 1

:: ::

A _____ is a formal presentation of a matter such as a complaint, indictment or bill of exchange. In early-medieval England, juries of _____ would hear inquests in order to establish whether someone should be presented for a crime.

Exam Probability: **Low**

5. *Answer choices:*

(see index for correct answer)

- a. Presentment
- b. empathy
- c. interpersonal communication
- d. deep-level diversity

Guidance: level 1

:: International trade ::

_____ involves the transfer of goods or services from one person or entity to another, often in exchange for money. A system or network that allows _____ is called a market.

Exam Probability: **High**

6. *Answer choices:*

(see index for correct answer)

- a. financial account
- b. Trade credit insurance
- c. Producer support estimate
- d. Quota share

Guidance: level 1

An _____ is an area of the production, distribution, or trade, and consumption of goods and services by different agents. Understood in its broadest sense, 'The _____ is defined as a social domain that emphasize the practices, discourses, and material expressions associated with the production, use, and management of resources'. Economic agents can be individuals, businesses, organizations, or governments. Economic transactions occur when two parties agree to the value or price of the transacted good or service, commonly expressed in a certain currency. However, monetary transactions only account for a small part of the economic domain.

Exam Probability: **Low**

7. *Answer choices:*

(see index for correct answer)

- a. deep-level diversity
- b. Economy
- c. information systems assessment
- d. surface-level diversity

Guidance: level 1

In contract law, rescission is an equitable remedy which allows a contractual party to cancel the contract. Parties may _____ if they are the victims of a vitiating factor, such as misrepresentation, mistake, duress, or undue influence. Rescission is the unwinding of a transaction. This is done to bring the parties, as far as possible, back to the position in which they were before they entered into a contract .

Exam Probability: **Low**

8. *Answer choices:*

(see index for correct answer)

- a. imperative
- b. empathy
- c. interpersonal communication
- d. Rescind

Guidance: level 1

:: ::

A _____ is a request to do something, most commonly addressed to a government official or public entity. _____ s to a deity are a form of prayer called supplication.

Exam Probability: **Low**

9. *Answer choices:*

(see index for correct answer)

- a. hierarchical perspective
- b. co-culture
- c. process perspective
- d. surface-level diversity

Guidance: level 1

:: Commercial item transport and distribution ::

A _____ is a commitment or expectation to perform some action in general or if certain circumstances arise. A _____ may arise from a system of ethics or morality, especially in an honor culture. Many duties are created by law, sometimes including a codified punishment or liability for non-performance. Performing one's _____ may require some sacrifice of self-interest.

Exam Probability: **Low**

10. *Answer choices:*

(see index for correct answer)

- a. Aeroscraft
- b. Duty
- c. Conveyor chain
- d. Blue Water Trucking

Guidance: level 1

:: Project management ::

> _____ is the right to exercise power, which can be formalized by a state and exercised by way of judges, appointed executives of government, or the ecclesiastical or priestly appointed representatives of a God or other deities.

Exam Probability: **Low**

11. *Answer choices:*

(see index for correct answer)

- a. Soft Costs
- b. Authority
- c. Precedence diagram method
- d. Project planning

Guidance: level 1

:: Forgery ::

_____ is a white-collar crime that generally refers to the false making or material alteration of a legal instrument with the specific intent to defraud anyone. Tampering with a certain legal instrument may be forbidden by law in some jurisdictions but such an offense is not related to _____ unless the tampered legal instrument was actually used in the course of the crime to defraud another person or entity. Copies, studio replicas, and reproductions are not considered forgeries, though they may later become forgeries through knowing and willful misrepresentations.

Exam Probability: **Medium**

12. *Answer choices:*

(see index for correct answer)

- a. Unapproved aircraft part
- b. Signature forgery
- c. Forgery Act
- d. Forgery

Guidance: level 1

:: ::

_____ is the study and management of exchange relationships. _____ is the business process of creating relationships with and satisfying customers. With its focus on the customer, _____ is one of the premier components of business management.

Exam Probability: **Low**

13. *Answer choices:*

(see index for correct answer)

- a. corporate values
- b. Marketing
- c. process perspective
- d. deep-level diversity

Guidance: level 1

:: Competition law ::

In competition law, a _____ is a market in which a particular product or service is sold. It is the intersection of a relevant product market and a relevant geographic market. The European Commission defines a _____ and its product and geographic components as follows.

Exam Probability: **Medium**

14. *Answer choices:*

(see index for correct answer)

- a. Marchfeld competition forum
- b. Legal Services Board
- c. Antitrust law

- d. Relevant market

Guidance: level 1

:: Psychometrics ::

_____ is a dynamic, structured, interactive process where a neutral third party assists disputing parties in resolving conflict through the use of specialized communication and negotiation techniques. All participants in _____ are encouraged to actively participate in the process. _____ is a "party-centered" process in that it is focused primarily upon the needs, rights, and interests of the parties. The mediator uses a wide variety of techniques to guide the process in a constructive direction and to help the parties find their optimal solution. A mediator is facilitative in that she/he manages the interaction between parties and facilitates open communication. _____ is also evaluative in that the mediator analyzes issues and relevant norms, while refraining from providing prescriptive advice to the parties.

Exam Probability: **Medium**

15. *Answer choices:*

(see index for correct answer)

- a. Person-fit analysis
- b. Polytomous Rasch model
- c. Intra-rater reliability
- d. Norm-referenced test

Guidance: level 1

:: ::

A _____ is an aggregate of fundamental principles or established precedents that constitute the legal basis of a polity, organisation or other type of entity, and commonly determine how that entity is to be governed.

Exam Probability: **High**

16. *Answer choices:*

(see index for correct answer)

- a. Constitution
- b. Sarbanes-Oxley act of 2002
- c. corporate values
- d. co-culture

Guidance: level 1

:: Legal reasoning ::

_____ is a Latin expression meaning on its first encounter or at first sight. The literal translation would be "at first face" or "at first appearance", from the feminine forms of primus and facies, both in the ablative case. In modern, colloquial and conversational English, a common translation would be "on the face of it". The term _____ is used in modern legal English to signify that upon initial examination, sufficient corroborating evidence appears to exist to support a case. In common law jurisdictions, _____ denotes evidence that, unless rebutted, would be sufficient to prove a particular proposition or fact. The term is used similarly in academic philosophy. Most legal proceedings, in most jurisdictions, require a _____ case to exist, following which proceedings may then commence to test it, and create a ruling.

Exam Probability: **Medium**

17. *Answer choices:*

(see index for correct answer)

- a. Prima facie
- b. Reasonable man
- c. Probable cause

Guidance: level 1

:: Asset ::

In financial accounting, an _____ is any resource owned by the business. Anything tangible or intangible that can be owned or controlled to produce value and that is held by a company to produce positive economic value is an _____ . Simply stated, _____ s represent value of ownership that can be converted into cash . The balance sheet of a firm records the monetary value of the _____ s owned by that firm. It covers money and other valuables belonging to an individual or to a business.

Exam Probability: **Medium**

18. *Answer choices:*
(see index for correct answer)

- a. Fixed asset
- b. Current asset

Guidance: level 1

:: Contract law ::

_____ is a legal process for collecting a monetary judgment on behalf of a plaintiff from a defendant. _____ allows the plaintiff to take the money or property of the debtor from the person or institution that holds that property . A similar legal mechanism called execution allows the seizure of money or property held directly by the debtor.

Exam Probability: **Medium**

19. *Answer choices:*

(see index for correct answer)

- a. Contingent contracts
- b. Interconnect agreement
- c. Garnishment
- d. Fundamental breach

Guidance: level 1

:: ::

In international relations, _____ is – from the perspective of governments – a voluntary transfer of resources from one country to another.

Exam Probability: **Low**

20. *Answer choices:*

(see index for correct answer)

- a. surface-level diversity
- b. Aid
- c. information systems assessment
- d. Sarbanes-Oxley act of 2002

Guidance: level 1

:: ::

Employment is a relationship between two parties, usually based on a contract where work is paid for, where one party, which may be a corporation, for profit, not-for-profit organization, co-operative or other entity is the employer and the other is the employee. Employees work in return for payment, which may be in the form of an hourly wage, by piecework or an annual salary, depending on the type of work an employee does or which sector she or he is working in. Employees in some fields or sectors may receive gratuities, bonus payment or stock options. In some types of employment, employees may receive benefits in addition to payment. Benefits can include health insurance, housing, disability insurance or use of a gym. Employment is typically governed by employment laws, regulations or legal contracts.

Exam Probability: **Medium**

21. *Answer choices:*

(see index for correct answer)

- a. hierarchical perspective
- b. similarity-attraction theory
- c. Personnel
- d. information systems assessment

Guidance: level 1

:: Legal doctrines and principles ::

_____ is a defense in the law of torts, which bars or reduces a plaintiff's right to recovery against a negligent tortfeasor if the defendant can demonstrate that the plaintiff voluntarily and knowingly assumed the risks at issue inherent to the dangerous activity in which he was participating at the time of his or her injury.

Exam Probability: **Low**

22. *Answer choices:*

(see index for correct answer)

- a. Act of state doctrine
- b. Mutual mistake
- c. negligence
- d. Nonacquiescence

Guidance: level 1

:: Financial regulatory authorities of the United States ::

The _____ is the revenue service of the United States federal government. The government agency is a bureau of the Department of the Treasury, and is under the immediate direction of the Commissioner of Internal Revenue, who is appointed to a five-year term by the President of the United States. The IRS is responsible for collecting taxes and administering the Internal Revenue Code, the main body of federal statutory tax law of the United States. The duties of the IRS include providing tax assistance to taxpayers and pursuing and resolving instances of erroneous or fraudulent tax filings. The IRS has also overseen various benefits programs, and enforces portions of the Affordable Care Act.

Exam Probability: **Low**

23. *Answer choices:*

(see index for correct answer)

- a. Internal Revenue Service
- b. Federal Deposit Insurance Corporation
- c. Farm Credit Administration
- d. Municipal Securities Rulemaking Board

Guidance: level 1

:: Legal doctrines and principles ::

In some common law jurisdictions, _____ is a defense to a tort claim based on negligence. If it is available, the defense completely bars plaintiffs from any recovery if they contribute to their own injury through their own negligence.

Exam Probability: **Medium**

24. *Answer choices:*

(see index for correct answer)

- a. Act of state doctrine
- b. Exclusionary rule
- c. Contributory negligence
- d. Mutual assent

Guidance: level 1

:: Business law ::

In the United States, the United Kingdom, Australia, Canada and South Africa, _____ relates to the doctrines of the law of agency. It is relevant particularly in corporate law and constitutional law. _____ refers to a situation where a reasonable third party would understand that an agent had authority to act. This means a principal is bound by the agent's actions, even if the agent had no actual authority, whether express or implied. It raises an estoppel because the third party is given an assurance, which he relies on and would be inequitable for the principal to deny the authority given. _____ can legally be found, even if actual authority has not been given.

Exam Probability: **Medium**

25. *Answer choices:*

(see index for correct answer)

- a. Board of directors
- b. Lease
- c. Tacit relocation
- d. Extraordinary resolution

Guidance: level 1

:: White-collar criminals ::

_____ refers to financially motivated, nonviolent crime committed by businesses and government professionals. It was first defined by the sociologist Edwin Sutherland in 1939 as "a crime committed by a person of respectability and high social status in the course of their occupation". Typical _____ s could include wage theft, fraud, bribery, Ponzi schemes, insider trading, labor racketeering, embezzlement, cybercrime, copyright infringement, money laundering, identity theft, and forgery. Lawyers can specialize in _____ .

Exam Probability: **Low**

26. *Answer choices:*

(see index for correct answer)

- a. Tongsun Park
- b. Du Jun

Guidance: level 1

:: ::

_____ is a process whereby a person assumes the parenting of another, usually a child, from that person's biological or legal parent or parents. Legal _____s permanently transfers all rights and responsibilities, along with filiation, from the biological parent or parents.

Exam Probability: **Low**

27. *Answer choices:*

(see index for correct answer)

- a. personal values
- b. open system
- c. similarity-attraction theory
- d. functional perspective

Guidance: level 1

:: ::

_____s and acquisitions are transactions in which the ownership of companies, other business organizations, or their operating units are transferred or consolidated with other entities. As an aspect of strategic management, M&A can allow enterprises to grow or downsize, and change the nature of their business or competitive position.

Exam Probability: **Low**

28. *Answer choices:*

(see index for correct answer)

- a. process perspective
- b. hierarchical
- c. functional perspective
- d. Merger

Guidance: level 1

:: Statutory law ::

_____ or statute law is written law set down by a body of legislature or by a singular legislator. This is as opposed to oral or customary law; or regulatory law promulgated by the executive or common law of the judiciary. Statutes may originate with national, state legislatures or local municipalities.

Exam Probability: **High**

29. *Answer choices:*

(see index for correct answer)

- a. statute law
- b. incorporation by reference

- c. Statutory Law
- d. Statute of repose

Guidance: level 1

:: Business ::

_____ is a trade policy that does not restrict imports or exports; it can also be understood as the free market idea applied to international trade. In government, _____ is predominantly advocated by political parties that hold liberal economic positions while economically left-wing and nationalist political parties generally support protectionism, the opposite of _____ .

Exam Probability: **High**

30. *Answer choices:*

(see index for correct answer)

- a. Open-book contract
- b. Auckland Chamber of Commerce
- c. Hellenic Australian Business Council
- d. Free trade

Guidance: level 1

:: ::

_____ is a concept of English common law and is a necessity for simple contracts but not for special contracts. The concept has been adopted by other common law jurisdictions, including the US.

Exam Probability: **Low**

31. *Answer choices:*

(see index for correct answer)

- a. Consideration
- b. Sarbanes-Oxley act of 2002
- c. co-culture
- d. process perspective

Guidance: level 1

:: ::

Credit is the trust which allows one party to provide money or resources to another party wherein the second party does not reimburse the first party immediately, but promises either to repay or return those resources at a later date. In other words, credit is a method of making reciprocity formal, legally enforceable, and extensible to a large group of unrelated people.

Exam Probability: **High**

32. *Answer choices:*

(see index for correct answer)

- a. Sarbanes-Oxley act of 2002
- b. similarity-attraction theory
- c. Consumer credit
- d. personal values

Guidance: level 1

:: ::

In English law, a _____ or _____ absolute is an estate in land, a form of freehold ownership. It is a way that real estate and land may be owned in common law countries, and is the highest possible ownership interest that can be held in real property. Allodial title is reserved to governments under a civil law structure. The rights of the _____ owner are limited by government powers of taxation, compulsory purchase, police power, and escheat, and it could also be limited further by certain encumbrances or conditions in the deed, such as, for example, a condition that required the land to be used as a public park, with a reversion interest in the grantor if the condition fails; this is a _____ conditional.

Exam Probability: **Medium**

33. *Answer choices:*
(see index for correct answer)

- a. open system
- b. Fee simple

- c. corporate values
- d. surface-level diversity

Guidance: level 1

:: ::

In regulatory jurisdictions that provide for it, _____ is a group of laws and organizations designed to ensure the rights of consumers as well as fair trade, competition and accurate information in the marketplace. The laws are designed to prevent the businesses that engage in fraud or specified unfair practices from gaining an advantage over competitors. They may also provides additional protection for those most vulnerable in society. _____ laws are a form of government regulation that aim to protect the rights of consumers. For example, a government may require businesses to disclose detailed information about products—particularly in areas where safety or public health is an issue, such as food.

Exam Probability: **High**

34. *Answer choices:*

(see index for correct answer)

- a. co-culture
- b. hierarchical perspective
- c. Consumer protection
- d. similarity-attraction theory

Guidance: level 1

:: Types of business entity ::

A _____, the basic form of partnership under common law, is in most countries an association of persons or an unincorporated company with the following major features.

Exam Probability: **Medium**

35. *Answer choices:*

(see index for correct answer)

- a. Globally integrated enterprise
- b. Kommanditselskab
- c. General partnership
- d. Anpartsselskab

Guidance: level 1

:: Commercial crimes ::

_____ is the process of concealing the origins of money obtained illegally by passing it through a complex sequence of banking transfers or commercial transactions. The overall scheme of this process returns the money to the launderer in an obscure and indirect way.

Exam Probability: **Low**

36. *Answer choices:*

(see index for correct answer)

- a. National White Collar Crime Center
- b. Money laundering
- c. False advertising
- d. Fence

Guidance: level 1

:: Legal doctrines and principles ::

In the United States, the _____ is a legal rule, based on constitutional law, that prevents evidence collected or analyzed in violation of the defendant`s constitutional rights from being used in a court of law. This may be considered an example of a prophylactic rule formulated by the judiciary in order to protect a constitutional right. The _____ may also, in some circumstances at least, be considered to follow directly from the constitutional language, such as the Fifth Amendment`s command that no person "shall be compelled in any criminal case to be a witness against himself" and that no person "shall be deprived of life, liberty or property without due process of law".

Exam Probability: **High**

37. *Answer choices:*

(see index for correct answer)

- a. Attractive nuisance doctrine
- b. Eminent domain
- c. Exclusionary rule
- d. Nonacquiescence

Guidance: level 1

:: ::

A contract is a legally-binding agreement which recognises and governs the rights and duties of the parties to the agreement. A contract is legally enforceable because it meets the requirements and approval of the law. An agreement typically involves the exchange of goods, services, money, or promises of any of those. In the event of breach of contract, the law awards the injured party access to legal remedies such as damages and cancellation.

Exam Probability: **Low**

38. *Answer choices:*

(see index for correct answer)

- a. deep-level diversity
- b. corporate values
- c. surface-level diversity
- d. Contract law

Guidance: level 1

:: Contract law ::

An _____ —or acceleration covenant— in the law of contracts, is a term that fully matures the performance due from a party upon a breach of the contract. Such clauses are most prevalent in mortgages and similar contracts to purchase real estate in installments.

Exam Probability: **Medium**

39. *Answer choices:*

(see index for correct answer)

- a. Co-signing
- b. Heads of Agreement
- c. Acceleration clause
- d. French contract law

Guidance: level 1

:: ::

The U.S. _____ is an independent agency of the United States federal government. The SEC holds primary responsibility for enforcing the federal securities laws, proposing securities rules, and regulating the securities industry, the nation's stock and options exchanges, and other activities and organizations, including the electronic securities markets in the United States.

Exam Probability: **Low**

40. *Answer choices:*

(see index for correct answer)

- a. imperative
- b. Securities and Exchange Commission
- c. Character
- d. surface-level diversity

Guidance: level 1

:: ::

_____ is that part of a civil law legal system which is part of the jus commune that involves relationships between individuals, such as the law of contracts or torts , and the law of obligations . It is to be distinguished from public law, which deals with relationships between both natural and artificial persons and the state, including regulatory statutes, penal law and other law that affects the public order. In general terms, _____ involves interactions between private citizens, whereas public law involves interrelations between the state and the general population.

Exam Probability: **Medium**

41. *Answer choices:*

(see index for correct answer)

- a. Sarbanes-Oxley act of 2002
- b. deep-level diversity
- c. Private law
- d. similarity-attraction theory

Guidance: level 1

:: ::

A federation is a political entity characterized by a union of partially self-governing provinces, states, or other regions under a central _____. In a federation, the self-governing status of the component states, as well as the division of power between them and the central government, is typically constitutionally entrenched and may not be altered by a unilateral decision of either party, the states or the federal political body. Alternatively, federation is a form of government in which sovereign power is formally divided between a central authority and a number of constituent regions so that each region retains some degree of control over its internal affairs. It is often argued that federal states where the central government has the constitutional authority to suspend a constituent state's government by invoking gross mismanagement or civil unrest, or to adopt national legislation that overrides or infringe on the constituent states' powers by invoking the central government's constitutional authority to ensure "peace and good government" or to implement obligations contracted under an international treaty, are not truly federal states.

Exam Probability: **Medium**

42. *Answer choices:*

(see index for correct answer)

- a. Federal government
- b. process perspective
- c. surface-level diversity
- d. information systems assessment

Guidance: level 1

:: ::

A _____, or trial by jury, is a lawful proceeding in which a jury makes a decision or findings of fact. It is distinguished from a bench trial in which a judge or panel of judges makes all decisions.

Exam Probability: **Low**

43. *Answer choices:*

(see index for correct answer)

- a. Jury Trial
- b. interpersonal communication
- c. hierarchical perspective
- d. similarity-attraction theory

Guidance: level 1

:: ::

A _____ loan or, simply, _____ is used either by purchasers of real property to raise funds to buy real estate, or alternatively by existing property owners to raise funds for any purpose, while putting a lien on the property being _____ d. The loan is "secured" on the borrower's property through a process known as _____ origination. This means that a legal mechanism is put into place which allows the lender to take possession and sell the secured property to pay off the loan in the event the borrower defaults on the loan or otherwise fails to abide by its terms. The word _____ is derived from a Law French term used in Britain in the Middle Ages meaning "death pledge" and refers to the pledge ending when either the obligation is fulfilled or the property is taken through foreclosure. A _____ can also be described as "a borrower giving consideration in the form of a collateral for a benefit ".

Exam Probability: **High**

44. Answer choices:

(see index for correct answer)

- a. open system
- b. Mortgage
- c. process perspective
- d. hierarchical

Guidance: level 1

_____ is an insurance that covers the whole or a part of the risk of a person incurring medical expenses, spreading the risk over a large number of persons. By estimating the overall risk of health care and health system expenses over the risk pool, an insurer can develop a routine finance structure, such as a monthly premium or payroll tax, to provide the money to pay for the health care benefits specified in the insurance agreement. The benefit is administered by a central organization such as a government agency, private business, or not-for-profit entity.

Exam Probability: **Medium**

45. *Answer choices:*

(see index for correct answer)

- a. corporate values
- b. imperative
- c. Character
- d. Health insurance

Guidance: level 1

:: Clauses of the United States Constitution ::

The _____ describes an enumerated power listed in the United States Constitution. The clause states that the United States Congress shall have power "To regulate Commerce with foreign Nations, and among the several States, and with the Indian Tribes." Courts and commentators have tended to discuss each of these three areas of commerce as a separate power granted to Congress. It is common to see the individual components of the _____ referred to under specific terms: the Foreign _____, the Interstate _____, and the Indian _____.

Exam Probability: **Low**

46. *Answer choices:*

(see index for correct answer)

- a. Double Jeopardy Clause
- b. Full faith and credit
- c. Commerce Clause

Guidance: level 1

:: ::

_____ is the administration of an organization, whether it is a business, a not-for-profit organization, or government body. _____ includes the activities of setting the strategy of an organization and coordinating the efforts of its employees to accomplish its objectives through the application of available resources, such as financial, natural, technological, and human resources. The term "_____" may also refer to those people who manage an organization.

Exam Probability: **Low**

47. *Answer choices:*

(see index for correct answer)

- a. process perspective
- b. surface-level diversity
- c. Management
- d. empathy

Guidance: level 1

:: United States federal public corruption crime ::

Mail fraud and _____ are federal crimes in the United States that involve mailing or electronically transmitting something associated with fraud. Jurisdiction is claimed by the federal government if the illegal activity crosses interstate or international borders.

Exam Probability: **Low**

48. *Answer choices:*

(see index for correct answer)

- a. RICO Act
- b. Racketeer Influenced and Corrupt Organizations Act

Guidance: level 1

:: Real property law ::

> _____ , sometimes colloquially described as 'squatter's rights', is a legal principle under which a person who does not have legal title to a piece of property—usually land—acquires legal ownership based on continuous possession or occupation of the land without the permission of its legal owner.

Exam Probability: **Low**

49. *Answer choices:*

(see index for correct answer)

- a. Contract for deed
- b. Adverse possession
- c. Deed in lieu of foreclosure
- d. Life estate

Guidance: level 1

:: Debt ::

A _____ is a party that has a claim on the services of a second party. It is a person or institution to whom money is owed. The first party, in general, has provided some property or service to the second party under the assumption that the second party will return an equivalent property and service. The second party is frequently called a debtor or borrower. The first party is called the _____ , which is the lender of property, service, or money.

Exam Probability: **Medium**

50. *Answer choices:*

(see index for correct answer)

- a. Debt crisis
- b. Extendible bond
- c. Paid outside closing
- d. Creditor

Guidance: level 1

:: ::

The _____ is an intergovernmental organization that is concerned with the regulation of international trade between nations. The WTO officially commenced on 1 January 1995 under the Marrakesh Agreement, signed by 124 nations on 15 April 1994, replacing the General Agreement on Tariffs and Trade , which commenced in 1948. It is the largest international economic organization in the world.

Exam Probability: **High**

51. *Answer choices:*

(see index for correct answer)

- a. World Trade Organization
- b. deep-level diversity
- c. co-culture
- d. personal values

Guidance: level 1

:: Business law ::

An _____ is an agreement in which a producer agrees to sell his or her entire production to the buyer, who in turn agrees to purchase the entire output. Example: an almond grower enters into an _____ with an almond packer; thus the producer has a "home" for output of nuts, and the packer of nuts is happy to try the particular product. The converse of this situation is a requirements contract, under which a seller agrees to supply the buyer with as much of a good or service as the buyer wants, in exchange for the buyer`s agreement not to buy that good or service elsewhere.

Exam Probability: **Low**

52. *Answer choices:*

(see index for correct answer)

- a. Business.gov
- b. Output contract
- c. Family and Medical Leave Act of 1993
- d. Double ticketing

Guidance: level 1

:: Monopoly (economics) ::

> _____ is a category of property that includes intangible creations of the human intellect. _____ encompasses two types of rights: industrial property rights and copyright. It was not until the 19th century that the term " _____ " began to be used, and not until the late 20th century that it became commonplace in the majority of the world.

Exam Probability: **High**

53. *Answer choices:*

(see index for correct answer)

- a. Eisenkammer Pirna
- b. Coercive monopoly
- c. Third-party access
- d. Cost per procedure

Guidance: level 1

:: ::

The _____ of 1933, also known as the 1933 Act, the _____, the Truth in _____, the Federal _____, and the `33 Act, was enacted by the United States Congress on May 27, 1933, during the Great Depression, after the stock market crash of 1929. Legislated pursuant to the Interstate Commerce Clause of the Constitution, it requires every offer or sale of securities that uses the means and instrumentalities of interstate commerce to be registered with the SEC pursuant to the 1933 Act, unless an exemption from registration exists under the law. The term "means and instrumentalities of interstate commerce" is extremely broad and it is virtually impossible to avoid the operation of the statute by attempting to offer or sell a security without using an "instrumentality" of interstate commerce. Any use of a telephone, for example, or the mails would probably be enough to subject the transaction to the statute.

Exam Probability: **Low**

54. *Answer choices:*

(see index for correct answer)

- a. surface-level diversity
- b. imperative
- c. Securities Act
- d. information systems assessment

Guidance: level 1

:: Insolvency ::

_____ is the state of being unable to pay the money owed, by a person or company, on time; those in a state of _____ are said to be insolvent. There are two forms: cash-flow _____ and balance-sheet _____ .

Exam Probability: **Low**

55. *Answer choices:*

(see index for correct answer)

- a. Conservatorship
- b. Insolvency
- c. Insolvency law of Russia
- d. Financial distress

Guidance: level 1

:: Legal doctrines and principles ::

In law, a _____ is an event sufficiently related to an injury that the courts deem the event to be the cause of that injury. There are two types of causation in the law: cause-in-fact, and proximate cause. Cause-in-fact is determined by the "but for" test: But for the action, the result would not have happened. The action is a necessary condition, but may not be a sufficient condition, for the resulting injury. A few circumstances exist where the but for test is ineffective. Since but-for causation is very easy to show, a second test is used to determine if an action is close enough to a harm in a "chain of events" to be legally valid. This test is called _____. _____ is a key principle of Insurance and is concerned with how the loss or damage actually occurred. There are several competing theories of _____. For an act to be deemed to cause a harm, both tests must be met; _____ is a legal limitation on cause-in-fact.

Exam Probability: **High**

56. *Answer choices:*

(see index for correct answer)

- a. Exclusionary rule
- b. Proximate cause
- c. Mutual mistake
- d. Res ipsa loquitur

Guidance: level 1

:: Writs ::

In common law, a _____ is a formal _____ ten order issued by a body with administrative or judicial jurisdiction; in modern usage, this body is generally a court. Warrants, prerogative _____ s, and subpoenas are common types of _____, but many forms exist and have existed.

Exam Probability: **Medium**

57. *Answer choices:*

(see index for correct answer)

- a. Writ of execution
- b. Qui tam
- c. Writ of assistance

Guidance: level 1

:: ::

A _____ is a person or firm who arranges transactions between a buyer and a seller for a commission when the deal is executed. A _____ who also acts as a seller or as a buyer becomes a principal party to the deal. Neither role should be confused with that of an agent—one who acts on behalf of a principal party in a deal.

Exam Probability: **High**

58. *Answer choices:*

(see index for correct answer)

- a. Broker
- b. levels of analysis
- c. similarity-attraction theory
- d. imperative

Guidance: level 1

The words "_____" and "testify" both derive from the Latin word testis, referring to the notion of a disinterested third-party witness.

Exam Probability: **High**

59. *Answer choices:*

(see index for correct answer)

- a. Testimony
- b. Sarbanes-Oxley act of 2002
- c. similarity-attraction theory
- d. Character

Guidance: level 1

Finance

Finance is a field that is concerned with the allocation (investment) of assets and liabilities over space and time, often under conditions of risk or uncertainty. Finance can also be defined as the science of money management. Participants in the market aim to price assets based on their risk level, fundamental value, and their expected rate of return. Finance can be split into three sub-categories: public finance, corporate finance and personal finance.

:: Asset ::

In financial accounting, an _____ is any resource owned by the business. Anything tangible or intangible that can be owned or controlled to produce value and that is held by a company to produce positive economic value is an _____ . Simply stated, _____ s represent value of ownership that can be converted into cash . The balance sheet of a firm records the monetary value of the _____ s owned by that firm. It covers money and other valuables belonging to an individual or to a business.

Exam Probability: **Medium**

1. *Answer choices:*
(see index for correct answer)

- a. Asset
- b. Current asset

Guidance: level 1

:: bad_topic ::

_____ refers to systematic approach to the governance and realization of value from the things that a group or entity is responsible for, over their whole life cycles. It may apply both to tangible assets and to intangible assets . _____ is a systematic process of developing, operating, maintaining, upgrading, and disposing of assets in the most cost-effective manner .

Exam Probability: **Low**

2. *Answer choices:*

(see index for correct answer)

- a. set model
- b. Asset management
- c. Cognitive neuroscience
- d. LTV Steel

Guidance: level 1

:: ::

_____ focuses on ratios, equities and debts. It is useful for portfolio management,distribution of dividend,capital raising,hedging and looking after fluctuations in foreign currency and product cycles.Financial managers are the people who will do research and based on the research, decide what sort of capital to obtain in order to fund the company's assets as well as maximizing the value of the firm for all the stakeholders. It also refers to the efficient and effective management of money in such a manner as to accomplish the objectives of the organization. It is the specialized function directly associated with the top management. The significance of this function is not seen in the `Line` but also in the capacity of the `Staff` in overall of a company. It has been defined differently by different experts in the field.

Exam Probability: **High**

3. *Answer choices:*

(see index for correct answer)

- a. Financial management
- b. imperative
- c. interpersonal communication
- d. empathy

Guidance: level 1

:: Costs ::

> In economics, _____ is the total economic cost of production and is made up of variable cost, which varies according to the quantity of a good produced and includes inputs such as labour and raw materials, plus fixed cost, which is independent of the quantity of a good produced and includes inputs that cannot be varied in the short term: fixed costs such as buildings and machinery, including sunk costs if any. Since cost is measured per unit of time, it is a flow variable.

Exam Probability: **Medium**

4. *Answer choices:*
(see index for correct answer)

- a. Cost per paper
- b. Total cost
- c. Prospective costs
- d. Cost reduction

Guidance: level 1

:: Asset ::

_____ s, also known as tangible assets or property, plant and equipment, is a term used in accounting for assets and property that cannot easily be converted into cash. This can be compared with current assets such as cash or bank accounts, described as liquid assets. In most cases, only tangible assets are referred to as fixed. IAS 16 defines _____ s as assets whose future economic benefit is probable to flow into the entity, whose cost can be measured reliably. _____ s belong to one of 2 types:"Freehold Assets" – assets which are purchased with legal right of ownership and used,and "Leasehold Assets" – assets used by owner without legal right for a particular period of time.

Exam Probability: **Low**

5. *Answer choices:*

(see index for correct answer)

- a. Fixed asset
- b. Asset

Guidance: level 1

:: Scheduling (computing) ::

Ageing or _____ is the process of becoming older. The term refers especially to human beings, many animals, and fungi, whereas for example bacteria, perennial plants and some simple animals are potentially biologically immortal. In the broader sense, ageing can refer to single cells within an organism which have ceased dividing or to the population of a species.

Exam Probability: **Low**

6. *Answer choices:*

(see index for correct answer)

- a. Aging
- b. Run queue
- c. Light-weight process
- d. Notation for theoretic scheduling problems

Guidance: level 1

:: Stock market ::

_____ or stock market launch is a type of public offering in which shares of a company are sold to institutional investors and usually also retail investors; an IPO is underwritten by one or more investment banks, who also arrange for the shares to be listed on one or more stock exchanges. Through this process, colloquially known as floating, or going public, a privately held company is transformed into a public company. _____ s can be used: to raise new equity capital for the company concerned; to monetize the investments of private shareholders such as company founders or private equity investors; and to enable easy trading of existing holdings or future capital raising by becoming publicly traded enterprises.

Exam Probability: **Low**

7. *Answer choices:*

(see index for correct answer)

- a. Lock-up period
- b. Prime Standard
- c. General Standard
- d. International Retail Service

Guidance: level 1

:: Generally Accepted Accounting Principles ::

Expenditure is an outflow of money to another person or group to pay for an item or service, or for a category of costs. For a tenant, rent is an _____ . For students or parents, tuition is an _____ . Buying food, clothing, furniture or an automobile is often referred to as an _____ . An _____ is a cost that is "paid" or "remitted", usually in exchange for something of value. Something that seems to cost a great deal is "expensive". Something that seems to cost little is "inexpensive". "_____ s of the table" are _____ s of dining, refreshments, a feast, etc.

Exam Probability: **Medium**

8. *Answer choices:*

(see index for correct answer)

- a. Provision
- b. Expense
- c. Cost principle
- d. Gross profit

Guidance: level 1

:: ::

_____ is the process of making predictions of the future based on past and present data and most commonly by analysis of trends. A commonplace example might be estimation of some variable of interest at some specified future date. Prediction is a similar, but more general term. Both might refer to formal statistical methods employing time series, cross-sectional or longitudinal data, or alternatively to less formal judgmental methods. Usage can differ between areas of application: for example, in hydrology the terms "forecast" and "_____" are sometimes reserved for estimates of values at certain specific future times, while the term "prediction" is used for more general estimates, such as the number of times floods will occur over a long period.

Exam Probability: **High**

9. *Answer choices:*

(see index for correct answer)

- a. functional perspective
- b. Sarbanes-Oxley act of 2002
- c. Forecasting
- d. process perspective

Guidance: level 1

:: Generally Accepted Accounting Principles ::

_____, or non-current liabilities, are liabilities that are due beyond a year or the normal operation period of the company. The normal operation period is the amount of time it takes for a company to turn inventory into cash. On a classified balance sheet, liabilities are separated between current and _____ to help users assess the company's financial standing in short-term and long-term periods. _____ give users more information about the long-term prosperity of the company, while current liabilities inform the user of debt that the company owes in the current period. On a balance sheet, accounts are listed in order of liquidity, so _____ come after current liabilities. In addition, the specific long-term liability accounts are listed on the balance sheet in order of liquidity. Therefore, an account due within eighteen months would be listed before an account due within twenty-four months. Examples of _____ are bonds payable, long-term loans, capital leases, pension liabilities, post-retirement healthcare liabilities, deferred compensation, deferred revenues, deferred income taxes, and derivative liabilities.

Exam Probability: **Medium**

10. *Answer choices:*

(see index for correct answer)

- a. Fixed investment
- b. Deferred income
- c. Long-term liabilities
- d. Engagement letter

Guidance: level 1

:: Manufacturing ::

_____ costs are all manufacturing costs that are related to the cost object but cannot be traced to that cost object in an economically feasible way.

Exam Probability: **High**

11. *Answer choices:*

(see index for correct answer)

- a. Dimensional metrology
- b. ISA-88
- c. Automated guided vehicle
- d. Manufacturing overhead

Guidance: level 1

:: Finance ::

A _____ , publicly-traded company, publicly-held company, publicly-listed company, or public limited company is a corporation whose ownership is dispersed among the general public in many shares of stock which are freely traded on a stock exchange or in over-the-counter markets. In some jurisdictions, public companies over a certain size must be listed on an exchange. A _____ can be listed or unlisted.

Exam Probability: **Low**

12. *Answer choices:*

(see index for correct answer)

- a. Debt capital
- b. Isoelastic utility
- c. SIMPLE Group
- d. Public company

Guidance: level 1

:: Accounting ::

_____ is a process of providing relief to shared service organization's cost centers that provide a product or service. In turn, the associated expense is assigned to internal clients' cost centers that consume the products and services. For example, the CIO may provide all IT services within the company and assign the costs back to the business units that consume each offering.

Exam Probability: **Medium**

13. *Answer choices:*

(see index for correct answer)

- a. Cost allocation
- b. Earnings surprise
- c. Teeming and lading
- d. AICPA Code of Professional Conduct

Guidance: level 1

:: Elementary geometry ::

The _____ is the front of an animal's head that features three of the head's sense organs, the eyes, nose, and mouth, and through which animals express many of their emotions. The _____ is crucial for human identity, and damage such as scarring or developmental deformities affects the psyche adversely.

Exam Probability: **Medium**

14. *Answer choices:*
(see index for correct answer)

- a. Face
- b. Equidistant
- c. Centre
- d. Multilateration

Guidance: level 1

:: Financial risk ::

_____ is any of various types of risk associated with financing, including financial transactions that include company loans in risk of default. Often it is understood to include only downside risk, meaning the potential for financial loss and uncertainty about its extent.

Exam Probability: **High**

15. *Answer choices:*

(see index for correct answer)

- a. Principled reasoning
- b. Expected return
- c. Financial risk
- d. Concentration risk

Guidance: level 1

:: Accounting terminology ::

In management accounting or _____ , managers use the provisions of accounting information in order to better inform themselves before they decide matters within their organizations, which aids their management and performance of control functions.

Exam Probability: **Medium**

16. *Answer choices:*

(see index for correct answer)

- a. Accounts payable
- b. Managerial accounting
- c. Fair value accounting
- d. Absorption costing

Guidance: level 1

:: Money ::

Cash and _____ s are the most liquid current assets found on a business's balance sheet. _____ s are short-term commitments "with temporarily idle cash and easily convertible into a known cash amount". An investment normally counts to be a _____ when it has a short maturity period of 90 days or less, and can be included in the cash and _____ s balance from the date of acquisition when it carries an insignificant risk of changes in the asset value; with more than 90 days maturity, the asset is not considered as cash and _____ s. Equity investments mostly are excluded from _____ s, unless they are essentially _____ s, for instance, if the preferred shares acquired within a short maturity period and with specified recovery date.

Exam Probability: **Medium**

17. *Answer choices:*

(see index for correct answer)

- a. Coin of account

- b. Cash equivalent
- c. Monetization
- d. Chained dollars

Guidance: level 1

:: Global systemically important banks ::

The _____ Corporation is an American multinational investment bank and financial services company based in Charlotte, North Carolina with central hubs in New York City, London, Hong Kong, Minneapolis, and Toronto. _____ was formed through NationsBank's acquisition of BankAmerica in 1998. It is the second largest banking institution in the United States, after JP Morgan Chase. As a part of the Big Four, it services approximately 10.73% of all American bank deposits, in direct competition with Citigroup, Wells Fargo, and JPMorgan Chase. Its primary financial services revolve around commercial banking, wealth management, and investment banking.

Exam Probability: **High**

18. *Answer choices:*

(see index for correct answer)

- a. UniCredit
- b. State Street Corporation
- c. Bank of America
- d. ING Group

Guidance: level 1

:: Debt ::

A _____ is a monetary amount owed to a creditor that is unlikely to be paid and, or which the creditor is not willing to take action to collect for various reasons, often due to the debtor not having the money to pay, for example due to a company going into liquidation or insolvency. There are various technical definitions of what constitutes a _____, depending on accounting conventions, regulatory treatment and the institution provisioning. In the USA, bank loans with more than ninety days' arrears become "problem loans". Accounting sources advise that the full amount of a _____ be written off to the profit and loss account or a provision for _____s as soon as it is foreseen.

Exam Probability: **Medium**

19. *Answer choices:*

(see index for correct answer)

- a. Default
- b. Odious debt
- c. Bad debt
- d. Credit cycle

Guidance: level 1

:: Manufacturing ::

_____s are goods that have completed the manufacturing process but have not yet been sold or distributed to the end user.

Exam Probability: **Low**

20. *Answer choices:*

(see index for correct answer)

- a. AGO system
- b. Telecommunications equipment
- c. OMAC
- d. Finished good

Guidance: level 1

:: Business economics ::

A _____ is a term used primarily in cost accounting to describe something to which costs are assigned. Common examples of _____s are: product lines, geographic territories, customers, departments or anything else for which management would like to quantify cost.

Exam Probability: **High**

21. *Answer choices:*

(see index for correct answer)

- a. Units of transportation measurement
- b. Inclusive business finance
- c. Nonprofit studies
- d. Cost object

Guidance: level 1

:: ::

_____ , often abbreviated as B/E in finance, is the point of balance making neither a profit nor a loss. The term originates in finance but the concept has been applied in other fields.

Exam Probability: **Low**

22. *Answer choices:*
(see index for correct answer)

- a. process perspective
- b. hierarchical perspective
- c. surface-level diversity
- d. co-culture

Guidance: level 1

:: Financial ratios ::

_____ is the difference between revenue and cost of goods sold divided by revenue. _____ is expressed as a percentage. Generally, it is calculated as the selling price of an item, less the cost of goods sold.
_____ is often used interchangeably with Gross Profit, but the terms are different. When speaking about a monetary amount, it is technically correct to use the term Gross Profit; when referring to a percentage or ratio, it is correct to use _____. In other words, _____ is a percentage value, while Gross Profit is a monetary value.

Exam Probability: **High**

23. *Answer choices:*

(see index for correct answer)

- a. Cash conversion cycle
- b. Expense ratio
- c. Days sales outstanding
- d. Gross margin

Guidance: level 1

:: ::

In production, research, retail, and accounting, a _____ is the value of money that has been used up to produce something or deliver a service, and hence is not available for use anymore. In business, the _____ may be one of acquisition, in which case the amount of money expended to acquire it is counted as _____. In this case, money is the input that is gone in order to acquire the thing. This acquisition _____ may be the sum of the _____ of production as incurred by the original producer, and further _____ s of transaction as incurred by the acquirer over and above the price paid to the producer. Usually, the price also includes a mark-up for profit over the _____ of production.

Exam Probability: **Medium**

24. *Answer choices:*

(see index for correct answer)

- a. personal values
- b. interpersonal communication
- c. levels of analysis
- d. Cost

Guidance: level 1

:: Costs ::

In microeconomic theory, the _____, or alternative cost, of making a particular choice is the value of the most valuable choice out of those that were not taken. In other words, opportunity that will require sacrifices.

Exam Probability: **Medium**

25. *Answer choices:*

(see index for correct answer)

- a. Further processing cost
- b. Incremental cost-effectiveness ratio
- c. Psychic cost
- d. Opportunity cost

Guidance: level 1

:: Derivatives (finance) ::

A _____ or _____ row is a line of closely spaced shrubs and sometimes trees, planted and trained to form a barrier or to mark the boundary of an area, such as between neighbouring properties. _____ s used to separate a road from adjoining fields or one field from another, and of sufficient age to incorporate larger trees, are known as _____ rows. Often they serve as windbreaks to improve conditions for the adjacent crops, as in bocage country. When clipped and maintained, _____ s are also a simple form of topiary.

Exam Probability: **Medium**

26. *Answer choices:*

(see index for correct answer)

- a. Hedge
- b. STIRT
- c. Iron butterfly
- d. underlying

Guidance: level 1

:: Mathematical finance ::

_____ is the value of an asset at a specific date. It measures the nominal future sum of money that a given sum of money is "worth" at a specified time in the future assuming a certain interest rate, or more generally, rate of return; it is the present value multiplied by the accumulation function. The value does not include corrections for inflation or other factors that affect the true value of money in the future. This is used in time value of money calculations.

Exam Probability: **High**

27. *Answer choices:*

(see index for correct answer)

- a. Econophysics
- b. Volatility risk premium
- c. Malliavin calculus
- d. AZFinText

Guidance: level 1

:: ::

In finance, return is a profit on an investment. It comprises any change in value of the investment, and/or cash flows which the investor receives from the investment, such as interest payments or dividends. It may be measured either in absolute terms or as a percentage of the amount invested. The latter is also called the holding period return.

Exam Probability: **High**

28. *Answer choices:*

(see index for correct answer)

- a. functional perspective
- b. Sarbanes-Oxley act of 2002
- c. Rate of return
- d. hierarchical perspective

Guidance: level 1

:: Accounting in the United States ::

_____ is the title of qualified accountants in numerous countries in the English-speaking world. In the United States, the CPA is a license to provide accounting services to the public. It is awarded by each of the 50 states for practice in that state. Additionally, almost every state has passed mobility laws to allow CPAs from other states to practice in their state. State licensing requirements vary, but the minimum standard requirements include passing the Uniform _____ Examination, 150 semester units of college education, and one year of accounting related experience.

Exam Probability: **High**

29. *Answer choices:*

(see index for correct answer)

- a. Other postemployment benefits
- b. Certified Government Financial Manager
- c. Certified Public Accountant
- d. Accounting Research Bulletins

Guidance: level 1

:: Accounting terminology ::

_____ or capital expense is the money a company spends to buy, maintain, or improve its fixed assets, such as buildings, vehicles, equipment, or land. It is considered a _____ when the asset is newly purchased or when money is used towards extending the useful life of an existing asset, such as repairing the roof.

Exam Probability: **High**

30. *Answer choices:*

(see index for correct answer)

- a. Accrued liabilities
- b. Share premium
- c. Accounts payable
- d. Basis of accounting

Guidance: level 1

:: Management accounting ::

_____ accounting is a traditional cost accounting method introduced in the 1920s, as an alternative for the traditional cost accounting method based on historical costs.

Exam Probability: **High**

31. *Answer choices:*

(see index for correct answer)

- a. Relevant cost
- b. Chartered Cost Accountant
- c. Standard cost
- d. Hedge accounting

Guidance: level 1

:: Currency ::

A _____ , in the most specific sense is money in any form when in use or circulation as a medium of exchange, especially circulating banknotes and coins. A more general definition is that a _____ is a system of money in common use, especially for people in a nation. Under this definition, US dollars, pounds sterling, Australian dollars, European euros, Russian rubles and Indian Rupees are examples of currencies. These various currencies are recognized as stores of value and are traded between nations in foreign exchange markets, which determine the relative values of the different currencies. Currencies in this sense are defined by governments, and each type has limited boundaries of acceptance.

Exam Probability: **Medium**

32. *Answer choices:*

(see index for correct answer)

- a. Demurrage
- b. Currency
- c. Unit of account
- d. Functional currency

Guidance: level 1

:: ::

_____ is a marketing communication that employs an openly sponsored, non-personal message to promote or sell a product, service or idea. Sponsors of _____ are typically businesses wishing to promote their products or services. _____ is differentiated from public relations in that an advertiser pays for and has control over the message. It differs from personal selling in that the message is non-personal, i.e., not directed to a particular individual. _____ is communicated through various mass media, including traditional media such as newspapers, magazines, television, radio, outdoor _____ or direct mail; and new media such as search results, blogs, social media, websites or text messages. The actual presentation of the message in a medium is referred to as an advertisement, or "ad" or advert for short.

Exam Probability: **Medium**

33. *Answer choices:*

(see index for correct answer)

- a. cultural
- b. Advertising
- c. imperative
- d. co-culture

Guidance: level 1

:: Money market instruments ::

_____ , in the global financial market, is an unsecured promissory note with a fixed maturity of not more than 270 days.

Exam Probability: **Medium**

34. *Answer choices:*

(see index for correct answer)

- a. Commercial paper
- b. Banker's acceptance

Guidance: level 1

:: ::

A _____ loan or, simply, _____ is used either by purchasers of real property to raise funds to buy real estate, or alternatively by existing property owners to raise funds for any purpose, while putting a lien on the property being _____ d. The loan is "secured" on the borrower's property through a process known as _____ origination. This means that a legal mechanism is put into place which allows the lender to take possession and sell the secured property to pay off the loan in the event the borrower defaults on the loan or otherwise fails to abide by its terms. The word _____ is derived from a Law French term used in Britain in the Middle Ages meaning "death pledge" and refers to the pledge ending when either the obligation is fulfilled or the property is taken through foreclosure. A _____ can also be described as "a borrower giving consideration in the form of a collateral for a benefit ".

Exam Probability: **Low**

35. *Answer choices:*

(see index for correct answer)

- a. co-culture
- b. cultural
- c. personal values
- d. hierarchical perspective

Guidance: level 1

:: Global systemically important banks ::

_____ Inc. or Citi is an American multinational investment bank and financial services corporation headquartered in New York City. The company was formed by the merger of banking giant Citicorp and financial conglomerate Travelers Group in 1998; Travelers was subsequently spun off from the company in 2002. _____ owns Citicorp, the holding company for Citibank, as well as several international subsidiaries.

Exam Probability: **Medium**

36. *Answer choices:*

(see index for correct answer)

- a. Citigroup
- b. Barclays
- c. Sumitomo Mitsui Banking Corporation
- d. Banco Bilbao Vizcaya Argentaria

Guidance: level 1

:: Pharmaceutical industry ::

A _____ is a document in which data collected for a clinical trial is first recorded. This data is usually later entered in the case report form. The International Conference on Harmonisation of Technical Requirements for Registration of Pharmaceuticals for Human Use guidelines define _____ s as "original documents, data, and records." _____ s contain source data, which is defined as "all information in original records and certified copies of original records of clinical findings, observations, or other activities in a clinical trial necessary for the reconstruction and evaluation of the trial."

Exam Probability: **Low**

37. *Answer choices:*
(see index for correct answer)

- a. Derwent Drug File
- b. Source document
- c. Microextrusion
- d. Tablet

Guidance: level 1

:: Management ::

The _____ is a strategy performance management tool – a semi-standard structured report, that can be used by managers to keep track of the execution of activities by the staff within their control and to monitor the consequences arising from these actions.

Exam Probability: **Low**

38. *Answer choices:*

(see index for correct answer)

- a. Executive compensation
- b. Unified interoperability
- c. Balanced scorecard
- d. Formula for change

Guidance: level 1

:: Generally Accepted Accounting Principles ::

_____ is the accounting classification of an account. It is part of double-entry book-keeping technique.

Exam Probability: **Low**

39. *Answer choices:*

(see index for correct answer)

- a. Generally accepted accounting principles
- b. Cost principle
- c. Normal balance
- d. Fixed investment

Guidance: level 1

:: Management accounting ::

> _____ is the process of recording, classifying, analyzing, summarizing, and allocating costs associated with a process, after that developing various courses of action to control the costs. Its goal is to advise the management on how to optimize business practices and processes based on cost efficiency and capability. _____ provides the detailed cost information that management needs to control current operations and plan for the future.

Exam Probability: **High**

40. *Answer choices:*

(see index for correct answer)

- a. Investment center
- b. Customer profitability
- c. Hedge accounting
- d. Management accounting

Guidance: level 1

:: Public finance ::

_____ is the process by which the monetary authority of a country, typically the central bank or currency board, controls either the cost of very short-term borrowing or the money supply, often targeting inflation rate or interest rate to ensure price stability and general trust in the currency.

Exam Probability: **Low**

41. *Answer choices:*

(see index for correct answer)

- a. Sovereign credit
- b. Preference revelation
- c. Right-financing
- d. Fiscal incidence

Guidance: level 1

:: Government bonds ::

A _____ or sovereign bond is a bond issued by a national government, generally with a promise to pay periodic interest payments called coupon payments and to repay the face value on the maturity date. The aim of a _____ is to support government spending. _____ s are usually denominated in the country's own currency, in which case the government cannot be forced to default, although it may choose to do so. If a government is close to default on its debt the media often refer to this as a sovereign debt crisis.

Exam Probability: **Medium**

42. *Answer choices:*

(see index for correct answer)

- a. Government bond
- b. Eurobonds
- c. Risk-free bond
- d. Gilt-edged

Guidance: level 1

:: Budgets ::

A _____ is a financial plan for a defined period, often one year. It may also include planned sales volumes and revenues, resource quantities, costs and expenses, assets, liabilities and cash flows. Companies, governments, families and other organizations use it to express strategic plans of activities or events in measurable terms.

Exam Probability: **High**

43. *Answer choices:*

(see index for correct answer)

- a. Budgeted cost of work scheduled
- b. Budget
- c. Budget constraint
- d. Marginal budgeting for bottlenecks

Guidance: level 1

:: Financial risk ::

The _____ on a financial investment is the expected value of its return. It is a measure of the center of the distribution of the random variable that is the return.

Exam Probability: **High**

44. *Answer choices:*

(see index for correct answer)

- a. Dynamic risk measure
- b. Operational risk management
- c. Credit scorecards
- d. Expected return

Guidance: level 1

:: ::

In financial markets, a share is a unit used as mutual funds, limited partnerships, and real estate investment trusts. The owner of _____ in the corporation/company is a shareholder of the corporation. A share is an indivisible unit of capital, expressing the ownership relationship between the company and the shareholder. The denominated value of a share is its face value, and the total of the face value of issued _____ represent the capital of a company, which may not reflect the market value of those _____ .

Exam Probability: **High**

45. *Answer choices:*

(see index for correct answer)

- a. Sarbanes-Oxley act of 2002
- b. Shares
- c. open system
- d. empathy

Guidance: level 1

:: Valuation (finance) ::

_____ refers to an assessment of the viability, stability, and profitability of a business, sub-business or project.

Exam Probability: **Low**

46. *Answer choices:*

(see index for correct answer)

- a. Loan modification
- b. Residual income valuation
- c. Financial analysis
- d. Investment value

Guidance: level 1

:: Generally Accepted Accounting Principles ::

The first published description of the process is found in Luca Pacioli's 1494 work Summa de arithmetica, in the section titled Particularis de Computis et Scripturis. Although he did not use the term, he essentially prescribed a technique similar to a post-closing _____ .

Exam Probability: **Low**

47. *Answer choices:*

(see index for correct answer)

- a. Normal balance
- b. Revenue recognition
- c. Trial balance
- d. Earnings before interest, taxes, depreciation, and amortization

Guidance: level 1

:: Business law ::

A _____, also known as the sole trader, individual entrepreneurship or proprietorship, is a type of enterprise that is owned and run by one person and in which there is no legal distinction between the owner and the business entity. A sole trader does not necessarily work `alone`—it is possible for the sole trader to employ other people.

Exam Probability: **High**

48. *Answer choices:*

(see index for correct answer)

- a. Official Assignee
- b. Forged endorsement
- c. Companies Acts
- d. Sole proprietorship

Guidance: level 1

:: Generally Accepted Accounting Principles ::

In business and accounting, _____ is an entity's income minus cost of goods sold, expenses and taxes for an accounting period. It is computed as the residual of all revenues and gains over all expenses and losses for the period, and has also been defined as the net increase in shareholders' equity that results from a company's operations. In the context of the presentation of financial statements, the IFRS Foundation defines _____ as synonymous with profit and loss. The difference between revenue and the cost of making a product or providing a service, before deducting overheads, payroll, taxation, and interest payments. This is different from operating income.

Exam Probability: **Medium**

49. *Answer choices:*

(see index for correct answer)

- a. Write-off
- b. Net income
- c. Operating profit
- d. Deferral

Guidance: level 1

:: Bonds (finance) ::

In finance, a _____ or convertible note or convertible debt is a type of bond that the holder can convert into a specified number of shares of common stock in the issuing company or cash of equal value. It is a hybrid security with debt- and equity-like features. It originated in the mid-19th century, and was used by early speculators such as Jacob Little and Daniel Drew to counter market cornering.

Exam Probability: **Low**

50. *Answer choices:*

(see index for correct answer)

- a. Convertible bond
- b. Recovery swap
- c. General obligation bond
- d. Bond credit rating

Guidance: level 1

:: ::

The U.S. _____ is an independent agency of the United States federal government. The SEC holds primary responsibility for enforcing the federal securities laws, proposing securities rules, and regulating the securities industry, the nation's stock and options exchanges, and other activities and organizations, including the electronic securities markets in the United States.

Exam Probability: **Medium**

51. *Answer choices:*

(see index for correct answer)

- a. hierarchical
- b. cultural
- c. functional perspective
- d. Securities and Exchange Commission

Guidance: level 1

:: International Financial Reporting Standards ::

_____, usually called IFRS, are standards issued by the IFRS Foundation and the International Accounting Standards Board to provide a common global language for business affairs so that company accounts are understandable and comparable across international boundaries. They are a consequence of growing international shareholding and trade and are particularly important for companies that have dealings in several countries. They are progressively replacing the many different national accounting standards. They are the rules to be followed by accountants to maintain books of accounts which are comparable, understandable, reliable and relevant as per the users internal or external. IFRS, with the exception of IAS 29 Financial Reporting in Hyperinflationary Economies and IFRIC 7 Applying the Restatement Approach under IAS 29, are authorized in terms of the historical cost paradigm. IAS 29 and IFRIC 7 are authorized in terms of the units of constant purchasing power paradigm.IAS 2 is related to inventories in this standard we talk about the stock its production process etcIFRS began as an attempt to harmonize accounting across the European Union but the value of harmonization quickly made the concept attractive around the world. However, it has been debated whether or not de facto harmonization has occurred. Standards that were issued by IASC are still within use today and go by the name International Accounting Standards , while standards issued by IASB are called IFRS. IAS were issued between 1973 and 2001 by the Board of the International Accounting Standards Committee . On 1 April 2001, the new International Accounting Standards Board took over from the IASC the responsibility for setting International Accounting Standards. During its first meeting the new Board adopted existing IAS and Standing Interpretations Committee standards . The IASB has continued to develop standards calling the new standards " _____ ".

Exam Probability: **Medium**

52. *Answer choices:*

(see index for correct answer)

- a. IAS 37
- b. IFRS Foundation
- c. IFRS 2

- d. International Financial Reporting Standards

Guidance: level 1

:: Accounting in the United States ::

The _____ is a private-sector, nonprofit corporation created by the Sarbanes–Oxley Act of 2002 to oversee the audits of public companies and other issuers in order to protect the interests of investors and further the public interest in the preparation of informative, accurate and independent audit reports. The PCAOB also oversees the audits of broker-dealers, including compliance reports filed pursuant to federal securities laws, to promote investor protection. All PCAOB rules and standards must be approved by the U.S. Securities and Exchange Commission .

Exam Probability: **Low**

53. *Answer choices:*

(see index for correct answer)

- a. Federal Accounting Standards Advisory Board
- b. Financial Accounting Foundation
- c. Governmental Accounting Standards Board
- d. Public Company Accounting Oversight Board

Guidance: level 1

:: ::

An _____ is an asset that lacks physical substance. It is defined in opposition to physical assets such as machinery and buildings. An _____ is usually very hard to evaluate. Patents, copyrights, franchises, goodwill, trademarks, and trade names. The general interpretation also includes software and other intangible computer based assets are all examples of _____ s. _____ s generally—though not necessarily—suffer from typical market failures of non-rivalry and non-excludability.

Exam Probability: **High**

54. *Answer choices:*

(see index for correct answer)

- a. Sarbanes-Oxley act of 2002
- b. deep-level diversity
- c. Intangible asset
- d. functional perspective

Guidance: level 1

:: Business law ::

A _____ is a group of people who jointly supervise the activities of an organization, which can be either a for-profit business, nonprofit organization, or a government agency. Such a board's powers, duties, and responsibilities are determined by government regulations and the organization's own constitution and bylaws. These authorities may specify the number of members of the board, how they are to be chosen, and how often they are to meet.

Exam Probability: **Low**

55. *Answer choices:*
(see index for correct answer)

- a. Board of directors
- b. Personal Property Security Act
- c. Rules of origin
- d. Financial Security Law of France

Guidance: level 1

:: Management ::

_____ is the identification, evaluation, and prioritization of risks followed by coordinated and economical application of resources to minimize, monitor, and control the probability or impact of unfortunate events or to maximize the realization of opportunities.

Exam Probability: **Medium**

56. Answer choices:

(see index for correct answer)

- a. Topple rate
- b. Organizational space
- c. Community-based management
- d. Customer Benefit Package

Guidance: level 1

:: Marketing ::

_____ is a financial mechanism in which a debtor obtains the right to delay payments to a creditor, for a defined period of time, in exchange for a charge or fee. Essentially, the party that owes money in the present purchases the right to delay the payment until some future date. The discount, or charge, is the difference between the original amount owed in the present and the amount that has to be paid in the future to settle the debt.

Exam Probability: **Low**

57. Answer choices:

(see index for correct answer)

- a. Lead management
- b. Concept testing
- c. Digital strategy
- d. Gift suite

Guidance: level 1

:: Accounting journals and ledgers ::

A _____, in accounting, is the logging of a transaction in an accounting journal that shows a company's debit and credit balances. The _____ can consist of several recordings, each of which is either a debit or a credit. The total of the debits must equal the total of the credits or the _____ is considered unbalanced. Journal entries can record unique items or recurring items such as depreciation or bond amortization. In accounting software, journal entries are usually entered using a separate module from accounts payable, which typically has its own subledger, that indirectly affects the general ledger. As a result, journal entries directly change the account balances on the general ledger. A properly documented _____ consists of the correct date, amount that will be debited, amount that will be credited, description of transaction, and unique reference number .

Exam Probability: **High**

58. *Answer choices:*

(see index for correct answer)

- a. Sales journal
- b. General journal
- c. Cash receipts journal
- d. Journal entry

Guidance: level 1

:: Project management ::

Some scenarios associate "this kind of planning" with learning "life skills". _____s are necessary, or at least useful, in situations where individuals need to know what time they must be at a specific location to receive a specific service, and where people need to accomplish a set of goals within a set time period.

Exam Probability: **High**

59. *Answer choices:*

(see index for correct answer)

- a. Project planning
- b. Elemental cost planning
- c. Schedule
- d. Participatory impact pathways analysis

Guidance: level 1

Human resource management

Human resource (HR) management is the strategic approach to the effective management of organization workers so that they help the business gain a competitive advantage. It is designed to maximize employee performance in service of an employer's strategic objectives. HR is primarily concerned with the management of people within organizations, focusing on policies and on systems. HR departments are responsible for overseeing employee-benefits design, employee recruitment, training and development, performance appraisal, and rewarding (e.g., managing pay and benefit systems). HR also concerns itself with organizational change and industrial relations, that is, the balancing of organizational practices with requirements arising from collective bargaining and from governmental laws.

:: Human resource management ::

_____ assesses whether a person performs a job well. _____, studied academically as part of industrial and organizational psychology, also forms a part of human resources management. Performance is an important criterion for organizational outcomes and success. John P. Campbell describes _____ as an individual-level variable, or something a single person does. This differentiates it from more encompassing constructs such as organizational performance or national performance, which are higher-level variables.

Exam Probability: **High**

1. *Answer choices:*
(see index for correct answer)

- a. Vendor on premises
- b. Salary
- c. Job performance
- d. Job knowledge

Guidance: level 1

:: Management ::

A _____ is a method or technique that has been generally accepted as superior to any alternatives because it produces results that are superior to those achieved by other means or because it has become a standard way of doing things, e.g., a standard way of complying with legal or ethical requirements.

Exam Probability: **Low**

2. *Answer choices:*

(see index for correct answer)

- a. Shrinkage
- b. Productive efficiency
- c. Porter five forces analysis
- d. Best practice

Guidance: level 1

:: ::

A _____ contract is a form of employment that carries fewer hours per week than a full-time job. They work in shifts. The shifts are often rotational. Workers are considered to be _____ if they commonly work fewer than 30 hours per week. According to the International Labour Organization, the number of _____ workers has increased from one-fourth to a half in the past 20 years in most developed countries, excluding the United States. There are many reasons for working _____ , including the desire to do so, having one's hours cut back by an employer and being unable to find a full-time job. The International Labour Organisation Convention 175 requires that _____ workers be treated no less favourably than full-time workers.

Exam Probability: **Low**

3. *Answer choices:*

(see index for correct answer)

- a. cultural
- b. personal values
- c. deep-level diversity
- d. Part-time

Guidance: level 1

:: Human resource management ::

_____ is a method of job analysis that was developed by the Employment and Training Administration of the United States Department of Labor. FJA produces standardized occupational information specific to the performance of the work and the performer.

Exam Probability: **Low**

4. *Answer choices:*

(see index for correct answer)

- a. Training and development
- b. Individual development plan
- c. Management development
- d. Talent management

Guidance: level 1

:: Life skills ::

_____, emotional leadership, emotional quotient and _____ quotient, is the capability of individuals to recognize their own emotions and those of others, discern between different feelings and label them appropriately, use emotional information to guide thinking and behavior, and manage and/or adjust emotions to adapt to environments or achieve one's goal.

Exam Probability: **Low**

5. *Answer choices:*

(see index for correct answer)

- a. Social intelligence
- b. Emotional intelligence
- c. multiple intelligence
- d. emotion work

Guidance: level 1

:: Behaviorism ::

In behavioral psychology, _____ is a consequence applied that will strengthen an organism's future behavior whenever that behavior is preceded by a specific antecedent stimulus. This strengthening effect may be measured as a higher frequency of behavior, longer duration, greater magnitude, or shorter latency. There are two types of _____, known as positive _____ and negative _____; positive is where by a reward is offered on expression of the wanted behaviour and negative is taking away an undesirable element in the persons environment whenever the desired behaviour is achieved.

Exam Probability: **Medium**

6. *Answer choices:*

(see index for correct answer)

- a. social facilitation
- b. Matching Law
- c. contingency management
- d. chaining

Guidance: level 1

:: Working time ::

The shift plan, rota or roster is the central component of a shift schedule in shift work. The schedule includes considerations of shift overlap, shift change times and alignment with the clock, vacation, training, shift differentials, holidays, etc. The shift plan determines the sequence of work and free days within a shift system.

Exam Probability: **High**

7. *Answer choices:*

(see index for correct answer)

- a. Holden v. Hardy
- b. Graveyard shift
- c. Blue laws in the United States
- d. Shift plan

Guidance: level 1

:: Human resource management ::

_____ are transactions in which the ownership of companies, other business organizations, or their operating units are transferred or consolidated with other entities. As an aspect of strategic management, M&A can allow enterprises to grow or downsize, and change the nature of their business or competitive position.

Exam Probability: **High**

8. *Answer choices:*

(see index for correct answer)

- a. T-shaped skills
- b. Training and development

- c. Talascend
- d. Mergers and acquisitions

Guidance: level 1

:: Sexual harassment in the United States ::

In law, a _____, reasonable man, or the man on the Clapham omnibus is a hypothetical person of legal fiction crafted by the courts and communicated through case law and jury instructions.

Exam Probability: **Medium**

9. *Answer choices:*

(see index for correct answer)

- a. Blakey v. Continental Airlines
- b. North Country
- c. Sandy Gallin
- d. Reasonable person

Guidance: level 1

:: Business ethics cases ::

_____, 477 U.S. 57, is a US labor law case, where the United States Supreme Court, in a 9-0 decision, recognized sexual harassment as a violation of Title VII of the Civil Rights Act of 1964. The case was the first of its kind to reach the Supreme Court and would redefine sexual harassment in the workplace.

Exam Probability: **Low**

10. *Answer choices:*

(see index for correct answer)

- a. Sandstorm report
- b. Firestone and Ford tire controversy
- c. Bank of Credit and Commerce International
- d. Libor scandal

Guidance: level 1

:: United States federal labor legislation ::

The _____ of 1967 is a US labor law that forbids employment discrimination against anyone at least 40 years of age in the United States. In 1967, the bill was signed into law by President Lyndon B. Johnson. The ADEA prevents age discrimination and provides equal employment opportunity under conditions that were not explicitly covered in Title VII of the Civil Rights Act of 1964. It also applies to the standards for pensions and benefits provided by employers, and requires that information concerning the needs of older workers be provided to the general public.

Exam Probability: **High**

11. *Answer choices:*

(see index for correct answer)

- a. Reliable Home Heating Act
- b. Federal Emergency Relief Administration
- c. Age Discrimination in Employment Act
- d. Erdman Act

Guidance: level 1

:: Recruitment ::

A _____ is a quantitative research method commonly employed in survey research. The aim of this approach is to ensure that each interview is presented with exactly the same questions in the same order. This ensures that answers can be reliably aggregated and that comparisons can be made with confidence between sample subgroups or between different survey periods.

Exam Probability: **High**

12. *Answer choices:*

(see index for correct answer)

- a. Realistic job preview
- b. Vacancy led recruitment

- c. Vetting
- d. Acqui-hiring

Guidance: level 1

:: Employment ::

The _____ is an individual's metaphorical "journey" through learning, work and other aspects of life. There are a number of ways to define _____ and the term is used in a variety of ways.

Exam Probability: **High**

13. *Answer choices:*

(see index for correct answer)

- a. Illicit work
- b. Career Pathways
- c. Psychological contract
- d. Contingent workforce

Guidance: level 1

:: Financial accounting ::

_____ is the intangible value of a business, covering its people, the value relating to its relationships, and everything that is left when the employees go home, of which intellectual property is but one component. It is the sum of everything everybody in a company knows that gives it a competitive edge. The term is used in academia in an attempt to account for the value of intangible assets not listed explicitly on a company's balance sheets. On a national level _____ refers to national intangible capital, NIC.A second meaning that is used in academia and was adopted in large corporations is focused on the recycling of knowledge via knowledge management and _____ management. Creating, shaping and updating the stock of _____ requires the formulation of a strategic vision, which blends together all three dimensions of _____ within the organisational context through exploration, exploitation, measurement, and disclosure. _____ is used in the context of assessing the wealth of organizations. A metric for the value of _____ is the amount by which the enterprise value of a firm exceeds the value of its tangible assets. Directly visible on corporate books is capital embodied in its physical assets and financial capital; however all three make up the value of an enterprise. Measuring the real value and the total performance of _____'s components is a critical part of running a company in the knowledge economy and Information Age. Understanding the _____ in an enterprise allows leveraging of its intellectual assets. For a corporation, the result will optimize its stock price.

Exam Probability: **High**

14. *Answer choices:*

(see index for correct answer)

- a. Intangibles
- b. Net worth
- c. Book value
- d. Holding gains

Guidance: level 1

:: Employment ::

_____ is measuring the output of a particular business process or procedure, then modifying the process or procedure to increase the output, increase efficiency, or increase the effectiveness of the process or procedure. _____ can be applied to either individual performance such as an athlete or organizational performance such as a racing team or a commercial business.

Exam Probability: **Medium**

15. *Answer choices:*

(see index for correct answer)

- a. Liaison job
- b. Performance improvement
- c. Virtual internship
- d. Work sharing

Guidance: level 1

:: Training ::

_____ is a phase of training needs analysis directed at identifying which individuals within an organization should receive training.

Exam Probability: **Medium**

16. *Answer choices:*

(see index for correct answer)

- a. Person Analysis
- b. Biography Work
- c. Boardcast
- d. Teletraining

Guidance: level 1

:: Self ::

_____ is a term that has been used in various psychology theories, often in different ways. The term was originally introduced by the organismic theorist Kurt Goldstein for the motive to realize one's full potential. In Goldstein's view, it is the organism's master motive, the only real motive: "the tendency to actualize itself as fully as possible is the basic drive ... the drive of _____." Carl Rogers similarly wrote of "the curative force in psychotherapy man's tendency to actualize himself, to become his potentialities ... to express and activate all the capacities of the organism." The concept was brought most fully to prominence in Abraham Maslow's hierarchy of needs theory as the final level of psychological development that can be achieved when all basic and mental needs are essentially fulfilled and the "actualization" of the full personal potential takes place, although he adapted this viewpoint later on in life to be more flexible.

Exam Probability: **Low**

17. *Answer choices:*

(see index for correct answer)

- a. a person
- b. Self-actualization
- c. Narcissism
- d. impression management

Guidance: level 1

:: ::

A _____ seeks to further a particular profession, the interests of individuals engaged in that profession and the public interest. In the United States, such an association is typically a nonprofit organization for tax purposes.

Exam Probability: **High**

18. *Answer choices:*

(see index for correct answer)

- a. hierarchical perspective
- b. empathy
- c. Professional association
- d. imperative

Guidance: level 1

:: Human resource management ::

A _____ is a group of people with different functional expertise working toward a common goal. It may include people from finance, marketing, operations, and human resources departments. Typically, it includes employees from all levels of an organization. Members may also come from outside an organization.

Exam Probability: **Low**

19. *Answer choices:*
(see index for correct answer)

- a. Job design
- b. Turnover
- c. Work activity management
- d. Cross-functional team

Guidance: level 1

:: ::

A _____ is a systematic way of determining the value/worth of a job in relation to other jobs in an organization. It tries to make a systematic comparison between jobs to assess their relative worth for the purpose of establishing a rational pay structure. _____ needs to be differentiated from job analysis. Job analysis is a systematic way of gathering information about a job. Every _____ method requires at least some basic job analysis in order to provide factual information about the jobs concerned. Thus, _____ begins with job analysis and ends at that point where the worth of a job is ascertained for achieving pay equity between jobs and different roles.

Exam Probability: **Medium**

20. *Answer choices:*

(see index for correct answer)

- a. similarity-attraction theory
- b. Character
- c. Job evaluation
- d. co-culture

Guidance: level 1

:: ::

A _____ is a technical analysis of a biological specimen, for example urine, hair, blood, breath, sweat, and/or oral fluid/saliva—to determine the presence or absence of specified parent drugs or their metabolites. Major applications of _____ ing include detection of the presence of performance enhancing steroids in sport, employers and parole/probation officers screening for drugs prohibited by law and police officers testing for the presence and concentration of alcohol in the blood commonly referred to as BAC . BAC tests are typically administered via a breathalyzer while urinalysis is used for the vast majority of _____ ing in sports and the workplace. Numerous other methods with varying degrees of accuracy, sensitivity , and detection periods exist.

Exam Probability: **High**

21. *Answer choices:*

(see index for correct answer)

- a. hierarchical perspective
- b. interpersonal communication
- c. levels of analysis
- d. Drug test

Guidance: level 1

:: Trade unions in the United States ::

The _____ is a labor union in the United States and Canada. Formed in 1903 by the merger of The Team Drivers International Union and The Teamsters National Union, the union now represents a diverse membership of blue-collar and professional workers in both the public and private sectors. The union had approximately 1.3 million members in 2013. Formerly known as the _____, Chauffeurs, Warehousemen and Helpers of America, the IBT is a member of the Change to Win Federation and Canadian Labour Congress.

Exam Probability: **High**

22. *Answer choices:*

(see index for correct answer)

- a. News Media Guild
- b. California Faculty Association
- c. Oregon Education Association
- d. International Brotherhood of Teamsters

Guidance: level 1

:: Personnel economics ::

In labor economics, the _____ hypothesis argues that wages, at least in some markets, form in a way that is not market-clearing. Specifically, it points to the incentive for managers to pay their employees more than the market-clearing wage in order to increase their productivity or efficiency, or reduce costs associated with turnover, in industries where the costs of replacing labor are high. This increased labor productivity and/or decreased costs pay for the higher wages.

Exam Probability: **High**

23. *Answer choices:*

(see index for correct answer)

- a. Luxury tax
- b. Work self-efficacy
- c. Personnel economics

Guidance: level 1

:: Unemployment in the United States ::

The _____ is a unit of the United States Department of Labor. It is the principal fact-finding agency for the U.S. government in the broad field of labor economics and statistics and serves as a principal agency of the U.S. Federal Statistical System. The BLS is a governmental statistical agency that collects, processes, analyzes, and disseminates essential statistical data to the American public, the U.S. Congress, other Federal agencies, State and local governments, business, and labor representatives. The BLS also serves as a statistical resource to the United States Department of Labor, and conducts research into how much families need to earn to be able to enjoy a decent standard of living.

Exam Probability: **Medium**

24. *Answer choices:*

(see index for correct answer)

- a. Average high cost multiple
- b. National Campaign Committee for Unemployment Insurance
- c. California unemployment statistics
- d. Bureau of Labor Statistics

Guidance: level 1

:: Employee relations ::

The _____ can be used to bring together employment and job-related information which employees need to know. It typically has three types of content.

Exam Probability: **Low**

25. *Answer choices:*
(see index for correct answer)

- a. employee stock ownership
- b. Industry Federation of the State of Rio de Janeiro
- c. Employee engagement
- d. Employee handbook

Guidance: level 1

:: ::

_____ was the plaintiff in the American employment discrimination case Ledbetter v. Goodyear Tire & Rubber Co. Congress passed a fair pay act in her name, the _____ Fair Pay Act of 2009. She has since become a women's equality activist, public speaker, and author. In 2011, Ledbetter was inducted into the National Women's Hall of Fame.

Exam Probability: **Medium**

26. *Answer choices:*

(see index for correct answer)

- a. process perspective
- b. Lilly Ledbetter
- c. hierarchical perspective
- d. information systems assessment

Guidance: level 1

:: Production and manufacturing ::

_____ is a set of techniques and tools for process improvement. Though as a shortened form it may be found written as 6S, it should not be confused with the methodology known as 6S.

Exam Probability: **Medium**

27. *Answer choices:*

(see index for correct answer)

- a. Wireless DNC
- b. Industrial engineering
- c. Six Sigma
- d. CTQ tree

Guidance: level 1

:: Human resource management ::

> _____ are the people who make up the workforce of an organization, business sector, or economy. "Human capital" is sometimes used synonymously with " _____ ", although human capital typically refers to a narrower effect. Likewise, other terms sometimes used include manpower, talent, labor, personnel, or simply people.

Exam Probability: **Low**

28. *Answer choices:*

(see index for correct answer)

- a. E-HRM
- b. Human resources
- c. Sham peer review
- d. Vendor on premises

Guidance: level 1

:: Trade unions ::

A _____ is an association of workers forming a legal unit or legal personhood, usually called a "bargaining unit", which acts as bargaining agent and legal representative for a unit of employees in all matters of law or right arising from or in the administration of a collective agreement. Labour unions typically fund the formal organisation, head office, and legal team functions of the labour union through regular fees or union dues. The delegate staff of the labour union representation in the workforce are made up of workplace volunteers who are appointed by members in democratic elections.

Exam Probability: **Medium**

29. *Answer choices:*

(see index for correct answer)

- a. Service model
- b. Vigilance committee
- c. Trade union
- d. Unfair list

Guidance: level 1

:: ::

_____, also known as drug abuse, is a patterned use of a drug in which the user consumes the substance in amounts or with methods which are harmful to themselves or others, and is a form of substance-related disorder. Widely differing definitions of drug abuse are used in public health, medical and criminal justice contexts. In some cases criminal or anti-social behaviour occurs when the person is under the influence of a drug, and long term personality changes in individuals may occur as well. In addition to possible physical, social, and psychological harm, use of some drugs may also lead to criminal penalties, although these vary widely depending on the local jurisdiction.

Exam Probability: **Low**

30. *Answer choices:*

(see index for correct answer)

- a. corporate values
- b. process perspective
- c. Substance abuse
- d. personal values

Guidance: level 1

:: Labour relations ::

A _____, also known as a post-entry closed shop, is a form of a union security clause. Under this, the employer agrees to either only hire labor union members or to require that any new employees who are not already union members become members within a certain amount of time. Use of the _____ varies widely from nation to nation, depending on the level of protection given trade unions in general.

Exam Probability: **Medium**

31. *Answer choices:*

(see index for correct answer)

- a. Worker center
- b. Review Body
- c. United Students Against Sweatshops
- d. Union shop

Guidance: level 1

:: Power (social and political) ::

In a notable study of power conducted by social psychologists John R. P. French and Bertram Raven in 1959, power is divided into five separate and distinct forms. In 1965 Raven revised this model to include a sixth form by separating the informational power base as distinct from the _____ base.

Exam Probability: **Medium**

32. Answer choices:

(see index for correct answer)

- a. need for power
- b. Referent power
- c. Hard power

Guidance: level 1

:: ::

> _____ is a form of development in which a person called a coach supports a learner or client in achieving a specific personal or professional goal by providing training and guidance. The learner is sometimes called a coachee. Occasionally, _____ may mean an informal relationship between two people, of whom one has more experience and expertise than the other and offers advice and guidance as the latter learns; but _____ differs from mentoring in focusing on specific tasks or objectives, as opposed to more general goals or overall development.

Exam Probability: **High**

33. Answer choices:

(see index for correct answer)

- a. corporate values
- b. empathy
- c. personal values

- d. Coaching

Guidance: level 1

:: ::

> _____ is the formal act of giving up or quitting one's office or position. A _____ can occur when a person holding a position gained by election or appointment steps down, but leaving a position upon the expiration of a term, or choosing not to seek an additional term, is not considered _____ .

Exam Probability: **Low**

34. *Answer choices:*

(see index for correct answer)

- a. imperative
- b. Resignation
- c. similarity-attraction theory
- d. levels of analysis

Guidance: level 1

:: Employment ::

_____ s are experiential learning opportunities, similar to internships but generally shorter, provided by partnerships between educational institutions and employers to give students short practical experiences in their field of study. In medicine it may refer to a visiting physician who is not part of the regular staff. In law, it usually refers to rigorous legal work opportunities undertaken by law students for law school credit and pay, similar to that of a junior attorney. It is derived from Latin externus and from English -ship.

Exam Probability: **High**

35. *Answer choices:*

(see index for correct answer)

- a. Work sharing
- b. Externship
- c. Jobless claims
- d. Nursing shortage

Guidance: level 1

:: Employment compensation ::

Compensation and benefits is a sub-discipline of human resources, focused on employee compensation and benefits policy-making. While compensation and benefits are tangible, there are intangible rewards such as recognition, work-life and development. Combined, these are referred to as _____ s. The term "compensation and benefits" refers to the discipline as well as the rewards themselves.

Exam Probability: **Low**

36. *Answer choices:*

(see index for correct answer)

- a. Golden handcuffs
- b. Anderson v. Mt. Clemens Pottery Co.
- c. Total Reward
- d. Lerman ratio

Guidance: level 1

:: Human resource management ::

A _____ is an outsourcing firm which provides services to small and medium sized businesses . Typically, the PEO offering may include human resource consulting, safety and risk mitigation services, payroll processing, employer payroll tax filing, workers' compensation insurance, health benefits, employers' practice and liability insurance , retirement vehicles , regulatory compliance assistance, workforce management technology, and training and development. The PEO enters into a contractual co-employment agreement with its clientele. Through co-employment, the PEO becomes the employer of record for tax purposes through filing payroll taxes under its own tax identification numbers.

Exam Probability: **Low**

37. *Answer choices:*

(see index for correct answer)

- a. Professional employer organization
- b. Four-day week
- c. Occupational burnout
- d. Pay in lieu of notice

Guidance: level 1

:: Human resource management ::

_____ is the application of information technology for both networking and supporting at least two individual or collective actors in their shared performing of HR activities.

Exam Probability: **Low**

38. *Answer choices:*
(see index for correct answer)

- a. E-HRM
- b. Competency-based recruitment
- c. Incentive program
- d. Flextime

Guidance: level 1

:: Management ::

In organizational studies, _____ is the efficient and effective development of an organization's resources when they are needed. Such resources may include financial resources, inventory, human skills, production resources, or information technology and natural resources.

Exam Probability: **Low**

39. *Answer choices:*

(see index for correct answer)

- a. Millennium software
- b. Business process interoperability
- c. Identity formation
- d. Resource management

Guidance: level 1

:: Recruitment ::

_____ is a specialized recruitment service which organizations pay to seek out and recruit highly qualified candidates for senior-level and executive jobs . Headhunters may also seek out and recruit other highly specialized and/or skilled positions in organizations for which there is strong competition in the job market for the top talent, such as senior data analysts or computer programmers. The method usually involves commissioning a third-party organization, typically an _____ firm, but possibly a standalone consultant or consulting firm, to research the availability of suitable qualified candidates working for competitors or related businesses or organizations. Having identified a shortlist of qualified candidates who match the client's requirements, the _____ firm may act as an intermediary to contact the individual and see if they might be interested in moving to a new employer. The _____ firm may also carry out initial screening of the candidate, negotiations on remuneration and benefits, and preparing the employment contract. In some markets there has been a move towards using _____ for lower positions driven by the fact that there are less candidates for some positions even on lower levels than executive.

Exam Probability: **Low**

40. *Answer choices:*

(see index for correct answer)

- a. Labour hire
- b. Executive search
- c. Silicon Milkroundabout
- d. Military recruitment

Guidance: level 1

:: Legal terms ::

_____, a form of alternative dispute resolution, is a way to resolve disputes outside the courts. The dispute will be decided by one or more persons, which renders the "_____ award". An _____ award is legally binding on both sides and enforceable in the courts.

Exam Probability: **Low**

41. *Answer choices:*

(see index for correct answer)

- a. Nota bene
- b. Arbitration
- c. Officious intermeddler
- d. Attendant circumstance

Guidance: level 1

:: Management ::

In the field of management, _____ involves the formulation and implementation of the major goals and initiatives taken by an organization's top management on behalf of owners, based on consideration of resources and an assessment of the internal and external environments in which the organization operates.

Exam Probability: **Low**

42. *Answer choices:*

(see index for correct answer)

- a. Managerial hubris
- b. Event management
- c. Plan
- d. Technology scouting

Guidance: level 1

:: Human resource management ::

_____ , also known as management by results , was first popularized by Peter Drucker in his 1954 book The Practice of Management. _____ is the process of defining specific objectives within an organization that management can convey to organization members, then deciding on how to achieve each objective in sequence. This process allows managers to take work that needs to be done one step at a time to allow for a calm, yet productive work environment. This process also helps organization members to see their accomplishments as they achieve each objective, which reinforces a positive work environment and a sense of achievement. An important part of MBO is the measurement and comparison of an employee's actual performance with the standards set. Ideally, when employees themselves have been involved with the goal-setting and choosing the course of action to be followed by them, they are more likely to fulfill their responsibilities. According to George S. Odiorne, the system of _____ can be described as a process whereby the superior and subordinate jointly identify common goals, define each individual's major areas of responsibility in terms of the results expected of him or her, and use these measures as guides for operating the unit and assessing the contribution of each of its members.

Exam Probability: **Medium**

43. *Answer choices:*

(see index for correct answer)

- a. Management by objectives
- b. Salary
- c. Employee value proposition
- d. Cross-training

Guidance: level 1

:: Multiple choice ::

> The _____ is a standardized psychometric test of adult personality and psychopathology. Psychologists and other mental health professionals use various versions of the MMPI to help develop treatment plans; assist with differential diagnosis; help answer legal questions ; screen job candidates during the personnel selection process; or as part of a therapeutic assessment procedure.

Exam Probability: **Low**

44. *Answer choices:*

(see index for correct answer)

- a. Minnesota Multiphasic Personality Inventory
- b. Eddy Test

- c. Eysenck Personality Questionnaire
- d. Millon Clinical Multiaxial Inventory

Guidance: level 1

:: Employment compensation ::

A _____ is a type of employee benefit plan offered in the United States pursuant to Section 125 of the Internal Revenue Code. Its name comes from the earliest such plans that allowed employees to choose between different types of benefits, similar to the ability of a customer to choose among available items in a cafeteria. Qualified _____ s are excluded from gross income. To qualify, a _____ must allow employees to choose from two or more benefits consisting of cash or qualified benefit plans. The Internal Revenue Code explicitly excludes deferred compensation plans from qualifying as a _____ subject to a gross income exemption. Section 125 also provides two exceptions.

Exam Probability: **Medium**

45. *Answer choices:*

(see index for correct answer)

- a. Golden handshake
- b. Cafeteria plan
- c. General Schedule
- d. Employee stock purchase plan

Guidance: level 1

:: Business ::

_____ is a trade policy that does not restrict imports or exports; it can also be understood as the free market idea applied to international trade. In government, _____ is predominantly advocated by political parties that hold liberal economic positions while economically left-wing and nationalist political parties generally support protectionism, the opposite of _____ .

Exam Probability: **Medium**

46. *Answer choices:*
(see index for correct answer)

- a. Office broker
- b. Legal governance, risk management, and compliance
- c. Business statistics
- d. Corporate social media

Guidance: level 1

:: Labour law ::

In law, _____ is to give an immediately secured right of present or future deployment. One has a vested right to an asset that cannot be taken away by any third party, even though one may not yet possess the asset. When the right, interest, or title to the present or future possession of a legal estate can be transferred to any other party, it is termed a vested interest.

Exam Probability: **Low**

47. *Answer choices:*

(see index for correct answer)

- a. Unfair dismissal
- b. Agency worker law
- c. Negligent retention
- d. Negligent hiring

Guidance: level 1

:: Financial statements ::

In financial accounting, a _____ or statement of financial position or statement of financial condition is a summary of the financial balances of an individual or organization, whether it be a sole proprietorship, a business partnership, a corporation, private limited company or other organization such as Government or not-for-profit entity. Assets, liabilities and ownership equity are listed as of a specific date, such as the end of its financial year. A _____ is often described as a "snapshot of a company's financial condition". Of the four basic financial statements, the _____ is the only statement which applies to a single point in time of a business' calendar year.

Exam Probability: **High**

48. *Answer choices:*

(see index for correct answer)

- a. Financial statement
- b. PnL Explained
- c. Financial report
- d. Balance sheet

Guidance: level 1

:: Human resource management ::

_____ is a process for identifying and developing new leaders who can replace old leaders when they leave, retire or die. _____ increases the availability of experienced and capable employees that are prepared to assume these roles as they become available. Taken narrowly, "replacement planning" for key roles is the heart of _____ .

Exam Probability: **Low**

49. *Answer choices:*

(see index for correct answer)

- a. Induction training
- b. Co-determination
- c. Chief human resources officer
- d. Workforce modeling

Guidance: level 1

:: Trade unions in the United States ::

_____ is a labor union in the United States and Canada with roughly 300,000 active members. The union's members work predominantly in the hotel, food service, laundry, warehouse, and casino gaming industries. The union was formed in 2004 by the merger of Union of Needletrades, Industrial, and Textile Employees and Hotel Employees and Restaurant Employees Union .

Exam Probability: **High**

50. *Answer choices:*

(see index for correct answer)

- a. American Guild of Musical Artists
- b. Graduate Employees%27 Organization
- c. State, County, and Municipal Workers of America
- d. Writers Guild of America, West

Guidance: level 1

:: Human resource management ::

_____, Inc. is an American office staffing company that operates globally. The company places employees at all levels in various sectors including financial services, information technology, and law. Also, its professional services include human resource and management consulting, outsourcing, recruitment, career transition, and vendor management. _____ was founded by William Russell Kelly in 1946 and is headquartered in Troy, Michigan. In 2015, the company reported 8,100 employees, $5.5 billion in revenue, and placed 550,000 employees to work in positions in various sectors, making it one of the world's largest staffing firms.

Exam Probability: **High**

51. *Answer choices:*

(see index for correct answer)

- a. Organizational culture
- b. Personal development planning

- c. Employment testing
- d. Kelly Services

Guidance: level 1

:: Parental leave ::

_____ is a type of employment discrimination that occurs when expectant women are fired, not hired, or otherwise discriminated against due to their pregnancy or intention to become pregnant. Common forms of _____ include not being hired due to visible pregnancy or likelihood of becoming pregnant, being fired after informing an employer of one's pregnancy, being fired after maternity leave, and receiving a pay dock due to pregnancy. Convention on the Elimination of All Forms of Discrimination against Women prohibits dismissal on the grounds of maternity or pregnancy and ensures right to maternity leave or comparable social benefits. The Maternity Protection Convention C 183 proclaims adequate protection for pregnancy as well. Though women have some protection in the United States because of the _____ Act of 1978, it has not completely curbed the incidence of _____ . The Equal Rights Amendment could ensure more robust sex equality ensuring that women and men could both work and have children at the same time.

Exam Probability: **High**

52. *Answer choices:*

(see index for correct answer)

- a. Pregnant Workers Directive
- b. Geduldig v. Aiello
- c. Sara Hlupekile Longwe

- d. Parental leave economics

Guidance: level 1

:: Systems thinking ::

In business management, a _____ is a company that facilitates the learning of its members and continuously transforms itself. The concept was coined through the work and research of Peter Senge and his colleagues.

Exam Probability: **Medium**

53. *Answer choices:*

(see index for correct answer)

- a. Delphi method
- b. The Letters of Utrecht
- c. Learning organization
- d. Scenario analysis

Guidance: level 1

:: Human resource management ::

_____ involves improving the effectiveness of organizations and the individuals and teams within them. Training may be viewed as related to immediate changes in organizational effectiveness via organized instruction, while development is related to the progress of longer-term organizational and employee goals. While _____ technically have differing definitions, the two are oftentimes used interchangeably and/or together. _____ has historically been a topic within applied psychology but has within the last two decades become closely associated with human resources management, talent management, human resources development, instructional design, human factors, and knowledge management.

Exam Probability: **Low**

54. *Answer choices:*

(see index for correct answer)

- a. Labour is not a commodity
- b. Training and development
- c. Cross-cultural capital
- d. Perceived organizational support

Guidance: level 1

:: Business law ::

_____ or employment relations is the multidisciplinary academic field that studies the employment relationship; that is, the complex interrelations between employers and employees, labor/trade unions, employer organizations and the state.

Exam Probability: **Low**

55. *Answer choices:*

(see index for correct answer)

- a. Arbitration award
- b. Perfection
- c. Industrial relations
- d. Articles of partnership

Guidance: level 1

:: Minimum wage ::

A _____ is the lowest remuneration that employers can legally pay their workers—the price floor below which workers may not sell their labor. Most countries had introduced _____ legislation by the end of the 20th century.

Exam Probability: **Low**

56. *Answer choices:*

(see index for correct answer)

- a. Minimum wage
- b. Guaranteed minimum income
- c. Minimum wage in Taiwan

- d. Minimum wage in the United States

Guidance: level 1

:: Human resource management ::

_____ , also known as organizational socialization, is management jargon first created in 1988 that refers to the mechanism through which new employees acquire the necessary knowledge, skills, and behaviors in order to become effective organizational members and insiders.

Exam Probability: **High**

57. *Answer choices:*

(see index for correct answer)

- a. Onboarding
- b. Competency-based job description
- c. Management by observation
- d. Focal Point Review

Guidance: level 1

:: Problem solving ::

A _____ is a unit or formation established to work on a single defined task or activity. Originally introduced by the United States Navy, the term has now caught on for general usage and is a standard part of NATO terminology. Many non-military organizations now create " _____ s" or task groups for temporary activities that might have once been performed by ad hoc committees.

Exam Probability: **Medium**

58. *Answer choices:*

(see index for correct answer)

- a. Syntegrity
- b. Objective approach
- c. Talking past each other
- d. Unified structured inventive thinking

Guidance: level 1

:: ::

A _____ is the ability to carry out a task with determined results often within a given amount of time, energy, or both. _____ s can often be divided into domain-general and domain-specific _____ s. For example, in the domain of work, some general _____ s would include time management, teamwork and leadership, self-motivation and others, whereas domain-specific _____ s would be used only for a certain job. _____ usually requires certain environmental stimuli and situations to assess the level of _____ being shown and used.

Exam Probability: **Medium**

59. *Answer choices:*

(see index for correct answer)

- a. Skill
- b. co-culture
- c. functional perspective
- d. information systems assessment

Guidance: level 1

Information systems

Information systems (IS) are formal, sociotechnical, organizational systems designed to collect, process, store, and distribute information. In a sociotechnical perspective Information Systems are composed by four components: technology, process, people and organizational structure.

:: Enterprise modelling ::

_____ are large-scale application software packages that support business processes, information flows, reporting, and data analytics in complex organizations. While ES are generally packaged enterprise application software systems they can also be bespoke, custom developed systems created to support a specific organization`s needs.

Exam Probability: **Medium**

1. *Answer choices:*

(see index for correct answer)

- a. ISO 19439
- b. Enterprise engineering
- c. Enterprise modelling
- d. Integrated enterprise modeling

Guidance: level 1

:: Computer file formats ::

_____ is a communication protocol for peer-to-peer file sharing which is used to distribute data and electronic files over the Internet.

Exam Probability: **Medium**

2. *Answer choices:*

(see index for correct answer)

- a. General content descriptor
- b. Execute Direct Access Program
- c. Tiny Tafel
- d. Unified Emulator Format

Guidance: level 1

:: Data collection ::

_____ is the application of data mining techniques to discover patterns from the World Wide Web. As the name proposes, this is information gathered by mining the web. It makes utilization of automated apparatuses to reveal and extricate data from servers and web2 reports, and it permits organizations to get to both organized and unstructured information from browser activities, server logs, website and link structure, page content and different sources.

Exam Probability: **High**

3. *Answer choices:*

(see index for correct answer)

- a. Web mining
- b. Synthetic Environment for Analysis and Simulations
- c. Global surveillance
- d. Data scraping

Guidance: level 1

:: World Wide Web ::

A _____ is a document that is suitable to act as a web resource on the World Wide Web. In order to graphically display a _____ , a web browser is needed. This is a type of software that can retrieve _____ s from the Internet. When accessed by a web browser it may be displayed as a _____ on a monitor or mobile device. Typical _____ s are hypertext documents which contain hyperlinks, often referred to as links, for browsing to other _____ s.

Exam Probability: **Low**

4. *Answer choices:*

(see index for correct answer)

- a. Web page
- b. Gateway
- c. Lockerz
- d. Social Semantic Web

Guidance: level 1

:: Automatic identification and data capture ::

_____ is the trademark for a type of matrix barcode first designed in 1994 for the automotive industry in Japan. A barcode is a machine-readable optical label that contains information about the item to which it is attached. In practice, _____ s often contain data for a locator, identifier, or tracker that points to a website or application. A _____ uses four standardized encoding modes to store data efficiently; extensions may also be used.

Exam Probability: **Medium**

5. *Answer choices:*

(see index for correct answer)

- a. QR code
- b. Digital Automated Identification SYstem
- c. Chipless RFID
- d. Wireless identification and sensing platform

Guidance: level 1

:: ::

_____ are interactive computer-mediated technologies that facilitate the creation and sharing of information, ideas, career interests and other forms of expression via virtual communities and networks. The variety of stand-alone and built-in _____ services currently available introduces challenges of definition; however, there are some common features.

Exam Probability: **Low**

6. *Answer choices:*

(see index for correct answer)

- a. levels of analysis
- b. open system

- c. Sarbanes-Oxley act of 2002
- d. deep-level diversity

Guidance: level 1

:: Computer access control protocols ::

> An _____ is a type of computer communications protocol or cryptographic protocol specifically designed for transfer of authentication data between two entities. It allows the receiving entity to authenticate the connecting entity as well as authenticate itself to the connecting entity by declaring the type of information needed for authentication as well as syntax. It is the most important layer of protection needed for secure communication within computer networks.

Exam Probability: **High**

7. *Answer choices:*

(see index for correct answer)

- a. Authentication protocol
- b. Kerberos
- c. POP before SMTP
- d. TACACS

Guidance: level 1

:: Fault tolerance ::

_____ is the property that enables a system to continue operating properly in the event of the failure of some of its components. If its operating quality decreases at all, the decrease is proportional to the severity of the failure, as compared to a naively designed system, in which even a small failure can cause total breakdown. _____ is particularly sought after in high-availability or life-critical systems. The ability of maintaining functionality when portions of a system break down is referred to as graceful degradation.

Exam Probability: **Low**

8. *Answer choices:*

(see index for correct answer)

- a. Dual modular redundancy
- b. Active redundancy
- c. Fault tolerance
- d. Hot swapping

Guidance: level 1

:: Information technology audit ::

_____ is the act of using a computer to take or alter electronic data, or to gain unlawful use of a computer or system. In the United States, _____ is specifically proscribed by the _____ and Abuse Act, which criminalizes computer-related acts under federal jurisdiction. Types of _____ include.

Exam Probability: **Low**

9. *Answer choices:*

(see index for correct answer)

- a. ACL
- b. David Coderre
- c. Computer fraud
- d. Computer forensics

Guidance: level 1

:: Systems theory ::

A _____ is a group of interacting or interrelated entities that form a unified whole. A _____ is delineated by its spatial and temporal boundaries, surrounded and influenced by its environment, described by its structure and purpose and expressed in its functioning.

Exam Probability: **Low**

10. *Answer choices:*

(see index for correct answer)

- a. decentralized system
- b. subsystem
- c. management system
- d. co-design

Guidance: level 1

:: Google services ::

> Google Ads is an online advertising platform developed by Google, where advertisers pay to display brief advertisements, service offerings, product listings, video content, and generate mobile application installs within the Google ad network to web users.

Exam Probability: **Medium**

11. *Answer choices:*

(see index for correct answer)

- a. Google Finance
- b. Google Safe Browsing
- c. AdWords
- d. Google Flights

Guidance: level 1

:: Costs ::

In economics, _____ is the total economic cost of production and is made up of variable cost, which varies according to the quantity of a good produced and includes inputs such as labour and raw materials, plus fixed cost, which is independent of the quantity of a good produced and includes inputs that cannot be varied in the short term: fixed costs such as buildings and machinery, including sunk costs if any. Since cost is measured per unit of time, it is a flow variable.

Exam Probability: **Medium**

12. *Answer choices:*

(see index for correct answer)

- a. Average cost
- b. Total cost
- c. Cost of poor quality
- d. Cost competitiveness of fuel sources

Guidance: level 1

:: E-commerce ::

_____, cybersecurity or information technology security is the protection of computer systems from theft or damage to their hardware, software or electronic data, as well as from disruption or misdirection of the services they provide.

Exam Probability: **Medium**

13. *Answer choices:*

(see index for correct answer)

- a. IDEAL
- b. Global Location Number
- c. TRADACOMS
- d. Computer security

Guidance: level 1

:: Content management systems ::

_____ is the textual, visual, or aural content that is encountered as part of the user experience on websites. It may include—among other things—text, images, sounds, videos, and animations.

Exam Probability: **High**

14. *Answer choices:*

(see index for correct answer)

- a. ThoughtFarmer
- b. Preservation metadata
- c. Composite C1
- d. Web content

Guidance: level 1

:: Identity management ::

_____ is the ability of an individual or group to seclude themselves, or information about themselves, and thereby express themselves selectively. The boundaries and content of what is considered private differ among cultures and individuals, but share common themes. When something is private to a person, it usually means that something is inherently special or sensitive to them. The domain of _____ partially overlaps with security, which can include the concepts of appropriate use, as well as protection of information. _____ may also take the form of bodily integrity.

Exam Probability: **Low**

15. *Answer choices:*

(see index for correct answer)

- a. Credential
- b. Mobile Signature Roaming
- c. User provisioning software
- d. Privacy

Guidance: level 1

:: Information technology management ::

_____ within quality management systems and information technology systems is a process—either formal or informal—used to ensure that changes to a product or system are introduced in a controlled and coordinated manner. It reduces the possibility that unnecessary changes will be introduced to a system without forethought, introducing faults into the system or undoing changes made by other users of software. The goals of a _____ procedure usually include minimal disruption to services, reduction in back-out activities, and cost-effective utilization of resources involved in implementing change.

Exam Probability: **Medium**

16. *Answer choices:*

(see index for correct answer)

- a. Software license server
- b. Change control
- c. Croquet Project
- d. Soluto

Guidance: level 1

:: Help desk ::

Data center management is the collection of tasks performed by those responsible for managing ongoing operation of a data center This includes Business service management and planning for the future.

Exam Probability: **Medium**

17. *Answer choices:*

(see index for correct answer)

- a. AetherPal
- b. Help desk
- c. KnowledgeBase Manager Pro
- d. Supportworks

Guidance: level 1

:: ::

A _____ is a structure / access pattern specific to data warehouse environments, used to retrieve client-facing data. The _____ is a subset of the data warehouse and is usually oriented to a specific business line or team. Whereas data warehouses have an enterprise-wide depth, the information in _____ s pertains to a single department. In some deployments, each department or business unit is considered the owner of its _____ including all the hardware, software and data. This enables each department to isolate the use, manipulation and development of their data. In other deployments where conformed dimensions are used, this business unit ownership will not hold true for shared dimensions like customer, product, etc.

Exam Probability: **Medium**

18. *Answer choices:*

(see index for correct answer)

- a. Data mart
- b. imperative
- c. similarity-attraction theory
- d. corporate values

Guidance: level 1

:: Network management ::

_____ is the process of administering and managing computer networks. Services provided by this discipline include fault analysis, performance management, provisioning of networks and maintaining the quality of service. Software that enables network administrators to perform their functions is called _____ software.

Exam Probability: **High**

19. *Answer choices:*

(see index for correct answer)

- a. Plixer International
- b. Network management

- c. Oracle Enterprise Manager Ops Center
- d. System Center Advisor

Guidance: level 1

:: Data quality ::

_____ or data cleaning is the process of detecting and correcting corrupt or inaccurate records from a record set, table, or database and refers to identifying incomplete, incorrect, inaccurate or irrelevant parts of the data and then replacing, modifying, or deleting the dirty or coarse data. _____ may be performed interactively with data wrangling tools, or as batch processing through scripting.

Exam Probability: **Medium**

20. *Answer choices:*
(see index for correct answer)

- a. Data validation
- b. Data cleansing
- c. Input mask
- d. Referential integrity

Guidance: level 1

:: Information technology management ::

_____ is the use of software to control machine tools and related ones in the manufacturing of workpieces. This is not the only definition for CAM, but it is the most common; CAM may also refer to the use of a computer to assist in all operations of a manufacturing plant, including planning, management, transportation and storage. Its primary purpose is to create a faster production process and components and tooling with more precise dimensions and material consistency, which in some cases, uses only the required amount of raw material, while simultaneously reducing energy consumption. CAM is now a system used in schools and lower educational purposes. CAM is a subsequent computer-aided process after computer-aided design and sometimes computer-aided engineering, as the model generated in CAD and verified in CAE can be input into CAM software, which then controls the machine tool. CAM is used in many schools alongside Computer-Aided Design to create objects.

Exam Probability: **High**

21. *Answer choices:*

(see index for correct answer)

- a. Trustworthy computing
- b. Computer-aided manufacturing
- c. High Availability Application Architecture
- d. Financial management for IT services

Guidance: level 1

:: Internet governance ::

A _____ is one of the domains at the highest level in the hierarchical Domain Name System of the Internet. The _____ names are installed in the root zone of the name space. For all domains in lower levels, it is the last part of the domain name, that is, the last label of a fully qualified domain name. For example, in the domain name www.example.com, the _____ is com. Responsibility for management of most _____ s is delegated to specific organizations by the Internet Corporation for Assigned Names and Numbers , which operates the Internet Assigned Numbers Authority , and is in charge of maintaining the DNS root zone.

Exam Probability: **Low**

22. *Answer choices:*

(see index for correct answer)

- a. Route server
- b. Pacific Islands ICT Policy and Strategic Plan
- c. Routing Assets Database
- d. Top-level domain

Guidance: level 1

:: Network analyzers ::

A _____, meaning "meat eater", is an organism that derives its energy and nutrient requirements from a diet consisting mainly or exclusively of animal tissue, whether through predation or scavenging. Animals that depend solely on animal flesh for their nutrient requirements are called obligate _____s while those that also consume non-animal food are called facultative _____s. Omnivores also consume both animal and non-animal food, and, apart from the more general definition, there is no clearly defined ratio of plant to animal material that would distinguish a facultative _____ from an omnivore. A _____ at the top of the food chain, not preyed upon by other animals, is termed an apex predator.

Exam Probability: **High**

23. *Answer choices:*

(see index for correct answer)

- a. Carnivore
- b. Ettercap
- c. Hping
- d. Packet crafting

Guidance: level 1

:: Management ::

A _____ describes the rationale of how an organization creates, delivers, and captures value, in economic, social, cultural or other contexts. The process of _____ construction and modification is also called _____ innovation and forms a part of business strategy.

Exam Probability: **Medium**

24. *Answer choices:*

(see index for correct answer)

- a. Board of governors
- b. Business model
- c. Job rotation
- d. Supply management

Guidance: level 1

:: Data management ::

A _____ is a place where you can store data. Commonly used to refer to a column in a database or a field in a data entry form or web form.

Exam Probability: **Medium**

25. *Answer choices:*

(see index for correct answer)

- a. Data field
- b. single sourcing
- c. CommVault Systems
- d. Database server

Guidance: level 1

:: E-commerce ::

A _____ is a plastic payment card that can be used instead of cash when making purchases. It is similar to a credit card, but unlike a credit card, the money is immediately transferred directly from the cardholder's bank account when performing a transaction.

Exam Probability: **Medium**

26. *Answer choices:*

(see index for correct answer)

- a. Shopping directory
- b. Transactional Link
- c. Debit card
- d. Electronic Commerce Directive

Guidance: level 1

:: Remote administration software ::

_____ is a protocol used on the Internet or local area network to provide a bidirectional interactive text-oriented communication facility using a virtual terminal connection. User data is interspersed in-band with _____ control information in an 8-bit byte oriented data connection over the Transmission Control Protocol.

Exam Probability: **Medium**

27. *Answer choices:*

(see index for correct answer)

- a. NetBus
- b. Proxy Networks, Inc.
- c. Telnet
- d. Ericom Software

Guidance: level 1

:: Marketing ::

_____ is a business model in which consumers create value and businesses consume that value. For example, when a consumer writes reviews or when a consumer gives a useful idea for new product development then that consumer is creating value for the business if the business adopts the input. In the C2B model, a reverse auction or demand collection model, enables buyers to name or demand their own price, which is often binding, for a specific good or service. Inside of a consumer to business market the roles involved in the transaction must be established and the consumer must offer something of value to the business.

Exam Probability: **High**

28. *Answer choices:*

(see index for correct answer)

- a. Consumer-to-business
- b. Mass-market theory
- c. Movie packaging
- d. Marketing mix

Guidance: level 1

:: Critical thinking ::

> In psychology, _____ is regarded as the cognitive process resulting in the selection of a belief or a course of action among several alternative possibilities. Every _____ process produces a final choice, which may or may not prompt action.

Exam Probability: **Low**

29. *Answer choices:*

(see index for correct answer)

- a. Proof
- b. Adviser
- c. Scholarly method

- d. Decision-making

Guidance: level 1

:: Sound recording ::

_____ is a medium for magnetic recording, made of a thin, magnetizable coating on a long, narrow strip of plastic film. It was developed in Germany in 1928, based on magnetic wire recording. Devices that record and play back audio and video using _____ are tape recorders and video tape recorders respectively. A device that stores computer data on _____ is known as a tape drive.

Exam Probability: **Medium**

30. *Answer choices:*

(see index for correct answer)

- a. Association for Recorded Sound Collections
- b. Experimental Talking Clock
- c. Audio letter
- d. Spill

Guidance: level 1

:: Information science ::

The United States National Forum on _____ defines _____ as "... the hyper ability to know when there is a need for information, to be able to identify, locate, evaluate, and effectively use that information for the issue or problem at hand." The American Library Association defines "_____" as a set of abilities requiring individuals to "recognize when information is needed and have the ability to locate, evaluate, and use effectively the needed information. Other definitions incorporate aspects of "skepticism, judgement, free thinking, questioning, and understanding..." or incorporate competencies that an informed citizen of an information society ought to possess to participate intelligently and actively in that society.

Exam Probability: **High**

31. *Answer choices:*

(see index for correct answer)

- a. ArchiMate
- b. Hydroinformatics
- c. Knowledge spillover
- d. Information literacy

Guidance: level 1

:: Reputation management ::

_____ refers to the influencing and controlling of an individual's or group's reputation. Originally a public relations term, the growth of the internet and social media, along with _____ companies, have made search results a core part of an individual's or group's reputation. Online _____, sometimes abbreviated as ORM, focuses on the management of product and service search website results. Ethical grey areas include mug shot removal sites, astroturfing customer review sites, censoring negative complaints, and using search engine optimization tactics to influence results.

Exam Probability: **Low**

32. *Answer choices:*

(see index for correct answer)

- a. Reputation management
- b. Raph Levien
- c. Distrust
- d. TrustedSource

Guidance: level 1

:: Business planning ::

_____ is an organization's process of defining its strategy, or direction, and making decisions on allocating its resources to pursue this strategy. It may also extend to control mechanisms for guiding the implementation of the strategy. _____ became prominent in corporations during the 1960s and remains an important aspect of strategic management. It is executed by strategic planners or strategists, who involve many parties and research sources in their analysis of the organization and its relationship to the environment in which it competes.

Exam Probability: **Low**

33. *Answer choices:*

(see index for correct answer)

- a. Stakeholder management
- b. Exit planning
- c. Customer Demand Planning
- d. Strategic planning

Guidance: level 1

:: Supply chain management ::

_____ is the removal of intermediaries in economics from a supply chain, or cutting out the middlemen in connection with a transaction or a series of transactions. Instead of going through traditional distribution channels, which had some type of intermediary, companies may now deal with customers directly, for example via the Internet. Hence, the use of factory direct and direct from the factory to mean the same thing.

Exam Probability: **Medium**

34. *Answer choices:*

(see index for correct answer)

- a. Revenue Technology Services
- b. Disintermediation
- c. RevPAR
- d. Dynamic discounting

Guidance: level 1

:: Market research ::

_____ is the action of defining, gathering, analyzing, and distributing intelligence about products, customers, competitors, and any aspect of the environment needed to support executives and managers in strategic decision making for an organization.

Exam Probability: **High**

35. *Answer choices:*

(see index for correct answer)

- a. INDEX
- b. IRI
- c. Coolhunting

- d. Competitive intelligence

Guidance: level 1

:: Data management ::

Data aggregation is the compiling of information from databases with intent to prepare combined datasets for data processing.

Exam Probability: **High**

36. *Answer choices:*
(see index for correct answer)

- a. DMAPI
- b. Information integration
- c. Data aggregator
- d. Address space

Guidance: level 1

:: Data management ::

_____ represents the business objects that contain the most valuable, agreed upon information shared across an organization. It can cover relatively static reference data, transactional, unstructured, analytical, hierarchical and metadata. It is the primary focus of the information technology discipline of _____ management.

Exam Probability: **Low**

37. *Answer choices:*

(see index for correct answer)

- a. Navigational database
- b. Scriptella
- c. Master data
- d. Grid-oriented storage

Guidance: level 1

:: Virtual reality ::

_____ is an experience taking place within simulated and immersive environments that can be similar to or completely different from the real world. Applications of _____ can include entertainment and educational purposes. Other, distinct types of VR style technology include augmented reality and mixed reality.

Exam Probability: **Medium**

38. *Answer choices:*

(see index for correct answer)

- a. 3DML
- b. Virtual reality
- c. Inverse kinematics
- d. Unreal Engine

Guidance: level 1

:: Commerce ::

_____, Inc. is an American media-services provider headquartered in Los Gatos, California, founded in 1997 by Reed Hastings and Marc Randolph in Scotts Valley, California. The company's primary business is its subscription-based streaming OTT service which offers online streaming of a library of films and television programs, including those produced in-house. As of April 2019, _____ had over 148 million paid subscriptions worldwide, including 60 million in the United States, and over 154 million subscriptions total including free trials. It is available almost worldwide except in mainland China as well as Syria, North Korea, and Crimea. The company also has offices in the Netherlands, Brazil, India, Japan, and South Korea. _____ is a member of the Motion Picture Association of America.

Exam Probability: **Low**

39. *Answer choices:*

(see index for correct answer)

- a. Third-party source
- b. Safe harbor
- c. Closed household economy
- d. Netflix

Guidance: level 1

:: ::

Collaborative software or _____ is application software designed to help people involved in a common task to achieve their goals. One of the earliest definitions of collaborative software is "intentional group processes plus software to support them".

Exam Probability: **High**

40. *Answer choices:*

(see index for correct answer)

- a. open system
- b. levels of analysis
- c. personal values
- d. Groupware

Guidance: level 1

:: Payment systems ::

A _____ is any system used to settle financial transactions through the transfer of monetary value. This includes the institutions, instruments, people, rules, procedures, standards, and technologies that make it exchange possible. A common type of _____ is called an operational network that links bank accounts and provides for monetary exchange using bank deposits. Some _____ s also include credit mechanisms, which are essentially a different aspect of payment.

Exam Probability: **High**

41. *Answer choices:*

(see index for correct answer)

- a. Payment system
- b. BIPS
- c. BASE24
- d. Direct corporate access

Guidance: level 1

:: Geographic information systems ::

_____ is the computational process of transforming a physical address description to a location on the Earth's surface. Reverse _____, on the other hand, converts geographic coordinates to a description of a location, usually the name of a place or an addressable location. _____ relies on a computer representation of address points, the street / road network, together with postal and administrative boundaries.

Exam Probability: **High**

42. *Answer choices:*

(see index for correct answer)

- a. Geography
- b. Conservation Geoportal
- c. British Cartographic Society
- d. National Land and Property Gazetteer

Guidance: level 1

:: ::

An _____ is system software that manages computer hardware and software resources and provides common services for computer programs.

Exam Probability: **Medium**

43. *Answer choices:*

(see index for correct answer)

- a. Operating system
- b. corporate values
- c. Sarbanes-Oxley act of 2002
- d. functional perspective

Guidance: level 1

:: Information systems ::

A _____ is an information system that supports business or organizational decision-making activities. DSSs serve the management, operations and planning levels of an organization and help people make decisions about problems that may be rapidly changing and not easily specified in advance—i.e. unstructured and semi-structured decision problems. _____ s can be either fully computerized or human-powered, or a combination of both.

Exam Probability: **Low**

44. *Answer choices:*

(see index for correct answer)

- a. Diablo Data Systems
- b. Complex event processing
- c. Decision support system
- d. Feral information systems

Guidance: level 1

:: ::

_____ is an American video-sharing website headquartered in San Bruno, California. Three former PayPal employees—Chad Hurley, Steve Chen, and Jawed Karim—created the service in February 2005. Google bought the site in November 2006 for US$1.65 billion; _____ now operates as one of Google's subsidiaries.

Exam Probability: **Low**

45. *Answer choices:*

(see index for correct answer)

- a. Sarbanes-Oxley act of 2002
- b. levels of analysis
- c. co-culture
- d. empathy

Guidance: level 1

:: Information technology ::

_____ is the use of computers to store, retrieve, transmit, and manipulate data, or information, often in the context of a business or other enterprise. IT is considered to be a subset of information and communications technology . An _____ system is generally an information system, a communications system or, more specifically speaking, a computer system – including all hardware, software and peripheral equipment – operated by a limited group of users.

Exam Probability: **Low**

46. *Answer choices:*

(see index for correct answer)

- a. Information technology
- b. Antlabs
- c. Micropipelining
- d. Information Technology Institute

Guidance: level 1

:: Information systems ::

_____s are information systems that are developed in response to corporate business initiative. They are intended to give competitive advantage to the organization. They may deliver a product or service that is at a lower cost, that is differentiated, that focuses on a particular market segment, or is innovative.

Exam Probability: **Low**

47. *Answer choices:*

(see index for correct answer)

- a. Electronic markets
- b. Strategic information system
- c. CGA
- d. Internavi

Guidance: level 1

:: Monopoly (economics) ::

A _____ exists when a specific person or enterprise is the only supplier of a particular commodity. This contrasts with a monopsony which relates to a single entity's control of a market to purchase a good or service, and with oligopoly which consists of a few sellers dominating a market. Monopolies are thus characterized by a lack of economic competition to produce the good or service, a lack of viable substitute goods, and the possibility of a high _____ price well above the seller's marginal cost that leads to a high _____ profit. The verb monopolise or monopolize refers to the process by which a company gains the ability to raise prices or exclude competitors. In economics, a _____ is a single seller. In law, a _____ is a business entity that has significant market power, that is, the power to charge overly high prices. Although monopolies may be big businesses, size is not a characteristic of a _____ . A small business may still have the power to raise prices in a small industry .

Exam Probability: **Low**

48. *Answer choices:*

(see index for correct answer)

- a. Wartime Law on Industrial Property
- b. Patent portfolio
- c. Monopoly
- d. Economies of scope

Guidance: level 1

:: Marketing by medium ::

_____, also called online marketing or Internet advertising or web advertising, is a form of marketing and advertising which uses the Internet to deliver promotional marketing messages to consumers. Many consumers find _____ disruptive and have increasingly turned to ad blocking for a variety of reasons. When software is used to do the purchasing, it is known as programmatic advertising.

Exam Probability: **Medium**

49. *Answer choices:*

(see index for correct answer)

- a. New media marketing
- b. Social intelligence architect
- c. Direct Text Marketing
- d. Social marketing intelligence

Guidance: level 1

:: Database management systems ::

A _____ is a type of data model that determines the logical structure of a database and fundamentally determines in which manner data can be stored, organized and manipulated. The most popular example of a _____ is the relational model, which uses a table-based format.

Exam Probability: **High**

50. *Answer choices:*

(see index for correct answer)

- a. Data definition language
- b. Relation
- c. Database model
- d. Relational calculus

Guidance: level 1

:: ::

A _____ is a system designed to capture, store, manipulate, analyze, manage, and present spatial or geographic data. GIS applications are tools that allow users to create interactive queries , analyze spatial information, edit data in maps, and present the results of all these operations. GIS sometimes refers to geographic information science , the science underlying geographic concepts, applications, and systems.

Exam Probability: **Medium**

51. *Answer choices:*

(see index for correct answer)

- a. Geographic information system
- b. Character
- c. cultural
- d. functional perspective

Guidance: level 1

:: Internet marketing ::

_____ is the process of increasing the quality and quantity of website traffic, increasing visibility of a website or a web page to users of a web search engine. SEO refers to the improvement of unpaid results , and excludes the purchase of paid placement.

Exam Probability: **High**

52. Answer choices:

(see index for correct answer)

- a. Post-click marketing
- b. Corporate blog
- c. Dynamic keyword insertion
- d. Search engine optimization

Guidance: level 1

:: ::

A _____ is an abstract model that organizes elements of data and standardizes how they relate to one another and to properties of the real world entities. For instance, a _____ may specify that the data element representing a car be composed of a number of other elements which, in turn, represent the color and size of the car and define its owner.

Exam Probability: **High**

53. Answer choices:

(see index for correct answer)

- a. open system
- b. empathy
- c. Data model
- d. Character

Guidance: level 1

:: Data collection ::

_____ is information that either does not have a pre-defined data model or is not organized in a pre-defined manner. Unstructured information is typically text-heavy, but may contain data such as dates, numbers, and facts as well. This results in irregularities and ambiguities that make it difficult to understand using traditional programs as compared to data stored in fielded form in databases or annotated in documents.

Exam Probability: **Low**

54. *Answer choices:*

(see index for correct answer)

- a. PowerLab
- b. Interpellation
- c. Unstructured data
- d. General Social Survey

Guidance: level 1

:: ::

_____ is a set of values of subjects with respect to qualitative or quantitative variables.

Exam Probability: **Low**

55. *Answer choices:*

(see index for correct answer)

- a. interpersonal communication
- b. empathy
- c. imperative
- d. Data

Guidance: level 1

:: Procurement practices ::

_____ or commercially available off-the-shelf products are packaged solutions which are then adapted to satisfy the needs of the purchasing organization, rather than the commissioning of custom-made, or bespoke, solutions. A related term, Mil-COTS, refers to COTS products for use by the U.S. military.

Exam Probability: **Medium**

56. *Answer choices:*

(see index for correct answer)

- a. Commercial off-the-shelf
- b. Construction by configuration

Guidance: level 1

:: Data privacy ::

_____ is the relationship between the collection and dissemination of data, technology, the public expectation of privacy, legal and political issues surrounding them. It is also known as data privacy or data protection.

Exam Probability: **Medium**

57. *Answer choices:*
(see index for correct answer)

- a. Exponential mechanism
- b. Information privacy
- c. Unclick
- d. Privacy Analytics

Guidance: level 1

:: ::

The _____ is a unit of digital information that most commonly consists of eight bits, representing a binary number. Historically, the _____ was the number of bits used to encode a single character of text in a computer and for this reason it is the smallest addressable unit of memory in many computer architectures.

Exam Probability: **High**

58. *Answer choices:*

(see index for correct answer)

- a. hierarchical perspective
- b. Byte
- c. process perspective
- d. interpersonal communication

Guidance: level 1

:: Networking hardware ::

A network interface controller is a computer hardware component that connects a computer to a computer network.

Exam Probability: **Medium**

59. *Answer choices:*

(see index for correct answer)

- a. bridging
- b. Network interface card
- c. Console server

Guidance: level 1

Marketing

Marketing is the study and management of exchange relationships. Marketing is the business process of creating relationships with and satisfying customers. With its focus on the customer, marketing is one of the premier components of business management.

Marketing is defined by the American Marketing Association as "the activity, set of institutions, and processes for creating, communicating, delivering, and exchanging offerings that have value for customers, clients, partners, and society at large."

:: Market research ::

_____ , an acronym for Information through Disguised Experimentation is an annual market research fair conducted by the students of IIM-Lucknow. Students create games and use various other simulated environments to capture consumers' subconscious thoughts. This innovative method of market research removes the sensitization effect that might bias peoples answers to questions. This ensures that the most truthful answers are captured to research questions. The games are designed in such a way that the observers can elicit all the required information just by observing and noting down the behaviour and the responses of the participants.

Exam Probability: **High**

1. *Answer choices:*

(see index for correct answer)

- a. Multivariate landing page optimization
- b. INDEX
- c. Sagacity segmentation
- d. Gerson Lehrman Group

Guidance: level 1

:: ::

_____ is change in the heritable characteristics of biological populations over successive generations. These characteristics are the expressions of genes that are passed on from parent to offspring during reproduction. Different characteristics tend to exist within any given population as a result of mutation, genetic recombination and other sources of genetic variation. _____ occurs when _____ary processes such as natural selection and genetic drift act on this variation, resulting in certain characteristics becoming more common or rare within a population. It is this process of _____ that has given rise to biodiversity at every level of biological organisation, including the levels of species, individual organisms and molecules.

Exam Probability: **High**

2. *Answer choices:*

(see index for correct answer)

- a. Evolution
- b. information systems assessment
- c. deep-level diversity
- d. co-culture

Guidance: level 1

:: ::

A _____ consists of one people who live in the same dwelling and share meals. It may also consist of a single family or another group of people. A dwelling is considered to contain multiple _____ s if meals or living spaces are not shared. The _____ is the basic unit of analysis in many social, microeconomic and government models, and is important to economics and inheritance.

Exam Probability: **Low**

3. *Answer choices:*

(see index for correct answer)

- a. information systems assessment
- b. Household
- c. deep-level diversity
- d. functional perspective

Guidance: level 1

:: Electronic feedback ::

_____ occurs when outputs of a system are routed back as inputs as part of a chain of cause-and-effect that forms a circuit or loop. The system can then be said to feed back into itself. The notion of cause-and-effect has to be handled carefully when applied to _____ systems.

Exam Probability: **Low**

4. *Answer choices:*

(see index for correct answer)

- a. Feedback
- b. Positive feedback

Guidance: level 1

:: Mereology ::

_____ , in the abstract, is what belongs to or with something, whether as an attribute or as a component of said thing. In the context of this article, it is one or more components , whether physical or incorporeal, of a person's estate; or so belonging to, as in being owned by, a person or jointly a group of people or a legal entity like a corporation or even a society. Depending on the nature of the _____ , an owner of _____ has the right to consume, alter, share, redefine, rent, mortgage, pawn, sell, exchange, transfer, give away or destroy it, or to exclude others from doing these things, as well as to perhaps abandon it; whereas regardless of the nature of the _____ , the owner thereof has the right to properly use it , or at the very least exclusively keep it.

Exam Probability: **Medium**

5. *Answer choices:*

(see index for correct answer)

- a. Mereological nihilism
- b. Property

- c. Mereotopology
- d. Gunk

Guidance: level 1

:: Direct marketing ::

_____ is a method of direct marketing in which a salesperson solicits prospective customers to buy products or services, either over the phone or through a subsequent face to face or Web conferencing appointment scheduled during the call. _____ can also include recorded sales pitches programmed to be played over the phone via automatic dialing.

Exam Probability: **Medium**

6. *Answer choices:*

(see index for correct answer)

- a. Peter Lemongello
- b. Ginsu
- c. World Perfume
- d. Telemarketing

Guidance: level 1

:: Advertising ::

_____ is the behavioral and cognitive process of selectively concentrating on a discrete aspect of information, whether deemed subjective or objective, while ignoring other perceivable information. It is a state of arousal. It is the taking possession by the mind in clear and vivid form of one out of what seem several simultaneous objects or trains of thought. Focalization, the concentration of consciousness, is of its essence. _____ has also been described as the allocation of limited cognitive processing resources.

Exam Probability: **Low**

7. *Answer choices:*

(see index for correct answer)

- a. Cidade Limpa
- b. One sheet
- c. Ad-ID
- d. Attention

Guidance: level 1

:: Packaging ::

In work place, _____ or job _____ means good ranking with the hypothesized conception of requirements of a role. There are two types of job _____ s: contextual and task. Task _____ is related to cognitive ability while contextual _____ is dependent upon personality. Task _____ are behavioral roles that are recognized in job descriptions and by remuneration systems, they are directly related to organizational _____ , whereas, contextual _____ are value based and additional behavioral roles that are not recognized in job descriptions and covered by compensation; they are extra roles that are indirectly related to organizational _____ . Citizenship _____ like contextual _____ means a set of individual activity/contribution that supports the organizational culture.

Exam Probability: **Medium**

8. *Answer choices:*

(see index for correct answer)

- a. Performance
- b. Flavor scalping
- c. Fair Packaging and Labeling Act
- d. Flexographic ink

Guidance: level 1

:: ::

A _____ is an organized collection of data, generally stored and accessed electronically from a computer system. Where _____ s are more complex they are often developed using formal design and modeling techniques.

Exam Probability: **High**

9. *Answer choices:*

(see index for correct answer)

- a. imperative
- b. Database
- c. co-culture
- d. empathy

Guidance: level 1

:: Consumer theory ::

A _____ is a technical term in psychology, economics and philosophy usually used in relation to choosing between alternatives. For example, someone prefers A over B if they would rather choose A than B.

Exam Probability: **Medium**

10. *Answer choices:*

(see index for correct answer)

- a. Expenditure function
- b. Induced consumption
- c. Supply and demand
- d. Permanent income hypothesis

Guidance: level 1

:: Trade associations ::

A _____ , also known as an industry trade group, business association, sector association or industry body, is an organization founded and funded by businesses that operate in a specific industry. An industry _____ participates in public relations activities such as advertising, education, political donations, lobbying and publishing, but its focus is collaboration between companies. Associations may offer other services, such as producing conferences, networking or charitable events or offering classes or educational materials. Many associations are non-profit organizations governed by bylaws and directed by officers who are also members.

Exam Probability: **Medium**

11. *Answer choices:*
(see index for correct answer)

- a. Africa Travel Association
- b. Trade Association Forum
- c. Japan Newspaper Publishers and Editors Association
- d. Trade association

Guidance: level 1

:: ::

_____ involves decision making. It can include judging the merits of multiple options and selecting one or more of them. One can make a _____ between imagined options or between real options followed by the corresponding action. For example, a traveler might choose a route for a journey based on the preference of arriving at a given destination as soon as possible. The preferred route can then follow from information such as the length of each of the possible routes, traffic conditions, etc. The arrival at a _____ can include more complex motivators such as cognition, instinct, and feeling.

Exam Probability: **Low**

12. *Answer choices:*

(see index for correct answer)

- a. levels of analysis
- b. deep-level diversity
- c. cultural
- d. hierarchical perspective

Guidance: level 1

:: ::

A _____ is an organization, usually a group of people or a company, authorized to act as a single entity and recognized as such in law. Early incorporated entities were established by charter. Most jurisdictions now allow the creation of new _____ s through registration.

Exam Probability: **Medium**

13. *Answer choices:*

(see index for correct answer)

- a. co-culture
- b. Corporation
- c. Character
- d. process perspective

Guidance: level 1

:: Costs ::

> In economics, _____ is the total economic cost of production and is made up of variable cost, which varies according to the quantity of a good produced and includes inputs such as labour and raw materials, plus fixed cost, which is independent of the quantity of a good produced and includes inputs that cannot be varied in the short term: fixed costs such as buildings and machinery, including sunk costs if any. Since cost is measured per unit of time, it is a flow variable.

Exam Probability: **High**

14. *Answer choices:*

(see index for correct answer)

- a. Implicit cost

- b. Cost of poor quality
- c. Total cost
- d. Cost competitiveness of fuel sources

Guidance: level 1

:: Business economics ::

In economics, _____ is demand for a factor of production or intermediate good that occurs as a result of the demand for another intermediate or final good. In essence, the demand for, say, a factor of production by a firm is dependent on the demand by consumers for the product produced by the firm. The term was first introduced by Alfred Marshall in his Principles of Economics in 1890.

Exam Probability: **Medium**

15. *Answer choices:*

(see index for correct answer)

- a. Derived demand
- b. Seasonal industry
- c. Kaizen costing
- d. Willingness to pay

Guidance: level 1

:: ::

_____ is the process whereby a business sets the price at which it will sell its products and services, and may be part of the business's marketing plan. In setting prices, the business will take into account the price at which it could acquire the goods, the manufacturing cost, the market place, competition, market condition, brand, and quality of product.

Exam Probability: **High**

16. *Answer choices:*

(see index for correct answer)

- a. cultural
- b. interpersonal communication
- c. Character
- d. Pricing

Guidance: level 1

:: ::

In the broadest sense, _____ is any practice which contributes to the sale of products to a retail consumer. At a retail in-store level, _____ refers to the variety of products available for sale and the display of those products in such a way that it stimulates interest and entices customers to make a purchase.

Exam Probability: **Medium**

17. *Answer choices:*

(see index for correct answer)

- a. Merchandising
- b. empathy
- c. levels of analysis
- d. interpersonal communication

Guidance: level 1

:: ::

_____ is an abstract concept of management of complex systems according to a set of rules and trends. In systems theory, these types of rules exist in various fields of biology and society, but the term has slightly different meanings according to context. For example.

Exam Probability: **High**

18. *Answer choices:*

(see index for correct answer)

- a. co-culture
- b. information systems assessment
- c. Regulation

- d. corporate values

Guidance: level 1

:: ::

_____ is a marketing communication that employs an openly sponsored, non-personal message to promote or sell a product, service or idea. Sponsors of _____ are typically businesses wishing to promote their products or services. _____ is differentiated from public relations in that an advertiser pays for and has control over the message. It differs from personal selling in that the message is non-personal, i.e., not directed to a particular individual. _____ is communicated through various mass media, including traditional media such as newspapers, magazines, television, radio, outdoor _____ or direct mail; and new media such as search results, blogs, social media, websites or text messages. The actual presentation of the message in a medium is referred to as an advertisement, or "ad" or advert for short.

Exam Probability: **High**

19. *Answer choices:*

(see index for correct answer)

- a. surface-level diversity
- b. Advertising
- c. information systems assessment
- d. levels of analysis

Guidance: level 1

:: Marketing ::

A _____ is the quantity of payment or compensation given by one party to another in return for one unit of goods or services.. A _____ is influenced by both production costs and demand for the product. A _____ may be determined by a monopolist or may be imposed on the firm by market conditions.

Exam Probability: **Low**

20. *Answer choices:*

(see index for correct answer)

- a. Penetration pricing
- b. Osborne effect
- c. Competitor indexing
- d. Price

Guidance: level 1

:: Marketing ::

A _____ is a group of customers within a business's serviceable available market at which a business aims its marketing efforts and resources. A _____ is a subset of the total market for a product or service. The _____ typically consists of consumers who exhibit similar characteristics and are considered most likely to buy a business's market offerings or are likely to be the most profitable segments for the business to service.

Exam Probability: **Medium**

21. *Answer choices:*

(see index for correct answer)

- a. Editorial calendar
- b. Inventory control
- c. The Cellar
- d. Target market

Guidance: level 1

:: Data analysis ::

_____ is a process of inspecting, cleansing, transforming, and modeling data with the goal of discovering useful information, informing conclusions, and supporting decision-making. _____ has multiple facets and approaches, encompassing diverse techniques under a variety of names, and is used in different business, science, and social science domains. In today's business world, _____ plays a role in making decisions more scientific and helping businesses operate more effectively.

Exam Probability: **Medium**

22. *Answer choices:*

(see index for correct answer)

- a. Data analysis
- b. Subgroup analysis
- c. Training set
- d. Health care analytics

Guidance: level 1

:: ::

_____ consists of using generic or ad hoc methods in an orderly manner to find solutions to problems. Some of the problem-solving techniques developed and used in philosophy, artificial intelligence, computer science, engineering, mathematics, or medicine are related to mental problem-solving techniques studied in psychology.

Exam Probability: **Medium**

23. *Answer choices:*

(see index for correct answer)

- a. interpersonal communication
- b. deep-level diversity

- c. empathy
- d. similarity-attraction theory

Guidance: level 1

:: ::

_____ is the practice of deliberately managing the spread of information between an individual or an organization and the public. _____ may include an organization or individual gaining exposure to their audiences using topics of public interest and news items that do not require direct payment. This differentiates it from advertising as a form of marketing communications. _____ is the idea of creating coverage for clients for free, rather than marketing or advertising. But now, advertising is also a part of greater PR Activities. An example of good _____ would be generating an article featuring a client, rather than paying for the client to be advertised next to the article. The aim of _____ is to inform the public, prospective customers, investors, partners, employees, and other stakeholders and ultimately persuade them to maintain a positive or favorable view about the organization, its leadership, products, or political decisions. _____ professionals typically work for PR and marketing firms, businesses and companies, government, and public officials as PIOs and nongovernmental organizations, and nonprofit organizations. Jobs central to _____ include account coordinator, account executive, account supervisor, and media relations manager.

Exam Probability: **Low**

24. *Answer choices:*

(see index for correct answer)

- a. open system
- b. process perspective
- c. levels of analysis
- d. Public relations

Guidance: level 1

:: Auctioneering ::

An _____ is a process of buying and selling goods or services by offering them up for bid, taking bids, and then selling the item to the highest bidder. The open ascending price _____ is arguably the most common form of _____ in use today. Participants bid openly against one another, with each subsequent bid required to be higher than the previous bid. An _____ eer may announce prices, bidders may call out their bids themselves, or bids may be submitted electronically with the highest current bid publicly displayed. In a Dutch _____ , the _____ eer begins with a high asking price for some quantity of like items; the price is lowered until a participant is willing to accept the _____ eer's price for some quantity of the goods in the lot or until the seller's reserve price is met. While _____ s are most associated in the public imagination with the sale of antiques, paintings, rare collectibles and expensive wines, _____ s are also used for commodities, livestock, radio spectrum and used cars. In economic theory, an _____ may refer to any mechanism or set of trading rules for exchange.

Exam Probability: **Medium**

25. *Answer choices:*

(see index for correct answer)

- a. Auction
- b. Unique bid auction
- c. Auto auction
- d. Japanese auction

Guidance: level 1

:: ::

An _____ is a systematic and independent examination of books, accounts, statutory records, documents and vouchers of an organization to ascertain how far the financial statements as well as non-financial disclosures present a true and fair view of the concern. It also attempts to ensure that the books of accounts are properly maintained by the concern as required by law. _____ing has become such a ubiquitous phenomenon in the corporate and the public sector that academics started identifying an "_____ Society". The _____ or perceives and recognises the propositions before them for examination, obtains evidence, evaluates the same and formulates an opinion on the basis of his judgement which is communicated through their _____ing report.

Exam Probability: **Medium**

26. *Answer choices:*

(see index for correct answer)

- a. levels of analysis
- b. corporate values
- c. imperative

- d. Audit

Guidance: level 1

:: ::

In communications and information processing, _____ is a system of rules to convert information—such as a letter, word, sound, image, or gesture—into another form or representation, sometimes shortened or secret, for communication through a communication channel or storage in a storage medium. An early example is the invention of language, which enabled a person, through speech, to communicate what they saw, heard, felt, or thought to others. But speech limits the range of communication to the distance a voice can carry, and limits the audience to those present when the speech is uttered. The invention of writing, which converted spoken language into visual symbols, extended the range of communication across space and time.

Exam Probability: **Medium**

27. *Answer choices:*

(see index for correct answer)

- a. Code
- b. hierarchical
- c. process perspective
- d. cultural

Guidance: level 1

:: Marketing analytics ::

_____ is a long-term, forward-looking approach to planning with the fundamental goal of achieving a sustainable competitive advantage. Strategic planning involves an analysis of the company's strategic initial situation prior to the formulation, evaluation and selection of market-oriented competitive position that contributes to the company's goals and marketing objectives.

Exam Probability: **Low**

28. *Answer choices:*

(see index for correct answer)

- a. Gross rating point
- b. Marketing performance measurement and management
- c. Marketing strategy
- d. Marketing effectiveness

Guidance: level 1

:: ::

_____ is a means of protection from financial loss. It is a form of risk management, primarily used to hedge against the risk of a contingent or uncertain loss

Exam Probability: **Medium**

29. *Answer choices:*

(see index for correct answer)

- a. process perspective
- b. imperative
- c. Insurance
- d. Sarbanes-Oxley act of 2002

Guidance: level 1

:: Market research ::

A _____ is a small, but demographically diverse group of people and whose reactions are studied especially in market research or political analysis in guided or open discussions about a new product or something else to determine the reactions that can be expected from a larger population. It is a form of qualitative research consisting of interviews in which a group of people are asked about their perceptions, opinions, beliefs, and attitudes towards a product, service, concept, advertisement, idea, or packaging. Questions are asked in an interactive group setting where participants are free to talk with other group members. During this process, the researcher either takes notes or records the vital points he or she is getting from the group. Researchers should select members of the _____ carefully for effective and authoritative responses.

Exam Probability: **High**

30. *Answer choices:*

(see index for correct answer)

- a. Cambashi
- b. Confidence interval
- c. Focus group
- d. Indian Readership Survey

Guidance: level 1

:: Marketing ::

_____s are structured marketing strategies designed by merchants to encourage customers to continue to shop at or use the services of businesses associated with each program. These programs exist covering most types of commerce, each one having varying features and rewards-schemes.

Exam Probability: **Medium**

31. *Answer choices:*

(see index for correct answer)

- a. Factor analysis
- b. Mass marketing
- c. Market environment
- d. Loyalty program

Guidance: level 1

:: Types of marketing ::

_____ was first defined as a form of marketing developed from direct response marketing campaigns which emphasizes customer retention and satisfaction, rather than a focus on sales transactions.

Exam Probability: **Low**

32. *Answer choices:*

(see index for correct answer)

- a. Account planning
- b. Limited edition candy
- c. Relationship marketing
- d. Project SCUM

Guidance: level 1

:: bad_topic ::

Sponsoring something is the act of supporting an event, activity, person, or organization financially or through the provision of products or services. The individual or group that provides the support, similar to a benefactor, is known as sponsor.

Exam Probability: **Medium**

33. *Answer choices:*

(see index for correct answer)

- a. Sponsorship
- b. Cognitive appraisal
- c. Wolverine Worldwide
- d. Sealy Corporation

Guidance: level 1

:: Problem solving ::

In other words, _____ is a situation where a group of people meet to generate new ideas and solutions around a specific domain of interest by removing inhibitions. People are able to think more freely and they suggest as many spontaneous new ideas as possible. All the ideas are noted down and those ideas are not criticized and after _____ session the ideas are evaluated. The term was popularized by Alex Faickney Osborn in the 1953 book Applied Imagination.

Exam Probability: **Medium**

34. Answer choices:

(see index for correct answer)

- a. Problem shaping
- b. Tar-Baby
- c. Rhetorical reason
- d. Brainstorming

Guidance: level 1

:: Direct marketing ::

> _____ is a form of advertising where organizations communicate directly to customers through a variety of media including cell phone text messaging, email, websites, online adverts, database marketing, fliers, catalog distribution, promotional letters, targeted television, newspapers, magazine advertisements, and outdoor advertising. Among practitioners, it is also known as direct response marketing.

Exam Probability: **Medium**

35. Answer choices:

(see index for correct answer)

- a. Database marketing
- b. Scentura
- c. Direct marketing
- d. Book of the Month Club

Guidance: level 1

:: ::

_____ is a process whereby a person assumes the parenting of another, usually a child, from that person's biological or legal parent or parents. Legal _____ s permanently transfers all rights and responsibilities, along with filiation, from the biological parent or parents.

Exam Probability: **Medium**

36. *Answer choices:*

(see index for correct answer)

- a. similarity-attraction theory
- b. Adoption
- c. empathy
- d. surface-level diversity

Guidance: level 1

:: ::

_____ Motor Company is an American multinational automaker that has its main headquarter in Dearborn, Michigan, a suburb of Detroit. It was founded by Henry _____ and incorporated on June 16, 1903. The company sells automobiles and commercial vehicles under the _____ brand and most luxury cars under the Lincoln brand. _____ also owns Brazilian SUV manufacturer Troller, an 8% stake in Aston Martin of the United Kingdom and a 32% stake in Jiangling Motors. It also has joint-ventures in China , Taiwan , Thailand , Turkey , and Russia . The company is listed on the New York Stock Exchange and is controlled by the _____ family; they have minority ownership but the majority of the voting power.

Exam Probability: **Low**

37. *Answer choices:*

(see index for correct answer)

- a. functional perspective
- b. information systems assessment
- c. Sarbanes-Oxley act of 2002
- d. Ford

Guidance: level 1

:: Market research ::

An _____ or lighthouse customer is an early customer of a given company, product, or technology. The term originates from Everett M. Rogers' Diffusion of Innovations .

Exam Probability: **High**

38. *Answer choices:*

(see index for correct answer)

- a. Sectoral analysis
- b. Consumer neuroscience
- c. Location intelligence
- d. Early adopter

Guidance: level 1

:: Cognitive dissonance ::

In the field of psychology, _____ is the mental discomfort experienced by a person who holds two or more contradictory beliefs, ideas, or values. This discomfort is triggered by a situation in which a person's belief clashes with new evidence perceived by the person. When confronted with facts that contradict beliefs, ideals, and values, people will try to find a way to resolve the contradiction to reduce their discomfort.

Exam Probability: **Low**

39. *Answer choices:*

(see index for correct answer)

- a. Self-refuting idea
- b. Cognitive dissonance

- c. Doublespeak
- d. The Fox and the Grapes

Guidance: level 1

:: Marketing ::

_____ is research conducted for a problem that has not been studied more clearly, intended to establish priorities, develop operational definitions and improve the final research design. _____ helps determine the best research design, data-collection method and selection of subjects. It should draw definitive conclusions only with extreme caution. Given its fundamental nature, _____ often relies on techniques such as.

Exam Probability: **High**

40. *Answer choices:*

(see index for correct answer)

- a. Exploratory research
- b. Call centre
- c. Market sector
- d. One Town One Product

Guidance: level 1

:: Health promotion ::

_____, as defined by the World _____ Organization, is "a state of complete physical, mental and social well-being and not merely the absence of disease or infirmity." This definition has been subject to controversy, as it may have limited value for implementation. _____ may be defined as the ability to adapt and manage physical, mental and social challenges throughout life.

Exam Probability: **High**

41. *Answer choices:*

(see index for correct answer)

- a. Integrated Management of Childhood Illness
- b. Myokine
- c. High-deductible health plan
- d. Health

Guidance: level 1

:: Marketing ::

_____ is a growth strategy that identifies and develops new market segments for current products. A _____ strategy targets non-buying customers in currently targeted segments. It also targets new customers in new segments.

Exam Probability: **Low**

42. *Answer choices:*

(see index for correct answer)

- a. Purchase funnel
- b. Disruptive innovation
- c. Marketing mix
- d. Market development

Guidance: level 1

:: Evaluation methods ::

> _____ is a scientific method of observation to gather non-numerical data. This type of research "refers to the meanings, concepts definitions, characteristics, metaphors, symbols, and description of things" and not to their "counts or measures." This research answers why and how a certain phenomenon may occur rather than how often. _____ approaches are employed across many academic disciplines, focusing particularly on the human elements of the social and natural sciences; in less academic contexts, areas of application include qualitative market research, business, service demonstrations by non-profits, and journalism.

Exam Probability: **High**

43. *Answer choices:*

(see index for correct answer)

- a. Economic impact analysis
- b. Most significant change technique

- c. Poll average
- d. Design science

Guidance: level 1

:: Goods ::

In most contexts, the concept of _____ denotes the conduct that should be preferred when posed with a choice between possible actions. _____ is generally considered to be the opposite of evil, and is of interest in the study of morality, ethics, religion and philosophy. The specific meaning and etymology of the term and its associated translations among ancient and contemporary languages show substantial variation in its inflection and meaning depending on circumstances of place, history, religious, or philosophical context.

Exam Probability: **Low**

44. *Answer choices:*

(see index for correct answer)

- a. Normal good
- b. Veblen good
- c. Good
- d. Durable good

Guidance: level 1

:: Management occupations ::

_____ ship is the process of designing, launching and running a new business, which is often initially a small business. The people who create these businesses are called _____ s.

Exam Probability: **Low**

45. *Answer choices:*

(see index for correct answer)

- a. entrepreneurial
- b. Corporate trainer
- c. Entrepreneur
- d. Deputy mayor

Guidance: level 1

:: Stock market ::

The _____ of a corporation is all of the shares into which ownership of the corporation is divided. In American English, the shares are commonly known as "_____s". A single share of the _____ represents fractional ownership of the corporation in proportion to the total number of shares. This typically entitles the _____ holder to that fraction of the company's earnings, proceeds from liquidation of assets, or voting power, often dividing these up in proportion to the amount of money each _____ holder has invested. Not all _____ is necessarily equal, as certain classes of _____ may be issued for example without voting rights, with enhanced voting rights, or with a certain priority to receive profits or liquidation proceeds before or after other classes of shareholders.

Exam Probability: **High**

46. *Answer choices:*

(see index for correct answer)

- a. Volume-weighted average price
- b. Stock
- c. Shadow stock
- d. OpenIPO

Guidance: level 1

:: Logistics ::

_____ is generally the detailed organization and implementation of a complex operation. In a general business sense, _____ is the management of the flow of things between the point of origin and the point of consumption in order to meet requirements of customers or corporations. The resources managed in _____ may include tangible goods such as materials, equipment, and supplies, as well as food and other consumable items. The _____ of physical items usually involves the integration of information flow, materials handling, production, packaging, inventory, transportation, warehousing, and often security.

Exam Probability: **High**

47. *Answer choices:*

(see index for correct answer)

- a. Logistics
- b. Hubs and Nodes
- c. Design for availability
- d. Navy lighterage pontoons

Guidance: level 1

:: ::

A _____ is a research instrument consisting of a series of questions for the purpose of gathering information from respondents. The _____ was invented by the Statistical Society of London in 1838.

Exam Probability: **Medium**

48. *Answer choices:*

(see index for correct answer)

- a. information systems assessment
- b. hierarchical perspective
- c. Character
- d. process perspective

Guidance: level 1

:: ::

In legal terminology, a _____ is any formal legal document that sets out the facts and legal reasons that the filing party or parties believes are sufficient to support a claim against the party or parties against whom the claim is brought that entitles the plaintiff to a remedy. For example, the Federal Rules of Civil Procedure that govern civil litigation in United States courts provide that a civil action is commenced with the filing or service of a pleading called a _____ . Civil court rules in states that have incorporated the Federal Rules of Civil Procedure use the same term for the same pleading.

Exam Probability: **Low**

49. *Answer choices:*

(see index for correct answer)

- a. information systems assessment
- b. personal values
- c. Complaint
- d. interpersonal communication

Guidance: level 1

:: Market research ::

_____ is the action of defining, gathering, analyzing, and distributing intelligence about products, customers, competitors, and any aspect of the environment needed to support executives and managers in strategic decision making for an organization.

Exam Probability: **Low**

50. *Answer choices:*
(see index for correct answer)

- a. Omnibus
- b. Media-Analyse
- c. CoolBrands
- d. Competitive intelligence

Guidance: level 1

_____ is the collection of techniques, skills, methods, and processes used in the production of goods or services or in the accomplishment of objectives, such as scientific investigation. _____ can be the knowledge of techniques, processes, and the like, or it can be embedded in machines to allow for operation without detailed knowledge of their workings. Systems applying _____ by taking an input, changing it according to the system's use, and then producing an outcome are referred to as _____ systems or technological systems.

Exam Probability: **Medium**

51. *Answer choices:*
(see index for correct answer)

- a. functional perspective
- b. open system
- c. Technology
- d. surface-level diversity

Guidance: level 1

In regulatory jurisdictions that provide for it, _____ is a group of laws and organizations designed to ensure the rights of consumers as well as fair trade, competition and accurate information in the marketplace. The laws are designed to prevent the businesses that engage in fraud or specified unfair practices from gaining an advantage over competitors. They may also provides additional protection for those most vulnerable in society. _____ laws are a form of government regulation that aim to protect the rights of consumers. For example, a government may require businesses to disclose detailed information about products—particularly in areas where safety or public health is an issue, such as food.

Exam Probability: **High**

52. *Answer choices:*

(see index for correct answer)

- a. corporate values
- b. Consumer Protection
- c. surface-level diversity
- d. imperative

Guidance: level 1

:: Data management ::

In computing, a _____ , also known as an enterprise _____ , is a system used for reporting and data analysis, and is considered a core component of business intelligence. DWs are central repositories of integrated data from one or more disparate sources. They store current and historical data in one single place that are used for creating analytical reports for workers throughout the enterprise.

Exam Probability: **High**

53. *Answer choices:*

(see index for correct answer)

- a. Data warehouse
- b. Data conditioning
- c. Single customer view
- d. Control break

Guidance: level 1

:: ::

In marketing jargon, product lining is offering several related products for sale individually. Unlike product bundling, where several products are combined into one group, which is then offered for sale as a units, product lining involves offering the products for sale separately. A line can comprise related products of various sizes, types, colors, qualities, or prices. Line depth refers to the number of subcategories a category has. Line consistency refers to how closely related the products that make up the line are. Line vulnerability refers to the percentage of sales or profits that are derived from only a few products in the line.

Exam Probability: **Medium**

54. *Answer choices:*

(see index for correct answer)

- a. open system
- b. Product line
- c. interpersonal communication
- d. empathy

Guidance: level 1

:: Advertising techniques ::

In promotion and of advertising, a _____ or show consists of a person's written or spoken statement extolling the virtue of a product. The term "_____" most commonly applies to the sales-pitches attributed to ordinary citizens, whereas the word "endorsement" usually applies to pitches by celebrities. _____ s can be part of communal marketing. Sometimes, the cartoon character can be a _____ in a commercial.

Exam Probability: **High**

55. *Answer choices:*

(see index for correct answer)

- a. Dolly Dimples
- b. Debranding
- c. FAST marketing
- d. Below the line

Guidance: level 1

:: ::

In logic and philosophy, an _____ is a series of statements, called the premises or premisses, intended to determine the degree of truth of another statement, the conclusion. The logical form of an _____ in a natural language can be represented in a symbolic formal language, and independently of natural language formally defined "_____ s" can be made in math and computer science.

Exam Probability: **High**

56. *Answer choices:*

(see index for correct answer)

- a. hierarchical perspective
- b. empathy
- c. surface-level diversity
- d. Argument

Guidance: level 1

:: Marketing ::

_____ is the process of using surveys to evaluate consumer acceptance of a new product idea prior to the introduction of a product to the market. It is important not to confuse _____ with advertising testing, brand testing and packaging testing; as is sometimes done. _____ focuses on the basic product idea, without the embellishments and puffery inherent in advertising.

Exam Probability: **High**

57. *Answer choices:*

(see index for correct answer)

- a. Beat-sheet
- b. Competitor indexing

- c. Concept testing
- d. Aspirational brand

Guidance: level 1

:: Marketing ::

_____ is multi-channel online marketing technique focused at reaching a specific audience on their smartphones, tablets, or any other related devices through websites, E-mail, SMS and MMS, social media, or mobile applications. _____ can provide customers with time and location sensitive, personalized information that promotes goods, services and ideas. In a more theoretical manner, academic Andreas Kaplan defines _____ as "any marketing activity conducted through a ubiquitous network to which consumers are constantly connected using a personal mobile device".

Exam Probability: **Low**

58. *Answer choices:*
(see index for correct answer)

- a. Product naming
- b. Fifth screen
- c. Generic brand
- d. Kano model

Guidance: level 1

:: Product development ::

In business and engineering, _____ covers the complete process of bringing a new product to market. A central aspect of NPD is product design, along with various business considerations. _____ is described broadly as the transformation of a market opportunity into a product available for sale. The product can be tangible or intangible, though sometimes services and other processes are distinguished from "products." NPD requires an understanding of customer needs and wants, the competitive environment, and the nature of the market. Cost, time and quality are the main variables that drive customer needs. Aiming at these three variables, innovative companies develop continuous practices and strategies to better satisfy customer requirements and to increase their own market share by a regular development of new products. There are many uncertainties and challenges which companies must face throughout the process. The use of best practices and the elimination of barriers to communication are the main concerns for the management of the NPD.

Exam Probability: **Medium**

59. *Answer choices:*

(see index for correct answer)

- a. Product design specification
- b. New product development
- c. Material selection
- d. Design for assembly

Guidance: level 1

Manufacturing

Manufacturing is the production of merchandise for use or sale using labor and machines, tools, chemical and biological processing, or formulation. The term may refer to a range of human activity, from handicraft to high tech, but is most commonly applied to industrial design, in which raw materials are transformed into finished goods on a large scale. Such finished goods may be sold to other manufacturers for the production of other, more complex products, such as aircraft, household appliances, furniture, sports equipment or automobiles, or sold to wholesalers, who in turn sell them to retailers, who then sell them to end users and consumers.

:: Industrial design ::

In physics and mathematics, the _____ of a mathematical space is informally defined as the minimum number of coordinates needed to specify any point within it. Thus a line has a _____ of one because only one coordinate is needed to specify a point on it for example, the point at 5 on a number line. A surface such as a plane or the surface of a cylinder or sphere has a _____ of two because two coordinates are needed to specify a point on it for example, both a latitude and longitude are required to locate a point on the surface of a sphere. The inside of a cube, a cylinder or a sphere is three-_____ al because three coordinates are needed to locate a point within these spaces.

Exam Probability: **High**

1. *Answer choices:*
(see index for correct answer)

- a. Humanscale
- b. User interface design
- c. Industrial design rights in the European Union
- d. Dimension

Guidance: level 1

:: ::

The _____ is a project plan of how the production budget will be spent over a given timescale, for every phase of a business project.

Exam Probability: **High**

2. *Answer choices:*

(see index for correct answer)

- a. similarity-attraction theory
- b. surface-level diversity
- c. Production schedule
- d. cultural

Guidance: level 1

:: ::

A _____ or till is a mechanical or electronic device for registering and calculating transactions at a point of sale. It is usually attached to a drawer for storing cash and other valuables. A modern _____ is usually attached to a printer that can print out receipts for record-keeping purposes.

Exam Probability: **Low**

3. *Answer choices:*

(see index for correct answer)

- a. Cash register
- b. process perspective
- c. empathy

- d. levels of analysis

Guidance: level 1

:: Risk analysis ::

> Supply-chain risk management is "the implementation of strategies to manage both everyday and exceptional risks along the supply chain based on continuous risk assessment with the objective of reducing vulnerability and ensuring continuity".

Exam Probability: **Low**

4. *Answer choices:*

(see index for correct answer)

- a. Unintended consequences
- b. Supply chain risk management
- c. Process decision program chart
- d. Qualitative risk analysis

Guidance: level 1

:: Quality ::

The _____ , formerly the _____ Control, is a knowledge-based global community of quality professionals, with nearly 80,000 members dedicated to promoting and advancing quality tools, principles, and practices in their workplaces and communities.

Exam Probability: **High**

5. *Answer choices:*

(see index for correct answer)

- a. Japanese quality
- b. The Partnership for Excellence
- c. American Society for Quality
- d. Quality of life

Guidance: level 1

:: Industries ::

The _____ comprises the companies that produce industrial chemicals. Central to the modern world economy, it converts raw materials into more than 70,000 different products. The plastics industry contains some overlap, as most chemical companies produce plastic as well as other chemicals.

Exam Probability: **Medium**

6. *Answer choices:*

(see index for correct answer)

- a. Chemical industry
- b. Alcohol industry
- c. Textile industry
- d. Radio industry

Guidance: level 1

:: Chemical reactions ::

A _____ is a process that leads to the chemical transformation of one set of chemical substances to another. Classically, _____ s encompass changes that only involve the positions of electrons in the forming and breaking of chemical bonds between atoms, with no change to the nuclei , and can often be described by a chemical equation. Nuclear chemistry is a sub-discipline of chemistry that involves the _____ s of unstable and radioactive elements where both electronic and nuclear changes can occur.

Exam Probability: **Medium**

7. *Answer choices:*

(see index for correct answer)

- a. Addition reaction
- b. Chemical reaction
- c. Bioorthogonal chemistry
- d. Neutralization

Guidance: level 1

:: Management ::

_____ is a method of quality control which employs statistical methods to monitor and control a process. This helps to ensure that the process operates efficiently, producing more specification-conforming products with less waste. SPC can be applied to any process where the "conforming product" output can be measured. Key tools used in SPC include run charts, control charts, a focus on continuous improvement, and the design of experiments. An example of a process where SPC is applied is manufacturing lines.

Exam Probability: **High**

8. *Answer choices:*

(see index for correct answer)

- a. Statistical process control
- b. Strategic group
- c. Value proposition
- d. Energy monitoring and targeting

Guidance: level 1

:: Quality awards ::

The _____ recognizes U.S. organizations in the business, health care, education, and nonprofit sectors for performance excellence. The Baldrige Award is the only formal recognition of the performance excellence of both public and private U.S. organizations given by the President of the United States. It is administered by the Baldrige Performance Excellence Program, which is based at and managed by the National Institute of Standards and Technology, an agency of the U.S. Department of Commerce.

Exam Probability: **Low**

9. *Answer choices:*
(see index for correct answer)

- a. The Deming Cup
- b. European Quality Award
- c. Malcolm Baldrige National Quality Award
- d. Philippine Quality Award

Guidance: level 1

:: Outsourcing ::

_____ is an institutional procurement process that continuously improves and re-evaluates the purchasing activities of a company. In the services industry, _____ refers to a service solution, sometimes called a strategic partnership, which is specifically customized to meet the client's individual needs. In a production environment, it is often considered one component of supply chain management. Modern supply chain management professionals have placed emphasis on defining the distinct differences between _____ and procurement. Procurement operations support tactical day-to-day transactions such as issuing Purchase Orders to suppliers, whereas _____ represents to strategic planning, supplier development, contract negotiation, supply chain infrastructure, and outsourcing models.

Exam Probability: **Low**

10. *Answer choices:*

(see index for correct answer)

- a. Service review
- b. Strategic sourcing
- c. Service-level agreement
- d. Application Management Services Framework

Guidance: level 1

:: Quality ::

_____ is a concept first outlined by quality expert Joseph M. Juran in publications, most notably Juran on _____ . Designing for quality and innovation is one of the three universal processes of the Juran Trilogy, in which Juran describes what is required to achieve breakthroughs in new products, services, and processes. Juran believed that quality could be planned, and that most quality crises and problems relate to the way in which quality was planned.

Exam Probability: **Medium**

11. *Answer choices:*

(see index for correct answer)

- a. Diamond clarity
- b. Ringtest
- c. Quality by Design
- d. Root cause

Guidance: level 1

:: Costs ::

In microeconomic theory, the _____ , or alternative cost, of making a particular choice is the value of the most valuable choice out of those that were not taken. In other words, opportunity that will require sacrifices.

Exam Probability: **High**

12. *Answer choices:*

(see index for correct answer)

- a. Sliding scale
- b. Economic cost
- c. Direct materials cost
- d. Opportunity cost

Guidance: level 1

:: E-commerce ::

_____ is the business-to-business or business-to-consumer or business-to-government purchase and sale of supplies, work, and services through the Internet as well as other information and networking systems, such as electronic data interchange and enterprise resource planning.

Exam Probability: **Medium**

13. *Answer choices:*

(see index for correct answer)

- a. Coinye
- b. E-procurement
- c. Dark store
- d. Spamvertising

Guidance: level 1

:: Promotion and marketing communications ::

The _____ of American Manufacturers, now ThomasNet, is an online platform for supplier discovery and product sourcing in the US and Canada. It was once known as the "big green books" and "Thomas Registry", and was a multi-volume directory of industrial product information covering 650,000 distributors, manufacturers and service companies within 67,000-plus industrial categories that is now published on ThomasNet.

Exam Probability: **Medium**

14. *Answer choices:*

(see index for correct answer)

- a. Reach
- b. Direct mail
- c. Sales promotion
- d. Thomas Register

Guidance: level 1

:: Business ::

The seller, or the provider of the goods or services, completes a sale in response to an acquisition, appropriation, requisition or a direct interaction with the buyer at the point of sale. There is a passing of title of the item, and the settlement of a price, in which agreement is reached on a price for which transfer of ownership of the item will occur. The seller, not the purchaser typically executes the sale and it may be completed prior to the obligation of payment. In the case of indirect interaction, a person who sells goods or service on behalf of the owner is known as a _____ man or _____ woman or _____ person, but this often refers to someone selling goods in a store/shop, in which case other terms are also common, including _____ clerk, shop assistant, and retail clerk.

Exam Probability: **Low**

15. *Answer choices:*

(see index for correct answer)

- a. Encore fellowships
- b. Architecture of Interoperable Information Systems
- c. Sales
- d. Corporate farming

Guidance: level 1

:: ::

_____ refers to a business or organization attempting to acquire goods or services to accomplish its goals. Although there are several organizations that attempt to set standards in the _____ process, processes can vary greatly between organizations. Typically the word "_____" is not used interchangeably with the word "procurement", since procurement typically includes expediting, supplier quality, and transportation and logistics in addition to _____ .

Exam Probability: **Medium**

16. *Answer choices:*

(see index for correct answer)

- a. hierarchical
- b. Purchasing
- c. functional perspective
- d. imperative

Guidance: level 1

:: Production and manufacturing ::

_____ was a management-led program to eliminate defects in industrial production that enjoyed brief popularity in American industry from 1964 to the early 1970s. Quality expert Philip Crosby later incorporated it into his "Absolutes of Quality Management" and it enjoyed a renaissance in the American automobile industry—as a performance goal more than as a program—in the 1990s. Although applicable to any type of enterprise, it has been primarily adopted within supply chains wherever large volumes of components are being purchased .

Exam Probability: **High**

17. *Answer choices:*

(see index for correct answer)

- a. Craft production
- b. Cellular manufacturing
- c. Zero Defects
- d. Continuous production

Guidance: level 1

:: Data interchange standards ::

_____ is the concept of businesses electronically communicating information that was traditionally communicated on paper, such as purchase orders and invoices. Technical standards for EDI exist to facilitate parties transacting such instruments without having to make special arrangements.

Exam Probability: **High**

18. *Answer choices:*

(see index for correct answer)

- a. ASC X12
- b. Data Interchange Standards Association
- c. Uniform Communication Standard

- d. Interaction protocol

Guidance: level 1

:: Management ::

A process is a unique combination of tools, materials, methods, and people engaged in producing a measurable output; for example a manufacturing line for machine parts. All processes have inherent statistical variability which can be evaluated by statistical methods.

Exam Probability: **Medium**

19. *Answer choices:*

(see index for correct answer)

- a. Commercial management
- b. Project management simulation
- c. Extended enterprise
- d. Matrix management

Guidance: level 1

:: Industrial processes ::

_____ is a technique involving the condensation of vapors and the return of this condensate to the system from which it originated. It is used in industrial and laboratory distillations. It is also used in chemistry to supply energy to reactions over a long period of time.

Exam Probability: **High**

20. *Answer choices:*

(see index for correct answer)

- a. Peroxide process
- b. Sinter Plant
- c. Sepro Mineral Systems
- d. Grainer evaporation process

Guidance: level 1

:: Quality management ::

_____ ensures that an organization, product or service is consistent. It has four main components: quality planning, quality assurance, quality control and quality improvement. _____ is focused not only on product and service quality, but also on the means to achieve it. _____ , therefore, uses quality assurance and control of processes as well as products to achieve more consistent quality.What a customer wants and is willing to pay for it determines quality. It is written or unwritten commitment to a known or unknown consumer in the market . Thus, quality can be defined as fitness for intended use or, in other words, how well the product performs its intended function

Exam Probability: **Low**

21. *Answer choices:*

(see index for correct answer)

- a. Flemish Quality Management Center
- b. ISO 9000
- c. Institute of Standards and Industrial Research of Iran
- d. Quality management

Guidance: level 1

:: Process management ::

_____ is a statistics package developed at the Pennsylvania State University by researchers Barbara F. Ryan, Thomas A. Ryan, Jr., and Brian L. Joiner in 1972. It began as a light version of OMNITAB 80, a statistical analysis program by NIST. Statistical analysis software such as _____ automates calculations and the creation of graphs, allowing the user to focus more on the analysis of data and the interpretation of results. It is compatible with other _____, Inc. software.

Exam Probability: **Low**

22. *Answer choices:*

(see index for correct answer)

- a. Artifact-centric business process model

- b. Minitab
- c. Business process discovery
- d. Revenue assurance

Guidance: level 1

:: Costs ::

The _____ is computed by dividing the total cost of goods available for sale by the total units available for sale. This gives a weighted-average unit cost that is applied to the units in the ending inventory.

Exam Probability: **High**

23. *Answer choices:*
(see index for correct answer)

- a. labor cost
- b. Average cost
- c. Khozraschyot
- d. Direct labor cost

Guidance: level 1

:: Business process ::

A committee is a body of one or more persons that is subordinate to a deliberative assembly. Usually, the assembly sends matters into a committee as a way to explore them more fully than would be possible if the assembly itself were considering them. Committees may have different functions and their type of work differ depending on the type of the organization and its needs.

Exam Probability: **High**

24. *Answer choices:*

(see index for correct answer)

- a. Business logic
- b. Steering committee
- c. Business process reengineering
- d. Business process validation

Guidance: level 1

:: Industrial equipment ::

_____ s are heat exchangers typically used to provide heat to the bottom of industrial distillation columns. They boil the liquid from the bottom of a distillation column to generate vapors which are returned to the column to drive the distillation separation. The heat supplied to the column by the _____ at the bottom of the column is removed by the condenser at the top of the column.

Exam Probability: **Low**

25. *Answer choices:*

(see index for correct answer)

- a. Reboiler
- b. Machine tool
- c. Recuperator
- d. Choke manifold

Guidance: level 1

:: Planning ::

_____ is a high level plan to achieve one or more goals under conditions of uncertainty. In the sense of the "art of the general," which included several subsets of skills including tactics, siegecraft, logistics etc., the term came into use in the 6th century C.E. in East Roman terminology, and was translated into Western vernacular languages only in the 18th century. From then until the 20th century, the word "_____" came to denote "a comprehensive way to try to pursue political ends, including the threat or actual use of force, in a dialectic of wills" in a military conflict, in which both adversaries interact.

Exam Probability: **High**

26. *Answer choices:*

(see index for correct answer)

- a. Territorialist School
- b. Cross-cultural differences in decision-making

- c. Fragplan
- d. Strategy

Guidance: level 1

:: Help desk ::

A high-explosive anti-tank warhead is a type of shaped charge explosive that uses the Munroe effect to penetrate thick tank armor. The warhead functions by having the explosive charge collapse a metal liner inside the warhead into a high-velocity superplastic jet. This superplastic jet is capable of penetrating armor steel to a depth of seven or more times the diameter of the charge but is usually used to immobilize or destroy tanks. Due to the way they work, they do not have to be fired as fast as an armor piercing shell, allowing less recoil. Contrary to a widespread misconception, the jet does not melt its way through armor, as its effect is purely kinetic in nature. The _____ warhead has become less effective against tanks and other armored vehicles due to the use of composite armor, explosive-reactive armor, and active protection systems which destroy the _____ warhead before it hits the tank. Even though _____ rounds are less effective against the heavy armor found on 2010s main battle tanks, _____ warheads remain a threat against less-armored parts of a main battle tank and against lighter armored vehicles or unarmored vehicles and helicopters.

Exam Probability: **Low**

27. *Answer choices:*
(see index for correct answer)

- a. HEAT
- b. Web Help Desk

- c. GLPI
- d. OTRS

Guidance: level 1

:: ::

_____ is a kind of action that occur as two or more objects have an effect upon one another. The idea of a two-way effect is essential in the concept of _____ , as opposed to a one-way causal effect. A closely related term is interconnectivity, which deals with the _____ s of _____ s within systems: combinations of many simple _____ s can lead to surprising emergent phenomena. _____ has different tailored meanings in various sciences. Changes can also involve _____ .

Exam Probability: **High**

28. *Answer choices:*

(see index for correct answer)

- a. interpersonal communication
- b. Interaction
- c. personal values
- d. deep-level diversity

Guidance: level 1

:: ::

An _____ is, most an organized examination or formal evaluation exercise. In engineering activities _____ involves the measurements, tests, and gauges applied to certain characteristics in regard to an object or activity. The results are usually compared to specified requirements and standards for determining whether the item or activity is in line with these targets, often with a Standard _____ Procedure in place to ensure consistent checking. _____ s are usually non-destructive.

Exam Probability: **Low**

29. *Answer choices:*

(see index for correct answer)

- a. Character
- b. personal values
- c. Inspection
- d. surface-level diversity

Guidance: level 1

:: Outsourcing ::

_____ is the practice of sourcing from the global market for goods and services across geopolitical boundaries. _____ often aims to exploit global efficiencies in the delivery of a product or service. These efficiencies include low cost skilled labor, low cost raw material and other economic factors like tax breaks and low trade tariffs. A large number of Information Technology projects and Services, including IS Applications and Mobile Apps and database services are outsourced globally to countries like Pakistan and India for more economical pricing.

Exam Probability: **High**

30. *Answer choices:*

(see index for correct answer)

- a. Chinggis Technologies
- b. MITIE Group
- c. Global sourcing
- d. Editorial process outsourcing

Guidance: level 1

:: Production and manufacturing ::

_____ is a comprehensive and rigorous industrial process by which a previously sold, leased, used, worn or non-functional product or part is returned to a 'like-new' or 'better-than-new' condition, from both a quality and performance perspective, through a controlled, reproducible and sustainable process.

Exam Probability: **High**

31. *Answer choices:*

(see index for correct answer)

- a. CTQ tree
- b. Turret lathe
- c. Cycle time variation
- d. Accelerated aging

Guidance: level 1

:: Consortia ::

A _____ is an association of two or more individuals, companies, organizations or governments with the objective of participating in a common activity or pooling their resources for achieving a common goal.

Exam Probability: **High**

32. *Answer choices:*

(see index for correct answer)

- a. PCI-SIG
- b. Consortium
- c. Open Source Development Labs
- d. CANARIE

Guidance: level 1

:: Supply chain management ::

_____ is the process of finding and agreeing to terms, and acquiring goods, services, or works from an external source, often via a tendering or competitive bidding process. _____ is used to ensure the buyer receives goods, services, or works at the best possible price when aspects such as quality, quantity, time, and location are compared. Corporations and public bodies often define processes intended to promote fair and open competition for their business while minimizing risks such as exposure to fraud and collusion.

Exam Probability: **High**

33. *Answer choices:*

(see index for correct answer)

- a. Global supply-chain finance
- b. Blinco Systems Inc.
- c. Procurement
- d. Symphony EYC

Guidance: level 1

:: Data management ::

_____ refers to a data-driven improvement cycle used for improving, optimizing and stabilizing business processes and designs. The _____ improvement cycle is the core tool used to drive Six Sigma projects. However, _____ is not exclusive to Six Sigma and can be used as the framework for other improvement applications.

Exam Probability: **Low**

34. *Answer choices:*

(see index for correct answer)

- a. Durability
- b. DMAIC
- c. single sourcing
- d. Data custodian

Guidance: level 1

:: Water ::

_____ is a transparent, tasteless, odorless, and nearly colorless chemical substance, which is the main constituent of Earth's streams, lakes, and oceans, and the fluids of most living organisms. It is vital for all known forms of life, even though it provides no calories or organic nutrients. Its chemical formula is H2O, meaning that each of its molecules contains one oxygen and two hydrogen atoms, connected by covalent bonds. _____ is the name of the liquid state of H2O at standard ambient temperature and pressure. It forms precipitation in the form of rain and aerosols in the form of fog. Clouds are formed from suspended droplets of _____ and ice, its solid state. When finely divided, crystalline ice may precipitate in the form of snow. The gaseous state of _____ is steam or _____ vapor. _____ moves continually through the _____ cycle of evaporation, transpiration, condensation, precipitation, and runoff, usually reaching the sea.

Exam Probability: **High**

35. *Answer choices:*

(see index for correct answer)

- a. Available water capacity
- b. Water
- c. Portable water tank
- d. Farm water

Guidance: level 1

:: Management ::

A _____ is an idea of the future or desired result that a person or a group of people envisions, plans and commits to achieve. People endeavor to reach _____ s within a finite time by setting deadlines.

Exam Probability: **Low**

36. *Answer choices:*

(see index for correct answer)

- a. Reverse innovation
- b. Sales outsourcing
- c. Social risk management
- d. Process capability

Guidance: level 1

:: Production and manufacturing ::

A BOM can define products as they are designed, as they are ordered, as they are built, or as they are maintained. The different types of BOMs depend on the business need and use for which they are intended. In process industries, the BOM is also known as the formula, recipe, or ingredients list. The phrase "bill of material" is frequently used by engineers as an adjective to refer not to the literal bill, but to the current production configuration of a product, to distinguish it from modified or improved versions under study or in test.

Exam Probability: **Medium**

37. *Answer choices:*

(see index for correct answer)

- a. Subir Chowdhury
- b. Simatic S5 PLC
- c. Value engineering
- d. Miniaturization

Guidance: level 1

:: ::

> _____ is the production of products for use or sale using labour and machines, tools, chemical and biological processing, or formulation. The term may refer to a range of human activity, from handicraft to high tech, but is most commonly applied to industrial design, in which raw materials are transformed into finished goods on a large scale. Such finished goods may be sold to other manufacturers for the production of other, more complex products, such as aircraft, household appliances, furniture, sports equipment or automobiles, or sold to wholesalers, who in turn sell them to retailers, who then sell them to end users and consumers.

Exam Probability: **Low**

38. *Answer choices:*

(see index for correct answer)

- a. deep-level diversity
- b. Sarbanes-Oxley act of 2002

- c. Manufacturing
- d. imperative

Guidance: level 1

:: Teams ::

A _____ usually refers to a group of individuals who work together from different geographic locations and rely on communication technology such as email, FAX, and video or voice conferencing services in order to collaborate. The term can also refer to groups or teams that work together asynchronously or across organizational levels. Powell, Piccoli and Ives define _____ s as "groups of geographically, organizationally and/or time dispersed workers brought together by information and telecommunication technologies to accomplish one or more organizational tasks." According to Ale Ebrahim et. al., _____ s can also be defined as "small temporary groups of geographically, organizationally and/or time dispersed knowledge workers who coordinate their work predominantly with electronic information and communication technologies in order to accomplish one or more organization tasks."

Exam Probability: **Low**

39. *Answer choices:*

(see index for correct answer)

- a. Team-building
- b. Virtual team

Guidance: level 1

:: Process management ::

A _____ is a diagram commonly used in chemical and process engineering to indicate the general flow of plant processes and equipment. The PFD displays the relationship between major equipment of a plant facility and does not show minor details such as piping details and designations. Another commonly used term for a PFD is a flowsheet.

Exam Probability: **Medium**

40. *Answer choices:*
(see index for correct answer)

- a. Acceptable quality limit
- b. Process flow diagram
- c. President%27s Quality Award
- d. Tampering

Guidance: level 1

:: Project management ::

A _____ is one of a series of numbered markers placed along a road or boundary at intervals of one mile or occasionally, parts of a mile. They are typically located at the side of the road or in a median or central reservation. They are alternatively known as mile markers, mileposts or mile posts . Mileage is the distance along the road from a fixed commencement point. Commonly the term " _____ " may also refer to markers placed at other distances, such as every kilometre.

Exam Probability: **Low**

41. *Answer choices:*

(see index for correct answer)

- a. Milestone
- b. Akihabara syndrome
- c. PRINCE2
- d. Elemental cost planning

Guidance: level 1

:: Time management ::

_____ is the process of planning and exercising conscious control of time spent on specific activities, especially to increase effectiveness, efficiency, and productivity. It involves a juggling act of various demands upon a person relating to work, social life, family, hobbies, personal interests and commitments with the finiteness of time. Using time effectively gives the person "choice" on spending/managing activities at their own time and expediency.

Exam Probability: **High**

42. *Answer choices:*

(see index for correct answer)

- a. Getting Things Done
- b. waiting room
- c. Sufficient unto the day is the evil thereof
- d. Time management

Guidance: level 1

:: Product management ::

_____ s, also known as Shewhart charts or process-behavior charts, are a statistical process control tool used to determine if a manufacturing or business process is in a state of control.

Exam Probability: **Low**

43. *Answer choices:*

(see index for correct answer)

- a. Crossing the Chasm
- b. Swing tag
- c. Product management
- d. Brand equity

Guidance: level 1

:: Management ::

In organizational studies, _____ is the efficient and effective development of an organization's resources when they are needed. Such resources may include financial resources, inventory, human skills, production resources, or information technology and natural resources.

Exam Probability: **Medium**

44. *Answer choices:*

(see index for correct answer)

- a. Business model
- b. Job rotation
- c. Resource management
- d. Enterprise smart grid

Guidance: level 1

:: Metalworking ::

A _____ is a round object with various uses. It is used in _____ games, where the play of the game follows the state of the _____ as it is hit, kicked or thrown by players. _____ s can also be used for simpler activities, such as catch or juggling. _____ s made from hard-wearing materials are used in engineering applications to provide very low friction bearings, known as _____ bearings. Black-powder weapons use stone and metal _____ s as projectiles.

Exam Probability: **Medium**

45. *Answer choices:*

(see index for correct answer)

- a. Cold-formed steel
- b. Spray forming
- c. Filing
- d. Chip formation

Guidance: level 1

:: Production and manufacturing ::

_____ is the production under license of technology developed elsewhere. It is an especially prominent commercial practice in developing nations, which often approach _____ as a starting point for indigenous industrial development.

Exam Probability: **Medium**

46. *Answer choices:*

(see index for correct answer)

- a. Enterprise control
- b. Simatic S5 PLC
- c. Nesting
- d. Licensed production

Guidance: level 1

:: Project management ::

Contemporary business and science treat as a _____ any undertaking, carried out individually or collaboratively and possibly involving research or design, that is carefully planned to achieve a particular aim.

Exam Probability: **Medium**

47. *Answer choices:*

(see index for correct answer)

- a. Operational bill
- b. Jeff Sutherland
- c. SQEP
- d. Project

Guidance: level 1

:: Industrial engineering ::

The _____ is the design of any task that aims to describe or explain the variation of information under conditions that are hypothesized to reflect the variation. The term is generally associated with experiments in which the design introduces conditions that directly affect the variation, but may also refer to the design of quasi-experiments, in which natural conditions that influence the variation are selected for observation.

Exam Probability: **Low**

48. *Answer choices:*
(see index for correct answer)

- a. Response surface methodology
- b. Society for Health Systems
- c. Pilot plant
- d. Indian Institution of Industrial Engineering

Guidance: level 1

:: Lean manufacturing ::

_____ is a Japanese term that means "mistake-proofing" or "inadvertent error prevention". A _____ is any mechanism in any process that helps an equipment operator avoid mistakes. Its purpose is to eliminate product defects by preventing, correcting, or drawing attention to human errors as they occur. The concept was formalised, and the term adopted, by Shigeo Shingo as part of the Toyota Production System. It was originally described as baka-yoke, but as this means "fool-proofing" the name was changed to the milder _____.

Exam Probability: **Medium**

49. *Answer choices:*

(see index for correct answer)

- a. Poka-yoke
- b. Overall equipment effectiveness
- c. Kaizen
- d. Frequent deliveries

Guidance: level 1

:: Infographics ::

The _____ is a form used to collect data in real time at the location where the data is generated. The data it captures can be quantitative or qualitative. When the information is quantitative, the _____ is sometimes called a tally sheet.

Exam Probability: **Medium**

50. *Answer choices:*

(see index for correct answer)

- a. Placard
- b. Hypergraphy
- c. Check sheet
- d. Motion chart

Guidance: level 1

:: Product development ::

In business and engineering, _____ covers the complete process of bringing a new product to market. A central aspect of NPD is product design, along with various business considerations. _____ is described broadly as the transformation of a market opportunity into a product available for sale. The product can be tangible or intangible , though sometimes services and other processes are distinguished from "products." NPD requires an understanding of customer needs and wants, the competitive environment, and the nature of the market.Cost, time and quality are the main variables that drive customer needs. Aiming at these three variables, innovative companies develop continuous practices and strategies to better satisfy customer requirements and to increase their own market share by a regular development of new products. There are many uncertainties and challenges which companies must face throughout the process. The use of best practices and the elimination of barriers to communication are the main concerns for the management of the NPD .

Exam Probability: **Low**

51. *Answer choices:*

(see index for correct answer)

- a. Virtual prototyping
- b. Y Media Labs
- c. Design brief
- d. Virtual product development

Guidance: level 1

:: Management ::

_____ is a category of business activity made possible by software tools that aim to provide customers with both independence from vendors and better means for engaging with vendors. These same tools can also apply to individuals' relations with other institutions and organizations.

Exam Probability: **High**

52. *Answer choices:*

(see index for correct answer)

- a. Failure demand
- b. Enterprise decision management
- c. Cross ownership
- d. Vendor relationship management

Guidance: level 1

:: Lean manufacturing ::

_____ is the Sino-Japanese word for "improvement". In business, _____ refers to activities that continuously improve all functions and involve all employees from the CEO to the assembly line workers. It also applies to processes, such as purchasing and logistics, that cross organizational boundaries into the supply chain. It has been applied in healthcare, psychotherapy, life-coaching, government, and banking.

Exam Probability: **Medium**

53. *Answer choices:*

(see index for correct answer)

- a. Kaizen
- b. No value added
- c. JobShopLean
- d. Lean CFP driven

Guidance: level 1

:: ::

_____ is the quantity of three-dimensional space enclosed by a closed surface, for example, the space that a substance or shape occupies or contains. _____ is often quantified numerically using the SI derived unit, the cubic metre. The _____ of a container is generally understood to be the capacity of the container; i. e., the amount of fluid that the container could hold, rather than the amount of space the container itself displaces. Three dimensional mathematical shapes are also assigned _____ s. _____ s of some simple shapes, such as regular, straight-edged, and circular shapes can be easily calculated using arithmetic formulas. _____ s of complicated shapes can be calculated with integral calculus if a formula exists for the shape's boundary. One-dimensional figures and two-dimensional shapes are assigned zero _____ in the three-dimensional space.

Exam Probability: **High**

54. *Answer choices:*

(see index for correct answer)

- a. interpersonal communication
- b. Character
- c. cultural
- d. Volume

Guidance: level 1

:: Casting (manufacturing) ::

A _____ is a regularity in the world, man-made design, or abstract ideas. As such, the elements of a _____ repeat in a predictable manner. A geometric _____ is a kind of _____ formed of geometric shapes and typically repeated like a wallpaper design.

Exam Probability: **Medium**

55. *Answer choices:*
(see index for correct answer)

- a. Plaster mold casting
- b. Full-mold casting
- c. Ceramic mold casting
- d. Die casting

Guidance: level 1

:: Business process ::

_____ is the value to an enterprise which is derived from the techniques, procedures, and programs that implement and enhance the delivery of goods and services. _____ is one of the three components of structural capital, itself a component of intellectual capital. _____ can be seen as the value of processes to any entity, whether for profit or not-for profit, but is most commonly used in reference to for-profit entities.

Exam Probability: **Low**

56. *Answer choices:*

(see index for correct answer)

- a. Software ecosystem
- b. Information technology outsourcing
- c. Extended Enterprise Modeling Language
- d. Sales process engineering

Guidance: level 1

:: Production and manufacturing ::

_____ is a set of techniques and tools for process improvement. Though as a shortened form it may be found written as 6S, it should not be confused with the methodology known as 6S.

Exam Probability: **Low**

57. *Answer choices:*

(see index for correct answer)

- a. Six Sigma
- b. Digital prototyping
- c. Queueing theory
- d. Digital materialization

Guidance: level 1

:: Management ::

_____ is a formal technique useful where many possible courses of action are competing for attention. In essence, the problem-solver estimates the benefit delivered by each action, then selects a number of the most effective actions that deliver a total benefit reasonably close to the maximal possible one.

Exam Probability: **Low**

58. *Answer choices:*

(see index for correct answer)

- a. Marketing science
- b. Product Development and Systems Engineering Consortium
- c. Personal offshoring
- d. Design management

Guidance: level 1

:: Commercial item transport and distribution ::

In commerce, supply-chain management , the management of the flow of goods and services, involves the movement and storage of raw materials, of work-in-process inventory, and of finished goods from point of origin to point of consumption. Interconnected or interlinked networks, channels and node businesses combine in the provision of products and services required by end customers in a supply chain. Supply-chain management has been defined as the "design, planning, execution, control, and monitoring of supply-chain activities with the objective of creating net value, building a competitive infrastructure, leveraging worldwide logistics, synchronizing supply with demand and measuring performance globally."SCM practice draws heavily from the areas of industrial engineering, systems engineering, operations management, logistics, procurement, information technology, and marketing and strives for an integrated approach. Marketing channels play an important role in supply-chain management. Current research in supply-chain management is concerned with topics related to sustainability and risk management, among others. Some suggest that the "people dimension" of SCM, ethical issues, internal integration, transparency/visibility, and human capital/talent management are topics that have, so far, been underrepresented on the research agenda.

Exam Probability: **Low**

59. *Answer choices:*

(see index for correct answer)

- a. Supply chain management
- b. Dautel
- c. Surface Freight Forwarder Deregulation Act of 1986
- d. Export Yellow Pages

Guidance: level 1

Commerce

Commerce relates to "the exchange of goods and services, especially on a large scale." It includes legal, economic, political, social, cultural and technological systems that operate in any country or internationally.

:: Payment systems ::

Amazon Pay is an online payments processing service that is owned by Amazon. Launched in 2007, Amazon Pay uses the consumer base of Amazon.com and focuses on giving users the option to pay with their Amazon accounts on external merchant websites. As of January 2019 the service is available in Austria, Belgium, Cyprus, Germany, Denmark, Spain, France, Hungary, Luxembourg, Republic of Ireland, India, Italy, Japan, Netherlands, Portugal, Sweden, United Kingdom, United States.

Exam Probability: **High**

1. *Answer choices:*

(see index for correct answer)

- a. Amazon Payments
- b. Adyen
- c. Google Wallet
- d. Cardsave

Guidance: level 1

:: E-commerce ::

E-commerce is the activity of buying or selling of products on online services or over the Internet. _____ draws on technologies such as mobile commerce, electronic funds transfer, supply chain management, Internet marketing, online transaction processing, electronic data interchange, inventory management systems, and automated data collection systems.

Exam Probability: **Low**

2. *Answer choices:*

(see index for correct answer)

- a. Electronic commerce
- b. Transactional Link

- c. SAF-T
- d. AsiaPay

Guidance: level 1

:: Business law ::

> A _____ is a group of people who jointly supervise the activities of an organization, which can be either a for-profit business, nonprofit organization, or a government agency. Such a board's powers, duties, and responsibilities are determined by government regulations and the organization's own constitution and bylaws. These authorities may specify the number of members of the board, how they are to be chosen, and how often they are to meet.

Exam Probability: **Medium**

3. *Answer choices:*

(see index for correct answer)

- a. Trusted Computing
- b. Negative option billing
- c. Arbitration clause
- d. Complex structured finance transactions

Guidance: level 1

:: Direct marketing ::

_____ is a form of advertising where organizations communicate directly to customers through a variety of media including cell phone text messaging, email, websites, online adverts, database marketing, fliers, catalog distribution, promotional letters, targeted television, newspapers, magazine advertisements, and outdoor advertising. Among practitioners, it is also known as direct response marketing.

Exam Probability: **Medium**

4. *Answer choices:*

(see index for correct answer)

- a. Caging
- b. Colony Brands
- c. Direct marketing
- d. A Common Reader

Guidance: level 1

:: Business law ::

The _____ , first published in 1952, is one of a number of Uniform Acts that have been established as law with the goal of harmonizing the laws of sales and other commercial transactions across the United States of America through UCC adoption by all 50 states, the District of Columbia, and the Territories of the United States.

Exam Probability: **Low**

5. *Answer choices:*

(see index for correct answer)

- a. Principal
- b. Ladenschlussgesetz
- c. Uniform Commercial Code
- d. Statutory authority

Guidance: level 1

:: ::

_____ or accountancy is the measurement, processing, and communication of financial information about economic entities such as businesses and corporations. The modern field was established by the Italian mathematician Luca Pacioli in 1494. _____ , which has been called the "language of business", measures the results of an organization`s economic activities and conveys this information to a variety of users, including investors, creditors, management, and regulators. Practitioners of _____ are known as accountants. The terms " _____ " and "financial reporting" are often used as synonyms.

Exam Probability: **Low**

6. *Answer choices:*

(see index for correct answer)

- a. interpersonal communication
- b. imperative
- c. Accounting
- d. cultural

Guidance: level 1

:: Real property law ::

A _____ is the grant of authority or rights, stating that the granter formally recognizes the prerogative of the recipient to exercise the rights specified. It is implicit that the granter retains superiority, and that the recipient admits a limited status within the relationship, and it is within that sense that _____ s were historically granted, and that sense is retained in modern usage of the term.

Exam Probability: **Medium**

7. *Answer choices:*

(see index for correct answer)

- a. Charter
- b. Nonpossessory interest in land
- c. Gavelkind
- d. Quia Emptores

Guidance: level 1

:: Commerce ::

_____ relates to "the exchange of goods and services, especially on a large scale". It includes legal, economic, political, social, cultural and technological systems that operate in a country or in international trade.

Exam Probability: **High**

8. *Answer choices:*
(see index for correct answer)

- a. Commerce
- b. V-commerce
- c. Trade in services statistics
- d. Defective on arrival

Guidance: level 1

:: Marketing ::

_____ is a concept introduced in a book of the same name in 1999 by marketing expert Seth Godin. _____ is a non-traditional marketing technique that advertises goods and services when advance consent is given.

Exam Probability: **High**

9. *Answer choices:*

(see index for correct answer)

- a. Branded asset management
- b. Permission marketing
- c. Jobbing house
- d. Marchitecture

Guidance: level 1

:: Commerce ::

> An _____ is a bank that offers card association branded payment cards directly to consumers. The name is derived from the practice of issuing payment to the acquiring bank on behalf of its customer.

Exam Probability: **Low**

10. *Answer choices:*

(see index for correct answer)

- a. PIN pad
- b. Issuing bank
- c. TradeCard
- d. Hong Kong Mercantile Exchange

Guidance: level 1

:: ::

In mathematics, computer science and operations research, mathematical optimization or mathematical programming is the selection of a best element from some set of available alternatives.

Exam Probability: **Medium**

11. *Answer choices:*

(see index for correct answer)

- a. Optimum
- b. hierarchical perspective
- c. Sarbanes-Oxley act of 2002
- d. functional perspective

Guidance: level 1

:: ::

A _____ is a person or firm who arranges transactions between a buyer and a seller for a commission when the deal is executed. A _____ who also acts as a seller or as a buyer becomes a principal party to the deal. Neither role should be confused with that of an agent—one who acts on behalf of a principal party in a deal.

Exam Probability: **Low**

12. *Answer choices:*

(see index for correct answer)

- a. Broker
- b. interpersonal communication
- c. process perspective
- d. information systems assessment

Guidance: level 1

:: Business terms ::

_____ ning is an organization's process of defining its strategy, or direction, and making decisions on allocating its resources to pursue this strategy. It may also extend to control mechanisms for guiding the implementation of the strategy. _____ ning became prominent in corporations during the 1960s and remains an important aspect of strategic management. It is executed by _____ ners or strategists, who involve many parties and research sources in their analysis of the organization and its relationship to the environment in which it competes.

Exam Probability: **Medium**

13. *Answer choices:*

(see index for correct answer)

- a. granular
- b. noncommercial
- c. operating cost
- d. year-to-date

Guidance: level 1

:: Auctioneering ::

An _____ is a process of buying and selling goods or services by offering them up for bid, taking bids, and then selling the item to the highest bidder. The open ascending price _____ is arguably the most common form of _____ in use today. Participants bid openly against one another, with each subsequent bid required to be higher than the previous bid. An _____ eer may announce prices, bidders may call out their bids themselves , or bids may be submitted electronically with the highest current bid publicly displayed. In a Dutch _____ , the _____ eer begins with a high asking price for some quantity of like items; the price is lowered until a participant is willing to accept the _____ eer's price for some quantity of the goods in the lot or until the seller's reserve price is met. While _____ s are most associated in the public imagination with the sale of antiques, paintings, rare collectibles and expensive wines, _____ s are also used for commodities, livestock, radio spectrum and used cars. In economic theory, an _____ may refer to any mechanism or set of trading rules for exchange.

Exam Probability: **Low**

14. *Answer choices:*

(see index for correct answer)

- a. Pie supper
- b. Wine auction
- c. AntiqueWeek
- d. Japanese auction

Guidance: level 1

:: Information retrieval ::

_____ is a technique used by recommender systems. _____ has two senses, a narrow one and a more general one.

Exam Probability: **High**

15. *Answer choices:*
(see index for correct answer)

- a. Hashtag
- b. Communication engine
- c. Collaborative filtering
- d. Discounted cumulative gain

Guidance: level 1

:: Manufacturing ::

A _____ is an object used to extend the ability of an individual to modify features of the surrounding environment. Although many animals use simple _____ s, only human beings, whose use of stone _____ s dates back hundreds of millennia, use _____ s to make other _____ s. The set of _____ s needed to perform different tasks that are part of the same activity is called gear or equipment.

Exam Probability: **Low**

16. *Answer choices:*

(see index for correct answer)

- a. Nanofoundry
- b. Ashery
- c. Tool
- d. By-product

Guidance: level 1

:: E-commerce ::

_____ is a United States-based payment gateway service provider allowing merchants to accept credit card and electronic check payments through their website and over an Internet Protocol connection. Founded in 1996, _____ is now a subsidiary of Visa Inc. Its service permits customers to enter credit card and shipping information directly onto a web page, in contrast to some alternatives that require the customer to sign up for a payment service before performing a transaction.

Exam Probability: **Low**

17. *Answer choices:*

(see index for correct answer)

- a. Paywall
- b. Authorize.Net
- c. SwapSimple
- d. Steam

Guidance: level 1

:: Marketing ::

_____ —an information- and communication-based electronic exchange environment—is a relatively new concept in marketing. Since physical boundaries no longer interfere with buy/sell decisions, the world has grown into several industry specific _____ s which are integration of marketplaces through sophisticated computer and telecommunication technologies. The term _____ was introduced by Jeffrey Rayport and John Sviokla in 1994 in their article "Managing in the _____ " that appeared in Harvard Business Review. In the article the authors distinguished between electronic and conventional markets. In a _____ , information and/or physical goods are exchanged, and transactions take place through computers and networks. These networks consist of blogs, forum threads, and micro-blogging services like Twitter. Businesses and their customers are enabled to create conversations and two-way communications about products and services. These conversations may also happen outside the sphere of control of a given business, when a marketing campaign or customer-service issue captures the attention of web-savvy consumers.

Exam Probability: **Medium**

18. *Answer choices:*

(see index for correct answer)

- a. Movement marketing
- b. Pricing science
- c. Industrial marketing
- d. Market environment

Guidance: level 1

:: Workplace ::

_____ is asystematic determination of a subject's merit, worth and significance, using criteria governed by a set of standards. It can assist an organization, program, design, project or any other intervention or initiative to assess any aim, realisable concept/proposal, or any alternative, to help in decision-making; or to ascertain the degree of achievement or value in regard to the aim and objectives and results of any such action that has been completed. The primary purpose of _____ , in addition to gaining insight into prior or existing initiatives, is to enable reflection and assist in the identification of future change.

Exam Probability: **Low**

19. *Answer choices:*

(see index for correct answer)

- a. Queen bee syndrome
- b. Evaluation
- c. Emotions in the workplace
- d. Workplace listening

Guidance: level 1

:: ::

_____ is an abstract concept of management of complex systems according to a set of rules and trends. In systems theory, these types of rules exist in various fields of biology and society, but the term has slightly different meanings according to context. For example.

Exam Probability: **Medium**

20. *Answer choices:*

(see index for correct answer)

- a. levels of analysis
- b. Sarbanes-Oxley act of 2002
- c. hierarchical perspective
- d. co-culture

Guidance: level 1

:: Export and import control ::

"_____" means the Government Service which is responsible for the administration of _____ law and the collection of duties and taxes and which also has the responsibility for the application of other laws and regulations relating to the importation, exportation, movement or storage of goods.

Exam Probability: **High**

21. *Answer choices:*

(see index for correct answer)

- a. Export of cryptography
- b. Bureau of Industry and Security
- c. Customs
- d. Export Management and Compliance Program

Guidance: level 1

:: ::

In law, an _____ is the process in which cases are reviewed, where parties request a formal change to an official decision. _____s function both as a process for error correction as well as a process of clarifying and interpreting law. Although appellate courts have existed for thousands of years, common law countries did not incorporate an affirmative right to _____ into their jurisprudence until the 19th century.

Exam Probability: **Medium**

22. *Answer choices:*

(see index for correct answer)

- a. corporate values
- b. surface-level diversity
- c. Sarbanes-Oxley act of 2002
- d. Appeal

Guidance: level 1

:: ::

In international relations, _____ is – from the perspective of governments – a voluntary transfer of resources from one country to another.

Exam Probability: **Medium**

23. *Answer choices:*

(see index for correct answer)

- a. personal values
- b. empathy
- c. similarity-attraction theory
- d. Aid

Guidance: level 1

:: E-commerce ::

_____ is the business-to-business or business-to-consumer or business-to-government purchase and sale of supplies, work, and services through the Internet as well as other information and networking systems, such as electronic data interchange and enterprise resource planning.

Exam Probability: **High**

24. *Answer choices:*

(see index for correct answer)

- a. E-procurement
- b. PagSeguro
- c. RapidBuyr
- d. GeBIZ

Guidance: level 1

:: Insolvency ::

_____ is a legal process through which people or other entities who cannot repay debts to creditors may seek relief from some or all of their debts. In most jurisdictions, _____ is imposed by a court order, often initiated by the debtor.

Exam Probability: **High**

25. *Answer choices:*

(see index for correct answer)

- a. Official Committee of Equity Security Holders
- b. George Samuel Ford
- c. Insolvency law of Russia
- d. Liquidator

Guidance: level 1

:: ::

A _____ , or also known as foreman, overseer, facilitator, monitor, area coordinator, or sometimes gaffer, is the job title of a low level management position that is primarily based on authority over a worker or charge of a workplace. A _____ can also be one of the most senior in the staff at the place of work, such as a Professor who oversees a PhD dissertation. Supervision, on the other hand, can be performed by people without this formal title, for example by parents. The term _____ itself can be used to refer to any personnel who have this task as part of their job description.

Exam Probability: **Low**

26. *Answer choices:*

(see index for correct answer)

- a. empathy
- b. co-culture
- c. information systems assessment
- d. Supervisor

Guidance: level 1

:: E-commerce ::

Customer to customer markets provide an innovative way to allow customers to interact with each other. Traditional markets require business to customer relationships, in which a customer goes to the business in order to purchase a product or service. In customer to customer markets, the business facilitates an environment where customers can sell goods or services to each other. Other types of markets include business to business and business to customer.

Exam Probability: **Low**

27. *Answer choices:*

(see index for correct answer)

- a. EFaktura
- b. Cyber Monday

- c. Consumer-to-consumer
- d. EPages

Guidance: level 1

:: Goods ::

In most contexts, the concept of _____ denotes the conduct that should be preferred when posed with a choice between possible actions. _____ is generally considered to be the opposite of evil, and is of interest in the study of morality, ethics, religion and philosophy. The specific meaning and etymology of the term and its associated translations among ancient and contemporary languages show substantial variation in its inflection and meaning depending on circumstances of place, history, religious, or philosophical context.

Exam Probability: **Low**

28. *Answer choices:*
(see index for correct answer)

- a. Refined goods
- b. Good
- c. Veblen good
- d. Credence good

Guidance: level 1

:: ::

In the broadest sense, _____ is any practice which contributes to the sale of products to a retail consumer. At a retail in-store level, _____ refers to the variety of products available for sale and the display of those products in such a way that it stimulates interest and entices customers to make a purchase.

Exam Probability: **High**

29. *Answer choices:*

(see index for correct answer)

- a. empathy
- b. Merchandising
- c. interpersonal communication
- d. cultural

Guidance: level 1

:: Data interchange standards ::

_____ is the concept of businesses electronically communicating information that was traditionally communicated on paper, such as purchase orders and invoices. Technical standards for EDI exist to facilitate parties transacting such instruments without having to make special arrangements.

Exam Probability: **Low**

30. *Answer choices:*

(see index for correct answer)

- a. Data Interchange Standards Association
- b. Common Alerting Protocol
- c. Domain Application Protocol
- d. Interaction protocol

Guidance: level 1

:: Economics terminology ::

_____ is the total receipts a seller can obtain from selling goods or services to buyers. It can be written as P × Q, which is the price of the goods multiplied by the quantity of the sold goods.

Exam Probability: **Low**

31. *Answer choices:*

(see index for correct answer)

- a. External costs
- b. Total revenue
- c. economic profit
- d. Physical capital

Guidance: level 1

:: ::

Regulatory economics is the economics of regulation. It is the application of law by government or independent administrative agencies for various purposes, including remedying market failure, protecting the environment, centrally-planning an economy, enriching well-connected firms, or benefiting politicians.

Exam Probability: **High**

32. *Answer choices:*

(see index for correct answer)

- a. deep-level diversity
- b. Economic regulation
- c. interpersonal communication
- d. hierarchical perspective

Guidance: level 1

:: ::

_____ are electronic transfer of money from one bank account to another, either within a single financial institution or across multiple institutions, via computer-based systems, without the direct intervention of bank staff.

Exam Probability: **Low**

33. *Answer choices:*

(see index for correct answer)

- a. open system
- b. personal values
- c. information systems assessment
- d. corporate values

Guidance: level 1

:: Trading posts of the Hanseatic League ::

_____ is a city and unitary authority area in North _____ shire, England, with a population of 208,200 as of 2017. Located at the confluence of the Rivers Ouse and Foss, it is the county town of the historic county of _____ shire and was the home of the House of _____ throughout its existence. The city is known for its famous historical landmarks such as _____ Minster and the city walls, as well as a variety of cultural and sporting activities, which makes it a popular tourist destination in England. The local authority is the City of _____ Council, a single tier governing body responsible for providing all local services and facilities throughout the city. The City of _____ local government district includes rural areas beyond the old city boundaries.

Exam Probability: **High**

34. *Answer choices:*

(see index for correct answer)

- a. Ipswich
- b. York
- c. Bruges
- d. Staraya Ladoga

Guidance: level 1

:: Industrial Revolution ::

The _____, now also known as the First _____, was the transition to new manufacturing processes in Europe and the US, in the period from about 1760 to sometime between 1820 and 1840. This transition included going from hand production methods to machines, new chemical manufacturing and iron production processes, the increasing use of steam power and water power, the development of machine tools and the rise of the mechanized factory system. The _____ also led to an unprecedented rise in the rate of population growth.

Exam Probability: **High**

35. *Answer choices:*

(see index for correct answer)

- a. Torr Vale Mill
- b. Grubb Family Iron Dynasty
- c. Jackshaft
- d. Industrial Revolution

Guidance: level 1

:: Commercial item transport and distribution ::

A _____ in common law countries is a person or company that transports goods or people for any person or company and that is responsible for any possible loss of the goods during transport. A _____ offers its services to the general public under license or authority provided by a regulatory body. The regulatory body has usually been granted "ministerial authority" by the legislation that created it. The regulatory body may create, interpret, and enforce its regulations upon the _____ with independence and finality, as long as it acts within the bounds of the enabling legislation.

Exam Probability: **High**

36. *Answer choices:*

(see index for correct answer)

- a. Common carrier
- b. Aeroscraft
- c. Green logistics
- d. Cargo scanning

Guidance: level 1

:: Fraud ::

In law, _____ is intentional deception to secure unfair or unlawful gain, or to deprive a victim of a legal right. _____ can violate civil law, a criminal law, or it may cause no loss of money, property or legal right but still be an element of another civil or criminal wrong. The purpose of _____ may be monetary gain or other benefits, for example by obtaining a passport, travel document, or driver's license, or mortgage _____, where the perpetrator may attempt to qualify for a mortgage by way of false statements.

Exam Probability: **High**

37. *Answer choices:*

(see index for correct answer)

- a. Swatting
- b. Fraud
- c. Pious fraud
- d. Deceptive advertising

Guidance: level 1

:: ::

According to the philosopher Piyush Mathur, "Tangibility is the property that a phenomenon exhibits if it has and/or transports mass and/or energy and/or momentum".

Exam Probability: **High**

38. *Answer choices:*

(see index for correct answer)

- a. Sarbanes-Oxley act of 2002
- b. personal values
- c. hierarchical
- d. imperative

Guidance: level 1

:: ::

_____ is the practice of deliberately managing the spread of information between an individual or an organization and the public. _____ may include an organization or individual gaining exposure to their audiences using topics of public interest and news items that do not require direct payment. This differentiates it from advertising as a form of marketing communications. _____ is the idea of creating coverage for clients for free, rather than marketing or advertising. But now, advertising is also a part of greater PR Activities. An example of good _____ would be generating an article featuring a client, rather than paying for the client to be advertised next to the article. The aim of _____ is to inform the public, prospective customers, investors, partners, employees, and other stakeholders and ultimately persuade them to maintain a positive or favorable view about the organization, its leadership, products, or political decisions. _____ professionals typically work for PR and marketing firms, businesses and companies, government, and public officials as PIOs and nongovernmental organizations, and nonprofit organizations. Jobs central to _____ include account coordinator, account executive, account supervisor, and media relations manager.

Exam Probability: **Low**

39. *Answer choices:*

(see index for correct answer)

- a. imperative
- b. similarity-attraction theory
- c. Public relations
- d. process perspective

Guidance: level 1

:: Commerce ::

A _____ is an employee within a company, business or other organization who is responsible at some level for buying or approving the acquisition of goods and services needed by the company. Responsible for buying the best quality products, goods and services for their company at the most competitive prices, _____ s work in a wide range of sectors for many different organizations. The position responsibilities may be the same as that of a buyer or purchasing agent, or may include wider supervisory or managerial responsibilities. A _____ may oversee the acquisition of materials needed for production, general supplies for offices and facilities, equipment, or construction contracts. A _____ often supervises purchasing agents and buyers, but in small companies the _____ may also be the purchasing agent or buyer. The _____ position may also carry the title "Procurement Manager" or in the public sector, "Procurement Officer". He or she can come from both an Engineering or Economics background.

Exam Probability: **High**

40. Answer choices:

(see index for correct answer)

- a. The Staple
- b. Bargaining power
- c. Recommerce
- d. Purchasing manager

Guidance: level 1

:: Generally Accepted Accounting Principles ::

In accounting, _____ is the income that a business have from its normal business activities, usually from the sale of goods and services to customers. _____ is also referred to as sales or turnover. Some companies receive _____ from interest, royalties, or other fees. _____ may refer to business income in general, or it may refer to the amount, in a monetary unit, earned during a period of time, as in "Last year, Company X had _____ of $42 million". Profits or net income generally imply total _____ minus total expenses in a given period. In accounting, in the balance statement it is a subsection of the Equity section and _____ increases equity, it is often referred to as the "top line" due to its position on the income statement at the very top. This is to be contrasted with the "bottom line" which denotes net income .

Exam Probability: **Low**

41. Answer choices:

(see index for correct answer)

- a. Deprival value
- b. Revenue
- c. Provision
- d. Generally Accepted Accounting Practice

Guidance: level 1

:: ::

> _____ is both a research area and a practical skill encompassing the ability of an individual or organization to "lead" or guide other individuals, teams, or entire organizations. Specialist literature debates various viewpoints, contrasting Eastern and Western approaches to _____, and also United States versus European approaches. U.S. academic environments define _____ as "a process of social influence in which a person can enlist the aid and support of others in the accomplishment of a common task".

Exam Probability: **Medium**

42. *Answer choices:*

(see index for correct answer)

- a. empathy
- b. functional perspective
- c. cultural
- d. Leadership

Guidance: level 1

:: Minimum wage ::

A _____ is the lowest remuneration that employers can legally pay their workers—the price floor below which workers may not sell their labor. Most countries had introduced _____ legislation by the end of the 20th century.

Exam Probability: **Low**

43. *Answer choices:*

(see index for correct answer)

- a. Minimum wage
- b. Minimum wage in Taiwan
- c. Working poor
- d. Minimum Wage Fairness Act

Guidance: level 1

:: Information technology management ::

B2B is often contrasted with business-to-consumer. In B2B commerce, it is often the case that the parties to the relationship have comparable negotiating power, and even when they do not, each party typically involves professional staff and legal counsel in the negotiation of terms, whereas B2C is shaped to a far greater degree by economic implications of information asymmetry. However, within a B2B context, large companies may have many commercial, resource and information advantages over smaller businesses. The United Kingdom government, for example, created the post of Small Business Commissioner under the Enterprise Act 2016 to "enable small businesses to resolve disputes" and "consider complaints by small business suppliers about payment issues with larger businesses that they supply."

Exam Probability: **High**

44. *Answer choices:*

(see index for correct answer)

- a. Website promotion
- b. Storage hypervisor
- c. Configuration Management
- d. e-HR

Guidance: level 1

:: ::

_____ is a type of government support for the citizens of that society. _____ may be provided to people of any income level, as with social security, but it is usually intended to ensure that the poor can meet their basic human needs such as food and shelter. _____ attempts to provide poor people with a minimal level of well-being, usually either a free- or a subsidized-supply of certain goods and social services, such as healthcare, education, and vocational training.

Exam Probability: **High**

45. *Answer choices:*

(see index for correct answer)

- a. corporate values
- b. Welfare
- c. empathy
- d. co-culture

Guidance: level 1

:: ::

A _____ is a person who trades in commodities produced by other people. Historically, a _____ is anyone who is involved in business or trade. _____ s have operated for as long as industry, commerce, and trade have existed. During the 16th-century, in Europe, two different terms for _____ s emerged: One term, meerseniers, described local traders such as bakers, grocers, etc.; while a new term, koopman (Dutch: koopman, described _____ s who operated on a global stage, importing and exporting goods over vast distances, and offering added-value services such as credit and finance.

Exam Probability: **Low**

46. *Answer choices:*

(see index for correct answer)

- a. deep-level diversity
- b. process perspective
- c. Character
- d. Merchant

Guidance: level 1

:: ::

_____ is "property consisting of land and the buildings on it, along with its natural resources such as crops, minerals or water; immovable property of this nature; an interest vested in this an item of real property, buildings or housing in general. Also: the business of _____ ; the profession of buying, selling, or renting land, buildings, or housing." It is a legal term used in jurisdictions whose legal system is derived from English common law, such as India, England, Wales, Northern Ireland, United States, Canada, Pakistan, Australia, and New Zealand.

Exam Probability: **Medium**

47. *Answer choices:*

(see index for correct answer)

- a. similarity-attraction theory
- b. hierarchical perspective
- c. Real estate
- d. information systems assessment

Guidance: level 1

:: Income ::

_____ is the application of disciplined analytics that predict consumer behaviour at the micro-market levels and optimize product availability and price to maximize revenue growth. The primary aim of _____ is selling the right product to the right customer at the right time for the right price and with the right pack. The essence of this discipline is in understanding customers' perception of product value and accurately aligning product prices, placement and availability with each customer segment.

Exam Probability: **Low**

48. *Answer choices:*

(see index for correct answer)

- a. Pay grade
- b. Real estate investing
- c. Revenue management
- d. Income Per User

Guidance: level 1

:: Materials ::

A _____, also known as a feedstock, unprocessed material, or primary commodity, is a basic material that is used to produce goods, finished products, energy, or intermediate materials which are feedstock for future finished products. As feedstock, the term connotes these materials are bottleneck assets and are highly important with regard to producing other products. An example of this is crude oil, which is a _____ and a feedstock used in the production of industrial chemicals, fuels, plastics, and pharmaceutical goods; lumber is a _____ used to produce a variety of products including all types of furniture. The term "_____" denotes materials in minimally processed or unprocessed in states; e.g., raw latex, crude oil, cotton, coal, raw biomass, iron ore, air, logs, or water i.e. "...any product of agriculture, forestry, fishing and any other mineral that is in its natural form or which has undergone the transformation required to prepare it for internationally marketing in substantial volumes."

Exam Probability: **Medium**

49. *Answer choices:*

(see index for correct answer)

- a. Raw material
- b. Ice substitute
- c. Refractory
- d. Composition leather

Guidance: level 1

:: ::

An _____ is a contingent motivator. Traditional _____s are extrinsic motivators which reward actions to yield a desired outcome. The effectiveness of traditional _____s has changed as the needs of Western society have evolved. While the traditional _____ model is effective when there is a defined procedure and goal for a task, Western society started to require a higher volume of critical thinkers, so the traditional model became less effective. Institutions are now following a trend in implementing strategies that rely on intrinsic motivations rather than the extrinsic motivations that the traditional _____s foster.

Exam Probability: **Medium**

50. *Answer choices:*

(see index for correct answer)

- a. surface-level diversity
- b. Incentive
- c. similarity-attraction theory
- d. cultural

Guidance: level 1

:: Summary statistics ::

_____ is the number of occurrences of a repeating event per unit of time. It is also referred to as temporal _____, which emphasizes the contrast to spatial _____ and angular _____. The period is the duration of time of one cycle in a repeating event, so the period is the reciprocal of the _____. For example: if a newborn baby's heart beats at a _____ of 120 times a minute, its period—the time interval between beats—is half a second. _____ is an important parameter used in science and engineering to specify the rate of oscillatory and vibratory phenomena, such as mechanical vibrations, audio signals, radio waves, and light.

Exam Probability: **Medium**

51. *Answer choices:*

(see index for correct answer)

- a. Multiple of the median
- b. Percentile
- c. Mean percentage error
- d. Five-number summary

Guidance: level 1

:: Consortia ::

A _____ is an association of two or more individuals, companies, organizations or governments with the objective of participating in a common activity or pooling their resources for achieving a common goal.

Exam Probability: **High**

52. *Answer choices:*

(see index for correct answer)

- a. Genomic Standards Consortium
- b. Consortium
- c. XBRL International
- d. RVU Alliance

Guidance: level 1

:: ::

_____ is a means of protection from financial loss. It is a form of risk management, primarily used to hedge against the risk of a contingent or uncertain loss

Exam Probability: **High**

53. *Answer choices:*

(see index for correct answer)

- a. co-culture
- b. Insurance
- c. interpersonal communication
- d. Sarbanes-Oxley act of 2002

Guidance: level 1

:: Packaging ::

In work place, _____ or job _____ means good ranking with the hypothesized conception of requirements of a role. There are two types of job _____ s: contextual and task. Task _____ is related to cognitive ability while contextual _____ is dependent upon personality. Task _____ are behavioral roles that are recognized in job descriptions and by remuneration systems, they are directly related to organizational _____, whereas, contextual _____ are value based and additional behavioral roles that are not recognized in job descriptions and covered by compensation; they are extra roles that are indirectly related to organizational _____ . Citizenship _____ like contextual _____ means a set of individual activity/contribution that supports the organizational culture.

Exam Probability: **Low**

54. *Answer choices:*
(see index for correct answer)

- a. Phillumeny
- b. Performance
- c. Vacuum packing
- d. Bag-in-box

Guidance: level 1

:: Price fixing convictions ::

_____ is the flag carrier airline of the United Kingdom, headquartered at Waterside, Harmondsworth. It is the second largest airline in the United Kingdom, based on fleet size and passengers carried, behind easyJet. The airline is based in Waterside near its main hub at London Heathrow Airport. In January 2011 BA merged with Iberia, creating the International Airlines Group , a holding company registered in Madrid, Spain. IAG is the world's third-largest airline group in terms of annual revenue and the second-largest in Europe. It is listed on the London Stock Exchange and in the FTSE 100 Index. _____ is the first passenger airline to have generated more than $1 billion on a single air route in a year .

Exam Probability: **High**

55. *Answer choices:*

(see index for correct answer)

- a. Northwest Airlines
- b. United States v. Archer Daniels Midland Co.
- c. Anheuser-Busch InBev
- d. Heineken International

Guidance: level 1

:: International trade ::

A _____ is a document issued by a carrier to acknowledge receipt of cargo for shipment. Although the term historically related only to carriage by sea, a _____ may today be used for any type of carriage of goods.

Exam Probability: **High**

56. *Answer choices:*

(see index for correct answer)

- a. National Foreign Trade Council
- b. Technology gap
- c. Revealed comparative advantage
- d. Certificate of origin

Guidance: level 1

:: ::

An _____ is an area of the production, distribution, or trade, and consumption of goods and services by different agents. Understood in its broadest sense, 'The _____ is defined as a social domain that emphasize the practices, discourses, and material expressions associated with the production, use, and management of resources'. Economic agents can be individuals, businesses, organizations, or governments. Economic transactions occur when two parties agree to the value or price of the transacted good or service, commonly expressed in a certain currency. However, monetary transactions only account for a small part of the economic domain.

Exam Probability: **High**

57. *Answer choices:*

(see index for correct answer)

- a. levels of analysis
- b. hierarchical perspective
- c. Sarbanes-Oxley act of 2002
- d. Economy

Guidance: level 1

:: Production economics ::

In microeconomics, _____ are the cost advantages that enterprises obtain due to their scale of operation, with cost per unit of output decreasing with increasing scale.

Exam Probability: **Medium**

58. *Answer choices:*

(see index for correct answer)

- a. Capitalist mode of production
- b. Economies of scale
- c. Capacity utilization
- d. Factor price

Guidance: level 1

:: Accounting source documents ::

An _____, bill or tab is a commercial document issued by a seller to a buyer, relating to a sale transaction and indicating the products, quantities, and agreed prices for products or services the seller had provided the buyer.

Exam Probability: **Low**

59. *Answer choices:*

(see index for correct answer)

- a. Remittance advice
- b. Credit memo
- c. Purchase order
- d. Banknote

Guidance: level 1

Business ethics

Business ethics (also known as corporate ethics) is a form of applied ethics or professional ethics, that examines ethical principles and moral or ethical problems that can arise in a business environment. It applies to all aspects of business conduct and is relevant to the conduct of individuals and entire organizations. These ethics originate from individuals, organizational statements or from the legal system. These norms, values, ethical, and unethical practices are what is used to guide business. They help those businesses maintain a better connection with their stakeholders.

:: Corporate scandals ::

_____ was a bank based in the Caribbean, which operated from 1986 to 2009 when it went into receivership. It was an affiliate of the Stanford Financial Group and failed when the its parent was seized by United States authorities in early 2009 as part of the investigation into Allen Stanford.

Exam Probability: **Low**

1. *Answer choices:*

(see index for correct answer)

- a. Milberg
- b. Product recall
- c. Lysine price-fixing conspiracy
- d. Patent encumbrance of large automotive NiMH batteries

Guidance: level 1

:: ::

_____ is the means to see, hear, or become aware of something or someone through our fundamental senses. The term _____ derives from the Latin word perceptio, and is the organization, identification, and interpretation of sensory information in order to represent and understand the presented information, or the environment.

Exam Probability: **High**

2. *Answer choices:*

(see index for correct answer)

- a. process perspective
- b. deep-level diversity
- c. interpersonal communication
- d. imperative

Guidance: level 1

:: Industrial ecology ::

> _____ is a strategy for reducing the amount of waste created and released into the environment, particularly by industrial facilities, agriculture, or consumers. Many large corporations view P2 as a method of improving the efficiency and profitability of production processes by technology advancements. Legislative bodies have enacted P2 measures, such as the _____ Act of 1990 and the Clean Air Act Amendments of 1990 by the United States Congress.

Exam Probability: **Medium**

3. *Answer choices:*

(see index for correct answer)

- a. Material flow analysis
- b. Extended producer responsibility
- c. Pollution Prevention

- d. Integrated chain management

Guidance: level 1

:: Leadership ::

_____ is a theory of leadership where a leader works with teams to identify needed change, creating a vision to guide the change through inspiration, and executing the change in tandem with committed members of a group; it is an integral part of the Full Range Leadership Model. _____ serves to enhance the motivation, morale, and job performance of followers through a variety of mechanisms; these include connecting the follower's sense of identity and self to a project and to the collective identity of the organization; being a role model for followers in order to inspire them and to raise their interest in the project; challenging followers to take greater ownership for their work, and understanding the strengths and weaknesses of followers, allowing the leader to align followers with tasks that enhance their performance.

Exam Probability: **Medium**

4. *Answer choices:*

(see index for correct answer)

- a. Spirit of Enniskillen Trust
- b. Transformational leadership
- c. Ethical leadership
- d. Leadership analysis

Guidance: level 1

:: ::

The Federal National Mortgage Association, commonly known as _____, is a United States government-sponsored enterprise and, since 1968, a publicly traded company. Founded in 1938 during the Great Depression as part of the New Deal, the corporation's purpose is to expand the secondary mortgage market by securitizing mortgage loans in the form of mortgage-backed securities, allowing lenders to reinvest their assets into more lending and in effect increasing the number of lenders in the mortgage market by reducing the reliance on locally based savings and loan associations. Its brother organization is the Federal Home Loan Mortgage Corporation, better known as Freddie Mac. As of 2018, _____ is ranked #21 on the Fortune 500 rankings of the largest United States corporations by total revenue.

Exam Probability: **High**

5. *Answer choices:*

(see index for correct answer)

- a. Fannie Mae
- b. personal values
- c. hierarchical
- d. hierarchical perspective

Guidance: level 1

:: Office work ::

_____ is the process and behavior in human interactions involving power and authority. It is also a tool to assess the operational capacity and to balance diverse views of interested parties. It is also known as office politics and organizational politics. It is the use of power and social networking within an organization to achieve changes that benefit the organization or individuals within it. Influence by individuals may serve personal interests without regard to their effect on the organization itself. Some of the personal advantages may include access to tangible assets, or intangible benefits such as status or pseudo-authority that influences the behavior of others. On the other hand, organizational politics can increase efficiency, form interpersonal relationships, expedite change, and profit the organization and its members simultaneously. Both individuals and groups may engage in office politics which can be highly destructive, as people focus on personal gains at the expense of the organization. "Self-serving political actions can negatively influence our social groupings, cooperation, information sharing, and many other organizational functions." Thus, it is vital to pay attention to organizational politics and create the right political landscape. "Politics is the lubricant that oils your organization's internal gears."
Office politics has also been described as "simply how power gets worked out on a practical, day-to-day basis."

Exam Probability: **Low**

6. *Answer choices:*

(see index for correct answer)

- a. Career woman
- b. Workplace politics
- c. Enterprise forms automation
- d. Small office/home office

Guidance: level 1

:: ::

> A _____ service is an online platform which people use to build social networks or social relationship with other people who share similar personal or career interests, activities, backgrounds or real-life connections.

Exam Probability: **Low**

7. *Answer choices:*

(see index for correct answer)

- a. personal values
- b. Social networking
- c. hierarchical
- d. hierarchical perspective

Guidance: level 1

:: Dutch inventions ::

> The Fairtrade certification initiative was created to form a new method for economic trade. This method takes an ethical standpoint, and considers the producers first.

Exam Probability: **Low**

8. Answer choices:

(see index for correct answer)

- a. Fairtrade
- b. Fair Trade Certified

Guidance: level 1

:: ::

A _____ is a proceeding by a party or parties against another in the civil court of law. The archaic term "suit in law" is found in only a small number of laws still in effect today. The term " _____ " is used in reference to a civil action brought in a court of law in which a plaintiff, a party who claims to have incurred loss as a result of a defendant's actions, demands a legal or equitable remedy. The defendant is required to respond to the plaintiff's complaint. If the plaintiff is successful, judgment is in the plaintiff's favor, and a variety of court orders may be issued to enforce a right, award damages, or impose a temporary or permanent injunction to prevent an act or compel an act. A declaratory judgment may be issued to prevent future legal disputes.

Exam Probability: **High**

9. Answer choices:

(see index for correct answer)

- a. cultural
- b. personal values

- c. Sarbanes-Oxley act of 2002
- d. Lawsuit

Guidance: level 1

:: ::

_____ is the collection of mechanisms, processes and relations by which corporations are controlled and operated. Governance structures and principles identify the distribution of rights and responsibilities among different participants in the corporation and include the rules and procedures for making decisions in corporate affairs. _____ is necessary because of the possibility of conflicts of interests between stakeholders, primarily between shareholders and upper management or among shareholders.

Exam Probability: **Low**

10. *Answer choices:*

(see index for correct answer)

- a. Corporate governance
- b. information systems assessment
- c. co-culture
- d. surface-level diversity

Guidance: level 1

:: United States federal labor legislation ::

The _____ of 1988 is a United States federal law that generally prevents employers from using polygraph tests, either for pre-employment screening or during the course of employment, with certain exemptions.

Exam Probability: **Medium**

11. *Answer choices:*

(see index for correct answer)

- a. Railway Labor Act
- b. National Apprenticeship Act
- c. Workforce Investment Act of 1998
- d. Contract Work Hours and Safety Standards Act

Guidance: level 1

:: Majority–minority relations ::

_____ , also known as reservation in India and Nepal, positive discrimination / action in the United Kingdom, and employment equity in Canada and South Africa, is the policy of promoting the education and employment of members of groups that are known to have previously suffered from discrimination. Historically and internationally, support for _____ has sought to achieve goals such as bridging inequalities in employment and pay, increasing access to education, promoting diversity, and redressing apparent past wrongs, harms, or hindrances.

Exam Probability: **Medium**

12. *Answer choices:*

(see index for correct answer)

- a. cultural dissonance
- b. cultural Relativism
- c. Affirmative action

Guidance: level 1

:: Monopoly (economics) ::

The _____ of 1890 was a United States antitrust law that regulates competition among enterprises, which was passed by Congress under the presidency of Benjamin Harrison.

Exam Probability: **Medium**

13. *Answer choices:*

(see index for correct answer)

- a. Bilateral monopoly
- b. Trust
- c. Building block model
- d. Sherman Antitrust Act

Guidance: level 1

:: Waste ::

_____ is any unwanted material in all forms that can cause harm. Many of today's household products such as televisions, computers and phones contain toxic chemicals that can pollute the air and contaminate soil and water. Disposing of such waste is a major public health issue.

Exam Probability: **Medium**

14. *Answer choices:*

(see index for correct answer)

- a. Post-consumer waste
- b. Business waste
- c. Controlled waste
- d. Bulky waste

Guidance: level 1

:: Anti-capitalism ::

_____ is a range of economic and social systems characterised by social ownership of the means of production and workers' self-management, as well as the political theories and movements associated with them. Social ownership can be public, collective or cooperative ownership, or citizen ownership of equity. There are many varieties of _____ and there is no single definition encapsulating all of them, with social ownership being the common element shared by its various forms.

Exam Probability: **Low**

15. *Answer choices:*

(see index for correct answer)

- a. Stalinism
- b. Green Left
- c. Derrick Jensen
- d. Socialism

Guidance: level 1

:: ::

_____ Ltd. is the world's 2nd largest offshore drilling contractor and is based in Vernier, Switzerland. The company has offices in 20 countries, including Switzerland, Canada, United States, Norway, Scotland, India, Brazil, Singapore, Indonesia and Malaysia.

Exam Probability: **Medium**

16. *Answer choices:*

(see index for correct answer)

- a. Transocean
- b. Character
- c. personal values
- d. similarity-attraction theory

Guidance: level 1

:: Electronic waste ::

_____ or e-waste describes discarded electrical or electronic devices. Used electronics which are destined for refurbishment, reuse, resale, salvage, recycling through material recovery, or disposal are also considered e-waste. Informal processing of e-waste in developing countries can lead to adverse human health effects and environmental pollution.

Exam Probability: **High**

17. *Answer choices:*

(see index for correct answer)

- a. ReGlobe
- b. Computer liquidator
- c. Electronic waste
- d. Global waste trade

Guidance: level 1

:: ::

_____ is the introduction of contaminants into the natural environment that cause adverse change. _____ can take the form of chemical substances or energy, such as noise, heat or light. Pollutants, the components of _____ , can be either foreign substances/energies or naturally occurring contaminants. _____ is often classed as point source or nonpoint source _____ .In 2015, _____ killed 9 million people in the world.

Exam Probability: **Medium**

18. *Answer choices:*

(see index for correct answer)

- a. imperative
- b. hierarchical perspective
- c. co-culture
- d. Pollution

Guidance: level 1

:: Price fixing convictions ::

_____ AG is a German multinational conglomerate company headquartered in Berlin and Munich and the largest industrial manufacturing company in Europe with branch offices abroad.

Exam Probability: **Medium**

19. *Answer choices:*

(see index for correct answer)

- a. High Noon Western Americana
- b. Hoffmann-La Roche
- c. Asahi Glass Co.
- d. Danish Christmas Tree Growers Association

Guidance: level 1

:: ::

A _____ is an organization, usually a group of people or a company, authorized to act as a single entity and recognized as such in law. Early incorporated entities were established by charter. Most jurisdictions now allow the creation of new _____ s through registration.

Exam Probability: **Medium**

20. *Answer choices:*

(see index for correct answer)

- a. cultural
- b. Sarbanes-Oxley act of 2002
- c. Corporation
- d. deep-level diversity

Guidance: level 1

:: Corporations law ::

A normal _____ consists of various departments that contribute to the company's overall mission and goals. Common departments include Marketing, [Finance, [[Operations managementOperations, Human Resource, and IT. These five divisions represent the major departments within a publicly traded company, though there are often smaller departments within autonomous firms. There is typically a CEO, and Board of Directors composed of the directors of each department. There are also company presidents, vice presidents, and CFOs. There is a great diversity in corporate forms as enterprises may range from single company to multi-corporate conglomerate. The four main _____ s are Functional, Divisional, Geographic, and the Matrix. Realistically, most corporations tend to have a "hybrid" structure, which is a combination of different models with one dominant strategy.

Exam Probability: **High**

21. *Answer choices:*

(see index for correct answer)

- a. United Kingdom company law

- b. Corporate structure
- c. Corporate law
- d. International Company and Commercial Law Review

Guidance: level 1

:: ::

A _____ is an astronomical body orbiting a star or stellar remnant that is massive enough to be rounded by its own gravity, is not massive enough to cause thermonuclear fusion, and has cleared its neighbouring region of _____ esimals.

Exam Probability: **Medium**

22. *Answer choices:*

(see index for correct answer)

- a. levels of analysis
- b. surface-level diversity
- c. hierarchical perspective
- d. interpersonal communication

Guidance: level 1

:: Confidence tricks ::

A _____ is a business model that recruits members via a promise of payments or services for enrolling others into the scheme, rather than supplying investments or sale of products. As recruiting multiplies, recruiting becomes quickly impossible, and most members are unable to profit; as such, _____ s are unsustainable and often illegal.

Exam Probability: **High**

23. *Answer choices:*

(see index for correct answer)

- a. Sucker list
- b. Art student scam
- c. DC Advertising
- d. Patent safe

Guidance: level 1

:: Leadership ::

_____ is leadership that is directed by respect for ethical beliefs and values and for the dignity and rights of others. It is thus related to concepts such as trust, honesty, consideration, charisma, and fairness.

Exam Probability: **Low**

24. *Answer choices:*

(see index for correct answer)

- a. Ethical leadership
- b. Strategic leadership
- c. Leadership analysis
- d. BTS Group

Guidance: level 1

:: Environmental economics ::

_____ is the process of people maintaining change in a balanced environment, in which the exploitation of resources, the direction of investments, the orientation of technological development and institutional change are all in harmony and enhance both current and future potential to meet human needs and aspirations. For many in the field, _____ is defined through the following interconnected domains or pillars: environment, economic and social, which according to Fritjof Capra is based on the principles of Systems Thinking. Sub-domains of sustainable development have been considered also: cultural, technological and political. While sustainable development may be the organizing principle for _____ for some, for others, the two terms are paradoxical. Sustainable development is the development that meets the needs of the present without compromising the ability of future generations to meet their own needs. Brundtland Report for the World Commission on Environment and Development introduced the term of sustainable development.

Exam Probability: **Low**

25. *Answer choices:*

(see index for correct answer)

- a. Sustainability
- b. Gas depletion
- c. Centre for Water Economics, Environment and Policy
- d. Hubbert peak theory

Guidance: level 1

:: ::

_____ is a non-governmental environmental organization with offices in over 39 countries and an international coordinating body in Amsterdam, the Netherlands. _____ was founded in 1971 by Irving Stowe, and Dorothy Stowe, Canadian and US ex-pat environmental activists. _____ states its goal is to "ensure the ability of the Earth to nurture life in all its diversity" and focuses its campaigning on worldwide issues such as climate change, deforestation, overfishing, commercial whaling, genetic engineering, and anti-nuclear issues. It uses direct action, lobbying, research, and ecotage to achieve its goals. The global organization does not accept funding from governments, corporations, or political parties, relying on three million individual supporters and foundation grants. _____ has a general consultative status with the United Nations Economic and Social Council and is a founding member of the INGO Accountability Charter, an international non-governmental organization that intends to foster accountability and transparency of non-governmental organizations.

Exam Probability: **High**

26. *Answer choices:*

(see index for correct answer)

- a. hierarchical
- b. Character
- c. imperative
- d. surface-level diversity

Guidance: level 1

:: Natural gas ::

_____ is a naturally occurring hydrocarbon gas mixture consisting primarily of methane, but commonly including varying amounts of other higher alkanes, and sometimes a small percentage of carbon dioxide, nitrogen, hydrogen sulfide, or helium. It is formed when layers of decomposing plant and animal matter are exposed to intense heat and pressure under the surface of the Earth over millions of years. The energy that the plants originally obtained from the sun is stored in the form of chemical bonds in the gas.

Exam Probability: **High**

27. *Answer choices:*

(see index for correct answer)

- a. Natural gas
- b. ISO 15971
- c. Natural-gas condensate
- d. Reid vapor pressure

Guidance: level 1

:: Criminal law ::

_____ is the body of law that relates to crime. It proscribes conduct perceived as threatening, harmful, or otherwise endangering to the property, health, safety, and moral welfare of people inclusive of one's self. Most _____ is established by statute, which is to say that the laws are enacted by a legislature. _____ includes the punishment and rehabilitation of people who violate such laws. _____ varies according to jurisdiction, and differs from civil law, where emphasis is more on dispute resolution and victim compensation, rather than on punishment or rehabilitation. Criminal procedure is a formalized official activity that authenticates the fact of commission of a crime and authorizes punitive or rehabilitative treatment of the offender.

Exam Probability: **Medium**

28. *Answer choices:*

(see index for correct answer)

- a. Mala prohibita
- b. Criminal law
- c. Self-incrimination
- d. mitigating factor

Guidance: level 1

:: Advertising techniques ::

The _____ is a story from the Trojan War about the subterfuge that the Greeks used to enter the independent city of Troy and win the war. In the canonical version, after a fruitless 10-year siege, the Greeks constructed a huge wooden horse, and hid a select force of men inside including Odysseus. The Greeks pretended to sail away, and the Trojans pulled the horse into their city as a victory trophy. That night the Greek force crept out of the horse and opened the gates for the rest of the Greek army, which had sailed back under cover of night. The Greeks entered and destroyed the city of Troy, ending the war.

Exam Probability: **High**

29. *Answer choices:*

(see index for correct answer)

- a. Trojan horse
- b. Roll-in
- c. Retail Radio
- d. Soft sell

Guidance: level 1

:: ::

The _____ Group is a global financial investment management and insurance company headquartered in Des Moines, Iowa.

Exam Probability: **Low**

30. *Answer choices:*

(see index for correct answer)

- a. empathy
- b. Principal Financial
- c. process perspective
- d. information systems assessment

Guidance: level 1

:: ::

_____ is a product prepared from the leaves of the _____ plant by curing them. The plant is part of the genus Nicotiana and of the Solanaceae family. While more than 70 species of _____ are known, the chief commercial crop is N. tabacum. The more potent variant N. rustica is also used around the world.

Exam Probability: **High**

31. *Answer choices:*

(see index for correct answer)

- a. deep-level diversity
- b. information systems assessment
- c. Tobacco
- d. Sarbanes-Oxley act of 2002

Guidance: level 1

:: Business ethics ::

The _____ are the names of two corporate codes of conduct, developed by the African-American preacher Rev. Leon Sullivan, promoting corporate social responsibility.

Exam Probability: **Low**

32. *Answer choices:*

(see index for correct answer)

- a. Sullivan principles
- b. Anti-consumerism
- c. Fair value
- d. Anti-sweatshop movement

Guidance: level 1

:: Statutory law ::

_____ or statute law is written law set down by a body of legislature or by a singular legislator. This is as opposed to oral or customary law; or regulatory law promulgated by the executive or common law of the judiciary. Statutes may originate with national, state legislatures or local municipalities.

Exam Probability: **Medium**

33. *Answer choices:*

(see index for correct answer)

- a. ratification
- b. Statutory law
- c. incorporation by reference
- d. Statute of repose

Guidance: level 1

:: False advertising law ::

The Lanham Act is the primary federal trademark statute of law in the United States. The Act prohibits a number of activities, including trademark infringement, trademark dilution, and false advertising.

Exam Probability: **Low**

34. *Answer choices:*

(see index for correct answer)

- a. Rebecca Tushnet
- b. Lanham Act

Guidance: level 1

:: ::

The _____ is an American stock exchange located at 11 Wall Street, Lower Manhattan, New York City, New York. It is by far the world's largest stock exchange by market capitalization of its listed companies at US$30.1 trillion as of February 2018. The average daily trading value was approximately US$169 billion in 2013. The NYSE trading floor is located at 11 Wall Street and is composed of 21 rooms used for the facilitation of trading. A fifth trading room, located at 30 Broad Street, was closed in February 2007. The main building and the 11 Wall Street building were designated National Historic Landmarks in 1978.

Exam Probability: **Medium**

35. *Answer choices:*
(see index for correct answer)

- a. hierarchical
- b. Sarbanes-Oxley act of 2002
- c. New York Stock Exchange
- d. cultural

Guidance: level 1

:: Cognitive biases ::

In personality psychology, _____ is the degree to which people believe that they have control over the outcome of events in their lives, as opposed to external forces beyond their control. Understanding of the concept was developed by Julian B. Rotter in 1954, and has since become an aspect of personality studies. A person's "locus" is conceptualized as internal or external.

Exam Probability: **Medium**

36. *Answer choices:*

(see index for correct answer)

- a. Base rate fallacy
- b. Cognitive closure
- c. Locus of control
- d. Illusion of external agency

Guidance: level 1

:: ::

A _____ is a set of rules, often written, with regards to clothing. _____ s are created out of social perceptions and norms, and vary based on purpose, circumstances and occasions. Different societies and cultures are likely to have different _____ s.

Exam Probability: **Medium**

37. *Answer choices:*

(see index for correct answer)

- a. Dress code
- b. interpersonal communication
- c. hierarchical
- d. Sarbanes-Oxley act of 2002

Guidance: level 1

:: ::

_____ is the practice of deliberately managing the spread of information between an individual or an organization and the public. _____ may include an organization or individual gaining exposure to their audiences using topics of public interest and news items that do not require direct payment. This differentiates it from advertising as a form of marketing communications. _____ is the idea of creating coverage for clients for free, rather than marketing or advertising. But now, advertising is also a part of greater PR Activities. An example of good _____ would be generating an article featuring a client, rather than paying for the client to be advertised next to the article. The aim of _____ is to inform the public, prospective customers, investors, partners, employees, and other stakeholders and ultimately persuade them to maintain a positive or favorable view about the organization, its leadership, products, or political decisions. _____ professionals typically work for PR and marketing firms, businesses and companies, government, and public officials as PIOs and nongovernmental organizations, and nonprofit organizations. Jobs central to _____ include account coordinator, account executive, account supervisor, and media relations manager.

Exam Probability: **Medium**

38. *Answer choices:*

(see index for correct answer)

- a. open system
- b. interpersonal communication
- c. Public relations
- d. Character

Guidance: level 1

:: Anti-Revisionism ::

_____, officially the German Democratic Republic, was a country that existed from 1949 to 1990, when the eastern portion of Germany was part of the Eastern Bloc during the Cold War. It described itself as a socialist "workers` and peasants` state", and the territory was administered and occupied by Soviet forces at the end of World War II — the Soviet Occupation Zone of the Potsdam Agreement, bounded on the east by the Oder–Neisse line. The Soviet zone surrounded West Berlin but did not include it; as a result, West Berlin remained outside the jurisdiction of the GDR.

Exam Probability: **Medium**

39. *Answer choices:*
(see index for correct answer)

- a. Hoxhaism
- b. Ho Chi Minh Thought
- c. East Germany
- d. Party of Labour of Albania

Guidance: level 1

:: Corporate governance ::

_____ refers to the practice of members of a corporate board of directors serving on the boards of multiple corporations. A person that sits on multiple boards is known as a multiple director. Two firms have a direct interlock if a director or executive of one firm is also a director of the other, and an indirect interlock if a director of each sits on the board of a third firm. This practice, although widespread and lawful, raises questions about the quality and independence of board decisions.

Exam Probability: **Medium**

40. *Answer choices:*

(see index for correct answer)

- a. King II
- b. Corporate headquarters
- c. InfoSTEP
- d. Interlocking directorate

Guidance: level 1

:: Culture ::

_____ is a society which is characterized by individualism, which is the prioritization or emphasis, of the individual over the entire group. _____ s are oriented around the self, being independent instead of identifying with a group mentality. They see each other as only loosely linked, and value personal goals over group interests. _____ s tend to have a more diverse population and are characterized with emphasis on personal achievements, and a rational assessment of both the beneficial and detrimental aspects of relationships with others. _____ s have such unique aspects of communication as being a low power-distance culture and having a low-context communication style. The United States, Australia, Great Britain, Canada, the Netherlands, and New Zealand have been identified as highly _____ s.

Exam Probability: **High**

41. *Answer choices:*

(see index for correct answer)

- a. Individualistic culture
- b. cultural framework
- c. Intracultural
- d. High-context

Guidance: level 1

:: Anti-competitive behaviour ::

_____ is a secret cooperation or deceitful agreement in order to deceive others, although not necessarily illegal, as a conspiracy. A secret agreement between two or more parties to limit open competition by deceiving, misleading, or defrauding others of their legal rights, or to obtain an objective forbidden by law typically by defrauding or gaining an unfair market advantage is an example of _____ . It is an agreement among firms or individuals to divide a market, set prices, limit production or limit opportunities.It can involve "unions, wage fixing, kickbacks, or misrepresenting the independence of the relationship between the colluding parties". In legal terms, all acts effected by _____ are considered void.

Exam Probability: **Low**

42. *Answer choices:*

(see index for correct answer)

- a. price maintenance
- b. Collusion
- c. Strategic entry deterrence
- d. Anti-siphoning laws in Australia

Guidance: level 1

:: Carbon finance ::

The _____ is an international treaty which extends the 1992 United Nations Framework Convention on Climate Change that commits state parties to reduce greenhouse gas emissions, based on the scientific consensus that global warming is occurring and it is extremely likely that human-made CO_2 emissions have predominantly caused it. The _____ was adopted in Kyoto, Japan on 11 December 1997 and entered into force on 16 February 2005. There are currently 192 parties to the Protocol.

Exam Probability: **High**

43. *Answer choices:*

(see index for correct answer)

- a. Verified Carbon Standard
- b. PopOffsets
- c. Carbon offset
- d. Trees for the Future

Guidance: level 1

:: Business ethics ::

_____ is an area of applied ethics which deals with the moral principles behind the operation and regulation of marketing. Some areas of _____ overlap with media ethics.

Exam Probability: **Low**

44. *Answer choices:*

(see index for correct answer)

- a. Corporate sustainability
- b. Anti-consumerism
- c. Marketing ethics
- d. Black Company

Guidance: level 1

:: Electronic feedback ::

_____ occurs when outputs of a system are routed back as inputs as part of a chain of cause-and-effect that forms a circuit or loop. The system can then be said to feed back into itself. The notion of cause-and-effect has to be handled carefully when applied to _____ systems.

Exam Probability: **Low**

45. *Answer choices:*

(see index for correct answer)

- a. Positive feedback
- b. feedback loop

Guidance: level 1

:: ::

The _____ is an institution of the European Union, responsible for proposing legislation, implementing decisions, upholding the EU treaties and managing the day-to-day business of the EU. Commissioners swear an oath at the European Court of Justice in Luxembourg City, pledging to respect the treaties and to be completely independent in carrying out their duties during their mandate. Unlike in the Council of the European Union, where members are directly and indirectly elected, and the European Parliament, where members are directly elected, the Commissioners are proposed by the Council of the European Union, on the basis of suggestions made by the national governments, and then appointed by the European Council after the approval of the European Parliament.

Exam Probability: **High**

46. *Answer choices:*

(see index for correct answer)

- a. interpersonal communication
- b. levels of analysis
- c. European Commission
- d. cultural

Guidance: level 1

:: Renewable energy ::

A _____ is a fuel that is produced through contemporary biological processes, such as agriculture and anaerobic digestion, rather than a fuel produced by geological processes such as those involved in the formation of fossil fuels, such as coal and petroleum, from prehistoric biological matter. If the source biomatter can regrow quickly, the resulting fuel is said to be a form of renewable energy.

Exam Probability: **High**

47. *Answer choices:*

(see index for correct answer)

- a. Thermal energy storage
- b. Biofuel
- c. Yield co
- d. Passive solar building design

Guidance: level 1

:: Business ::

_____ , or built-in obsolescence, in industrial design and economics is a policy of planning or designing a product with an artificially limited useful life, so that it becomes obsolete after a certain period of time. The rationale behind this strategy is to generate long-term sales volume by reducing the time between repeat purchases .

Exam Probability: **Medium**

48. *Answer choices:*

(see index for correct answer)

- a. Customer experience
- b. For-profit charity
- c. Business
- d. Planned obsolescence

Guidance: level 1

:: United States federal defense and national security legislation ::

The USA _____ is an Act of the U.S. Congress that was signed into law by President George W. Bush on October 26, 2001. The title of the Act is a contrived three letter initialism preceding a seven letter acronym, which in combination stand for Uniting and Strengthening America by Providing Appropriate Tools Required to Intercept and Obstruct Terrorism Act of 2001. The acronym was created by a 23 year old Congressional staffer, Chris Kyle.

Exam Probability: **Medium**

49. *Answer choices:*

(see index for correct answer)

- a. USA PATRIOT Act
- b. Export Administration Act

Guidance: level 1

:: Toxicology ::

_____ or lead-based paint is paint containing lead. As pigment, lead chromate , Lead oxide, , and lead carbonate are the most common forms. Lead is added to paint to accelerate drying, increase durability, maintain a fresh appearance, and resist moisture that causes corrosion. It is one of the main health and environmental hazards associated with paint. In some countries, lead continues to be added to paint intended for domestic use, whereas countries such as the U.S. and the UK have regulations prohibiting this, although _____ may still be found in older properties painted prior to the introduction of such regulations. Although lead has been banned from household paints in the United States since 1978, paint used in road markings may still contain it. Alternatives such as water-based, lead-free traffic paint are readily available, and many states and federal agencies have changed their purchasing contracts to buy these instead.

Exam Probability: **Low**

50. *Answer choices:*

(see index for correct answer)

- a. Lead paint
- b. Committee on Toxicity
- c. Toxicophore
- d. Klimisch score

Guidance: level 1

:: ::

:::: was a philosopher during the Classical period in Ancient Greece, the founder of the Lyceum and the Peripatetic school of philosophy and Aristotelian tradition. Along with his teacher Plato, he is considered the "Father of Western Philosophy". His writings cover many subjects – including physics, biology, zoology, metaphysics, logic, ethics, aesthetics, poetry, theatre, music, rhetoric, psychology, linguistics, economics, politics and government. _____ provided a complex synthesis of the various philosophies existing prior to him, and it was above all from his teachings that the West inherited its intellectual lexicon, as well as problems and methods of inquiry. As a result, his philosophy has exerted a unique influence on almost every form of knowledge in the West and it continues to be a subject of contemporary philosophical discussion.

Exam Probability: **Low**

51. *Answer choices:*

(see index for correct answer)

- a. co-culture
- b. interpersonal communication
- c. process perspective
- d. cultural

Guidance: level 1

:: ::

The _____ was a severe worldwide economic depression that took place mostly during the 1930s, beginning in the United States. The timing of the _____ varied across nations; in most countries it started in 1929 and lasted until the late-1930s. It was the longest, deepest, and most widespread depression of the 20th century. In the 21st century, the _____ is commonly used as an example of how intensely the world`s economy can decline.

Exam Probability: **Low**

52. *Answer choices:*

(see index for correct answer)

- a. functional perspective
- b. interpersonal communication
- c. empathy
- d. deep-level diversity

Guidance: level 1

:: Business ethics ::

_____ is a type of harassment technique that relates to a sexual nature and the unwelcome or inappropriate promise of rewards in exchange for sexual favors. _____ includes a range of actions from mild transgressions to sexual abuse or assault. Harassment can occur in many different social settings such as the workplace, the home, school, churches, etc. Harassers or victims may be of any gender.

Exam Probability: **High**

53. *Answer choices:*

(see index for correct answer)

- a. Conscious business
- b. Sweatshop
- c. Minority business enterprise
- d. Sexual harassment

Guidance: level 1

:: ::

Competition law is a law that promotes or seeks to maintain market competition by regulating anti-competitive conduct by companies. Competition law is implemented through public and private enforcement. Competition law is known as " _____ law" in the United States for historical reasons, and as "anti-monopoly law" in China and Russia. In previous years it has been known as trade practices law in the United Kingdom and Australia. In the European Union, it is referred to as both _____ and competition law.

Exam Probability: **High**

54. *Answer choices:*

(see index for correct answer)

- a. Sarbanes-Oxley act of 2002

- b. imperative
- c. Antitrust
- d. cultural

Guidance: level 1

:: Management ::

The term _____ refers to measures designed to increase the degree of autonomy and self-determination in people and in communities in order to enable them to represent their interests in a responsible and self-determined way, acting on their own authority. It is the process of becoming stronger and more confident, especially in controlling one`s life and claiming one`s rights. _____ as action refers both to the process of self-_____ and to professional support of people, which enables them to overcome their sense of powerlessness and lack of influence, and to recognize and use their resources. To do work with power.

Exam Probability: **Low**

55. *Answer choices:*
(see index for correct answer)

- a. Empowerment
- b. Stewardship theory
- c. Enterprise planning system
- d. Personal offshoring

Guidance: level 1

:: Trade unions ::

A _____ was a group formed of private citizens to administer law and order where they considered governmental structures to be inadequate. The term is commonly associated with the frontier areas of the American West in the mid-19th century, where groups attacked cattle rustlers and gangs, and people at gold mining claims. As non-state organizations no functioning checks existed to protect against excessive force or safeguard due process from the committees. In the years prior to the Civil War, some committees worked to free slaves and transport them to freedom.

Exam Probability: **Medium**

56. *Answer choices:*

(see index for correct answer)

- a. Vigilance committee
- b. Unionized cooperative
- c. Scope clause
- d. Union democracy

Guidance: level 1

:: Competition regulators ::

The _____ is an independent agency of the United States government, established in 1914 by the _____ Act. Its principal mission is the promotion of consumer protection and the elimination and prevention of anticompetitive business practices, such as coercive monopoly. It is headquartered in the _____ Building in Washington, D.C.

Exam Probability: **Medium**

57. *Answer choices:*

(see index for correct answer)

- a. Competition and Markets Authority
- b. Competition Authority
- c. Federal Trade Commission
- d. Jersey Competition Regulatory Authority

Guidance: level 1

:: Professional ethics ::

In the mental health field, a _____ is a situation where multiple roles exist between a therapist, or other mental health practitioner, and a client. _____ s are also referred to as multiple relationships, and these two terms are used interchangeably in the research literature. The American Psychological Association Ethical Principles of Psychologists and Code of Conduct is a resource that outlines ethical standards and principles to which practitioners are expected to adhere. Standard 3.05 of the APA ethics code outlines the definition of multiple relationships. Dual or multiple relationships occur when.

Exam Probability: **Low**

58. Answer choices:

(see index for correct answer)

- a. Dual relationship
- b. professional conduct
- c. Continuous professional development

Guidance: level 1

:: Business ethics ::

> _____ is a type of international private business self-regulation. While once it was possible to describe CSR as an internal organisational policy or a corporate ethic strategy, that time has passed as various international laws have been developed and various organisations have used their authority to push it beyond individual or even industry-wide initiatives. While it has been considered a form of corporate self-regulation for some time, over the last decade or so it has moved considerably from voluntary decisions at the level of individual organisations, to mandatory schemes at regional, national and even transnational levels.

Exam Probability: **High**

59. Answer choices:

(see index for correct answer)

- a. United Nations Global Compact

- b. TG Soft
- c. Foreign official
- d. Ethical consumerism

Guidance: level 1

Accounting

Accounting or accountancy is the measurement, processing, and communication of financial information about economic entities such as businesses and corporations. The modern field was established by the Italian mathematician Luca Pacioli in 1494. Accounting, which has been called the "language of business", measures the results of an organization's economic activities and conveys this information to a variety of users, including investors, creditors, management, and regulators.

:: Classification systems ::

_____ is the practice of comparing business processes and performance metrics to industry bests and best practices from other companies. Dimensions typically measured are quality, time and cost.

Exam Probability: **Low**

1. *Answer choices:*

(see index for correct answer)

- a. Biological classification
- b. Chinese Classification of Mental Disorders
- c. Benchmarking
- d. Structural Classification of Proteins database

Guidance: level 1

:: Insolvency ::

_____ is the process in accounting by which a company is brought to an end in the United Kingdom, Republic of Ireland and United States. The assets and property of the company are redistributed. _____ is also sometimes referred to as winding-up or dissolution, although dissolution technically refers to the last stage of _____ . The process of _____ also arises when customs, an authority or agency in a country responsible for collecting and safeguarding customs duties, determines the final computation or ascertainment of the duties or drawback accruing on an entry.

Exam Probability: **Medium**

2. *Answer choices:*

(see index for correct answer)

- a. Insolvency law of Russia
- b. Liquidation
- c. Bankruptcy
- d. Debt consolidation

Guidance: level 1

:: Taxation ::

_____ is a type of tax law that allows a person to give assets to his or her spouse with reduced or no tax imposed upon the transfer. Some _____ laws even apply to transfers made postmortem. The right to receive property conveys ownership for tax purposes. A decree of divorce transfers the right to that property by reason of the marriage and is also a transfer within a marriage. It makes no difference whether the property itself or equivalent compensation is transferred before, or after the decree dissolves the marriage. There is no U.S. estate and gift tax on transfers of any amount between spouses, whether during their lifetime or at death. There is an important exceptions for non-citizens. The U.S. federal Estate and gift tax _____ is only available if the surviving spouse is a U.S. citizen. For a surviving spouse who is not a U.S. citizen a bequest through a Qualified Domestic Trust defers estate tax until principal is distributed by the trustee, a U.S. citizen or corporation who also withholds the estate tax. Income on principal distributed to the surviving spouse is taxed as individual income. If the surviving spouse becomes a U.S. citizen, principal remaining in a Qualifying Domestic Trust may then be distributed without further tax.

Exam Probability: **Low**

3. *Answer choices:*

(see index for correct answer)

- a. Value capture
- b. African Tax Administration Forum
- c. Marital deduction
- d. Tax break

Guidance: level 1

:: Taxation in the United States ::

Basis, as used in United States tax law, is the original cost of property, adjusted for factors such as depreciation. When property is sold, the taxpayer pays/ taxes on a capital gain/ that equals the amount realized on the sale minus the sold property's basis.

Exam Probability: **Medium**

4. *Answer choices:*

(see index for correct answer)

- a. Cost basis
- b. Itemized
- c. Half-year convention
- d. Carryover basis

Guidance: level 1

:: Management accounting ::

In economics, _____ s, indirect costs or overheads are business expenses that are not dependent on the level of goods or services produced by the business. They tend to be time-related, such as interest or rents being paid per month, and are often referred to as overhead costs. This is in contrast to variable costs, which are volume-related and unknown at the beginning of the accounting year. For a simple example, such as a bakery, the monthly rent for the baking facilities, and the monthly payments for the security system and basic phone line are _____ s, as they do not change according to how much bread the bakery produces and sells. On the other hand, the wage costs of the bakery are variable, as the bakery will have to hire more workers if the production of bread increases. Economists reckon _____ as a entry barrier for new entrepreneurs.

Exam Probability: **High**

5. *Answer choices:*

(see index for correct answer)

- a. Overhead
- b. Certified Management Accountants of Canada
- c. Fixed cost
- d. Throughput accounting

Guidance: level 1

:: Management accounting ::

_____ is a professional business study of Accounts and management in which we learn importance of accounts in our management system.

Exam Probability: **High**

6. *Answer choices:*
(see index for correct answer)

- a. Accounting management
- b. Dual overhead rate
- c. Activity-based management
- d. Chartered Institute of Management Accountants

Guidance: level 1

:: Taxation ::

_____ refers to the base upon which an income tax system imposes tax. Generally, it includes some or all items of income and is reduced by expenses and other deductions. The amounts included as income, expenses, and other deductions vary by country or system. Many systems provide that some types of income are not taxable and some expenditures not deductible in computing _____. Some systems base tax on _____ of the current period, and some on prior periods. _____ may refer to the income of any taxpayer, including individuals and corporations, as well as entities that themselves do not pay tax, such as partnerships, in which case it may be called "net profit".

Exam Probability: **Low**

7. *Answer choices:*

(see index for correct answer)

- a. Taxable income
- b. Tax advisor
- c. Tax break
- d. Tax policy

Guidance: level 1

:: Finance ::

_____ , in finance and accounting, means stated value or face value. From this come the expressions at par , over par and under par .

Exam Probability: **Medium**

8. *Answer choices:*

(see index for correct answer)

- a. Par value
- b. Debt capital
- c. Minority interest
- d. Replicating strategy

Guidance: level 1

:: Generally Accepted Accounting Principles ::

_____s is an accounting term that refers to groups of accounts serving to express the cost of goods and service allocatable within a business or manufacturing organization. The principle behind the pool is to correlate direct and indirect costs with a specified cost driver, so to find out the total sum of expenses related to the manufacture of a product.

Exam Probability: **Medium**

9. *Answer choices:*

(see index for correct answer)

- a. Cost pool
- b. Historical cost
- c. Net income
- d. Net realizable value

Guidance: level 1

:: Financial ratios ::

A _____ or accounting ratio is a relative magnitude of two selected numerical values taken from an enterprise's financial statements. Often used in accounting, there are many standard ratios used to try to evaluate the overall financial condition of a corporation or other organization. _____ s may be used by managers within a firm, by current and potential shareholders of a firm, and by a firm's creditors. Financial analysts use _____ s to compare the strengths and weaknesses in various companies. If shares in a company are traded in a financial market, the market price of the shares is used in certain _____ s.

Exam Probability: **High**

10. *Answer choices:*

(see index for correct answer)

- a. Omega ratio
- b. Like for like
- c. Financial ratio
- d. Return on equity

Guidance: level 1

:: Information systems ::

_____ are formal, sociotechnical, organizational systems designed to collect, process, store, and distribute information. In a sociotechnical perspective, _____ are composed by four components: task, people, structure, and technology.

Exam Probability: **Low**

11. *Answer choices:*

(see index for correct answer)

- a. TOPS
- b. Control flow diagram
- c. Information engineering
- d. Student information system

Guidance: level 1

:: ::

An _____ is a systematic and independent examination of books, accounts, statutory records, documents and vouchers of an organization to ascertain how far the financial statements as well as non-financial disclosures present a true and fair view of the concern. It also attempts to ensure that the books of accounts are properly maintained by the concern as required by law. _____ ing has become such a ubiquitous phenomenon in the corporate and the public sector that academics started identifying an " _____ Society". The _____ or perceives and recognises the propositions before them for examination, obtains evidence, evaluates the same and formulates an opinion on the basis of his judgement which is communicated through their _____ ing report.

Exam Probability: **Low**

12. *Answer choices:*

(see index for correct answer)

- a. surface-level diversity
- b. process perspective
- c. corporate values
- d. similarity-attraction theory

Guidance: level 1

:: Labor terms ::

_____ , often called DI or disability income insurance, or income protection, is a form of insurance that insures the beneficiary's earned income against the risk that a disability creates a barrier for a worker to complete the core functions of their work. For example, the worker may suffer from an inability to maintain composure in the case of psychological disorders or an injury, illness or condition that causes physical impairment or incapacity to work. It encompasses paid sick leave, short-term disability benefits , and long-term disability benefits . Statistics show that in the US a disabling accident occurs, on average, once every second. In fact, nearly 18.5% of Americans are currently living with a disability, and 1 out of every 4 persons in the US workforce will suffer a disabling injury before retirement.

Exam Probability: **Medium**

13. *Answer choices:*
(see index for correct answer)

- a. Civilian noninstitutional population

- b. Civilian workers
- c. Disability insurance
- d. Deflator

Guidance: level 1

:: Inventory ::

_____ is a system of inventory in which updates are made on a periodic basis. This differs from perpetual inventory systems, where updates are made as seen fit.

Exam Probability: **Medium**

14. *Answer choices:*

(see index for correct answer)

- a. Spare part
- b. Decomposition
- c. Stock-taking
- d. Cost of goods available for sale

Guidance: level 1

:: Management accounting ::

_____ are costs that are not directly accountable to a cost object. _____ may be either fixed or variable. _____ include administration, personnel and security costs. These are those costs which are not directly related to production. Some _____ may be overhead. But some overhead costs can be directly attributed to a project and are direct costs.

Exam Probability: **Low**

15. *Answer choices:*

(see index for correct answer)

- a. Institute of Management Accountants
- b. Certified Management Accountant
- c. Overhead
- d. Indirect costs

Guidance: level 1

:: ::

The _____ of 1934 is a law governing the secondary trading of securities in the United States of America. A landmark of wide-ranging legislation, the Act of '34 and related statutes form the basis of regulation of the financial markets and their participants in the United States. The 1934 Act also established the Securities and Exchange Commission, the agency primarily responsible for enforcement of United States federal securities law.

Exam Probability: **Medium**

16. *Answer choices:*

(see index for correct answer)

- a. surface-level diversity
- b. Securities Exchange Act
- c. hierarchical
- d. empathy

Guidance: level 1

:: Accounting ::

_____ are key sources of information and evidence used to prepare, verify and/or audit the financial statements. They also include documentation to prove asset ownership for creation of liabilities and proof of monetary and non monetary transactions.

Exam Probability: **Medium**

17. *Answer choices:*

(see index for correct answer)

- a. amortisation
- b. Bookkeeping
- c. Accounting records
- d. History of accounting

Guidance: level 1

:: ::

The _____ of 1938 29 U.S.C. § 203 is a United States labor law that creates the right to a minimum wage, and "time-and-a-half" overtime pay when people work over forty hours a week. It also prohibits most employment of minors in "oppressive child labor". It applies to employees engaged in interstate commerce or employed by an enterprise engaged in commerce or in the production of goods for commerce, unless the employer can claim an exemption from coverage.

Exam Probability: **High**

18. *Answer choices:*

(see index for correct answer)

- a. deep-level diversity
- b. Fair Labor Standards Act
- c. corporate values
- d. imperative

Guidance: level 1

:: Management accounting ::

_____ is an approach to determine a product's life-cycle cost which should be sufficient to develop specified functionality and quality, while ensuring its desired profit. It involves setting a target cost by subtracting a desired profit margin from a competitive market price. A target cost is the maximum amount of cost that can be incurred on a product, however, the firm can still earn the required profit margin from that product at a particular selling price. _____ decomposes the target cost from product level to component level. Through this decomposition, _____ spreads the competitive pressure faced by the company to product's designers and suppliers. _____ consists of cost planning in the design phase of production as well as cost control throughout the resulting product life cycle. The cardinal rule of _____ is to never exceed the target cost. However, the focus of _____ is not to minimize costs, but to achieve a desired level of cost reduction determined by the _____ process.

Exam Probability: **High**

19. *Answer choices:*

(see index for correct answer)

- a. Notional profit
- b. Institute of Cost and Management Accountants of Bangladesh
- c. Target costing
- d. Dual overhead rate

Guidance: level 1

:: Economic globalization ::

_____ is an agreement in which one company hires another company to be responsible for a planned or existing activity that is or could be done internally, and sometimes involves transferring employees and assets from one firm to another.

Exam Probability: **Low**

20. *Answer choices:*

(see index for correct answer)

- a. reshoring
- b. global financial

Guidance: level 1

:: Business models ::

A _____ is a company that owns enough voting stock in another firm to control management and operation by influencing or electing its board of directors. The company is deemed a subsidiary of the _____ .

Exam Probability: **High**

21. *Answer choices:*

(see index for correct answer)

- a. Copy to China

- b. Parent company
- c. Product-service system
- d. Micro-enterprise

Guidance: level 1

:: Expense ::

_____ relates to the cost of borrowing money. It is the price that a lender charges a borrower for the use of the lender's money. On the income statement, _____ can represent the cost of borrowing money from banks, bond investors, and other sources. _____ is different from operating expense and CAPEX, for it relates to the capital structure of a company, and it is usually tax-deductible.

Exam Probability: **Low**

22. *Answer choices:*

(see index for correct answer)

- a. Business overhead expense disability insurance
- b. Interest expense
- c. Freight expense
- d. Operating expense

Guidance: level 1

:: Financial ratios ::

_____ is a financial ratio that indicates the percentage of a company's assets that are provided via debt. It is the ratio of total debt and total assets.

Exam Probability: **High**

23. *Answer choices:*

(see index for correct answer)

- a. Put/call ratio
- b. Debt service ratio
- c. Return on assets
- d. Asset turnover

Guidance: level 1

:: Financial ratios ::

_____ or interest coverage ratio is a measure of a company's ability to honor its debt payments. It may be calculated as either EBIT or EBITDA divided by the total interest payable.

Exam Probability: **Medium**

24. *Answer choices:*

(see index for correct answer)

- a. Return on capital
- b. Debt service coverage ratio
- c. CASA ratio
- d. Times interest earned

Guidance: level 1

:: Accounting organizations ::

The _____ promotes accounting education, research and practice. Founded in 1916 as the American Association of University Instructors in Accounting, its present name was adopted in 1936. The Association is a voluntary group of persons interested in accounting education and research.

Exam Probability: **High**

25. *Answer choices:*

(see index for correct answer)

- a. Accounting Hall of Fame
- b. Institute for Truth in Accounting
- c. Taxand
- d. American Accounting Association

Guidance: level 1

:: Manufacturing ::

_____s are goods that have completed the manufacturing process but have not yet been sold or distributed to the end user.

Exam Probability: **Medium**

26. *Answer choices:*

(see index for correct answer)

- a. Finished good
- b. Eneas
- c. Axiomatic design
- d. Manufacturing Engineering Centre

Guidance: level 1

:: Free accounting software ::

A _____ is the principal book or computer file for recording and totaling economic transactions measured in terms of a monetary unit of account by account type, with debits and credits in separate columns and a beginning monetary balance and ending monetary balance for each account.

Exam Probability: **Medium**

27. *Answer choices:*

(see index for correct answer)

- a. HomeBank
- b. GnuCash
- c. Ledger
- d. JFin

Guidance: level 1

:: ::

A _____, in the word's original meaning, is a sheet of paper on which one performs work. They come in many forms, most commonly associated with children's school work assignments, tax forms, and accounting or other business environments. Software is increasingly taking over the paper-based _____.

Exam Probability: **Low**

28. *Answer choices:*

(see index for correct answer)

- a. Worksheet
- b. imperative
- c. open system

- d. similarity-attraction theory

Guidance: level 1

:: Asset ::

In financial accounting, an _____ is any resource owned by the business. Anything tangible or intangible that can be owned or controlled to produce value and that is held by a company to produce positive economic value is an _____ . Simply stated, _____ s represent value of ownership that can be converted into cash . The balance sheet of a firm records the monetary value of the _____ s owned by that firm. It covers money and other valuables belonging to an individual or to a business.

Exam Probability: **Low**

29. *Answer choices:*
(see index for correct answer)

- a. Current asset
- b. Asset

Guidance: level 1

:: ::

The _____ is a private, non-profit organization standard-setting body whose primary purpose is to establish and improve Generally Accepted Accounting Principles within the United States in the public's interest. The Securities and Exchange Commission designated the FASB as the organization responsible for setting accounting standards for public companies in the US. The FASB replaced the American Institute of Certified Public Accountants' Accounting Principles Board on July 1, 1973.

Exam Probability: **Medium**

30. *Answer choices:*

(see index for correct answer)

- a. open system
- b. Financial Accounting Standards Board
- c. interpersonal communication
- d. deep-level diversity

Guidance: level 1

:: Credit cards ::

A _____ is a payment card issued to users to enable the cardholder to pay a merchant for goods and services based on the cardholder's promise to the card issuer to pay them for the amounts plus the other agreed charges. The card issuer creates a revolving account and grants a line of credit to the cardholder, from which the cardholder can borrow money for payment to a merchant or as a cash advance.

Exam Probability: **Medium**

31. *Answer choices:*

(see index for correct answer)

- a. Credit card
- b. MasterCard
- c. Fuel card
- d. CardLab

Guidance: level 1

:: Payment systems ::

A _____ is a bond of the redeemable transaction type which is worth a certain monetary value and which may be spent only for specific reasons or on specific goods. Examples include housing, travel, and food _____ s. The term _____ is also a synonym for receipt and is often used to refer to receipts used as evidence of, for example, the declaration that a service has been performed or that an expenditure has been made. _____ is a tourist guide for using services with a guarantee of payment by the agency.

Exam Probability: **Medium**

32. *Answer choices:*

(see index for correct answer)

- a. Square, Inc.

- b. BPAY
- c. Monexgroup
- d. Immediate Payment Service

Guidance: level 1

:: ::

_____ are electronic transfer of money from one bank account to another, either within a single financial institution or across multiple institutions, via computer-based systems, without the direct intervention of bank staff.

Exam Probability: **Low**

33. *Answer choices:*

(see index for correct answer)

- a. process perspective
- b. personal values
- c. hierarchical
- d. Electronic funds transfer

Guidance: level 1

:: Income ::

_____ is a ratio between the net profit and cost of investment resulting from an investment of some resources. A high ROI means the investment's gains favorably to its cost. As a performance measure, ROI is used to evaluate the efficiency of an investment or to compare the efficiencies of several different investments. In purely economic terms, it is one way of relating profits to capital invested. _____ is a performance measure used by businesses to identify the efficiency of an investment or number of different investments.

Exam Probability: **Low**

34. *Answer choices:*

(see index for correct answer)

- a. Trinity study
- b. Giganomics
- c. Return on investment
- d. Income earner

Guidance: level 1

:: Generally Accepted Accounting Principles ::

In accounting, _____ is the income that a business have from its normal business activities, usually from the sale of goods and services to customers. _____ is also referred to as sales or turnover. Some companies receive _____ from interest, royalties, or other fees. _____ may refer to business income in general, or it may refer to the amount, in a monetary unit, earned during a period of time, as in "Last year, Company X had _____ of $42 million". Profits or net income generally imply total _____ minus total expenses in a given period. In accounting, in the balance statement it is a subsection of the Equity section and _____ increases equity, it is often referred to as the "top line" due to its position on the income statement at the very top. This is to be contrasted with the "bottom line" which denotes net income .

Exam Probability: **Medium**

35. *Answer choices:*

(see index for correct answer)

- a. Gross profit
- b. Write-off
- c. Engagement letter
- d. Revenue

Guidance: level 1

:: Stock market ::

_____ is a form of corporate equity ownership, a type of security. The terms voting share and ordinary share are also used frequently in other parts of the world; "_____" being primarily used in the United States. They are known as Equity shares or Ordinary shares in the UK and other Commonwealth realms. This type of share gives the stockholder the right to share in the profits of the company, and to vote on matters of corporate policy and the composition of the members of the board of directors.

Exam Probability: **Low**

36. *Answer choices:*

(see index for correct answer)

- a. General Standard
- b. Common stock
- c. Green chip
- d. Stock

Guidance: level 1

:: ::

An _____ is an asset that lacks physical substance. It is defined in opposition to physical assets such as machinery and buildings. An _____ is usually very hard to evaluate. Patents, copyrights, franchises, goodwill, trademarks, and trade names. The general interpretation also includes software and other intangible computer based assets are all examples of _____ s. _____ s generally—though not necessarily—suffer from typical market failures of non-rivalry and non-excludability.

Exam Probability: **Low**

37. *Answer choices:*

(see index for correct answer)

- a. empathy
- b. personal values
- c. hierarchical perspective
- d. Intangible asset

Guidance: level 1

:: Accounting software ::

_____ is an accounting software package developed and marketed by Intuit. _____ products are geared mainly toward small and medium-sized businesses and offer on-premises accounting applications as well as cloud-based versions that accept business payments, manage and pay bills, and payroll functions.

Exam Probability: **High**

38. *Answer choices:*

(see index for correct answer)

- a. Costpoint
- b. QuickBooks

- c. Intacct
- d. Fortora Fresh Finance

Guidance: level 1

:: Income taxes ::

An _____ is a tax imposed on individuals or entities that varies with respective income or profits . _____ generally is computed as the product of a tax rate times taxable income. Taxation rates may vary by type or characteristics of the taxpayer.

Exam Probability: **Low**

39. *Answer choices:*

(see index for correct answer)

- a. Dual income tax
- b. Papal income tax
- c. Income taxes in Canada
- d. Income tax

Guidance: level 1

:: ::

_____ is the process of making predictions of the future based on past and present data and most commonly by analysis of trends. A commonplace example might be estimation of some variable of interest at some specified future date. Prediction is a similar, but more general term. Both might refer to formal statistical methods employing time series, cross-sectional or longitudinal data, or alternatively to less formal judgmental methods. Usage can differ between areas of application: for example, in hydrology the terms "forecast" and "_____" are sometimes reserved for estimates of values at certain specific future times, while the term "prediction" is used for more general estimates, such as the number of times floods will occur over a long period.

Exam Probability: **High**

40. *Answer choices:*

(see index for correct answer)

- a. Sarbanes-Oxley act of 2002
- b. hierarchical
- c. Forecasting
- d. interpersonal communication

Guidance: level 1

:: Generally Accepted Accounting Principles ::

_____ is a small amount of discretionary funds in the form of cash used for expenditures where it is not sensible to make any disbursement by cheque, because of the inconvenience and costs of writing, signing, and then cashing the cheque.

Exam Probability: **Medium**

41. *Answer choices:*

(see index for correct answer)

- a. Petty cash
- b. Cash method of accounting
- c. Pro forma
- d. Expense

Guidance: level 1

:: Management accounting ::

In finance, the _____ or net present worth applies to a series of cash flows occurring at different times. The present value of a cash flow depends on the interval of time between now and the cash flow. It also depends on the discount rate. NPV accounts for the time value of money. It provides a method for evaluating and comparing capital projects or financial products with cash flows spread over time, as in loans, investments, payouts from insurance contracts plus many other applications.

Exam Probability: **High**

42. *Answer choices:*

(see index for correct answer)

- a. Management accounting

- b. Grenzplankostenrechnung
- c. Certified Management Accountants of Canada
- d. Net present value

Guidance: level 1

:: Budgets ::

_____ is a method of budgeting in which all expenses must be justified and approved for each new period. Developed by Peter Pyhrr in the 1970s, _____ starts from a "zero base" at the beginning of every budget period, analyzing needs and costs of every function within an organization and allocating funds accordingly, regardless of how much money has previously been budgeted to any given line item.

Exam Probability: **High**

43. *Answer choices:*

(see index for correct answer)

- a. Film budgeting
- b. Budget set
- c. Programme budgeting
- d. Zero-based budgeting

Guidance: level 1

:: Insurance terms ::

A _____ in the broadest sense is a natural person or other legal entity who receives money or other benefits from a benefactor. For example, the _____ of a life insurance policy is the person who receives the payment of the amount of insurance after the death of the insured.

Exam Probability: **High**

44. *Answer choices:*

(see index for correct answer)

- a. Copayment
- b. Additional insured
- c. Pro rata
- d. Beneficiary

Guidance: level 1

:: Financial ratios ::

The _____ shows the percentage of how profitable a company's assets are in generating revenue.

Exam Probability: **High**

45. Answer choices:

(see index for correct answer)

- a. Capital employed
- b. Capital recovery factor
- c. Return on assets
- d. Debt-to-capital ratio

Guidance: level 1

:: ::

_____ is the collection of mechanisms, processes and relations by which corporations are controlled and operated. Governance structures and principles identify the distribution of rights and responsibilities among different participants in the corporation and include the rules and procedures for making decisions in corporate affairs. _____ is necessary because of the possibility of conflicts of interests between stakeholders, primarily between shareholders and upper management or among shareholders.

Exam Probability: **High**

46. Answer choices:

(see index for correct answer)

- a. corporate values
- b. information systems assessment
- c. imperative

- d. Corporate governance

Guidance: level 1

:: Types of business entity ::

A _____ is a partnership in which some or all partners have limited liabilities. It therefore can exhibit elements of partnerships and corporations. In a LLP, each partner is not responsible or liable for another partner's misconduct or negligence. This is an important difference from the traditional partnership under the UK Partnership Act 1890, in which each partner has joint and several liability. In a LLP, some or all partners have a form of limited liability similar to that of the shareholders of a corporation. Unlike corporate shareholders, the partners have the right to manage the business directly. In contrast, corporate shareholders must elect a board of directors under the laws of various state charters. The board organizes itself and hires corporate officers who then have as "corporate" individuals the legal responsibility to manage the corporation in the corporation's best interest. A LLP also contains a different level of tax liability from that of a corporation.

Exam Probability: **Low**

47. *Answer choices:*
(see index for correct answer)

- a. Limited liability partnership
- b. Off-budget enterprise
- c. Globally integrated enterprise
- d. Virtual limited liability company

Guidance: level 1

:: Management accounting ::

_____ , or dollar contribution per unit, is the selling price per unit minus the variable cost per unit. "Contribution" represents the portion of sales revenue that is not consumed by variable costs and so contributes to the coverage of fixed costs. This concept is one of the key building blocks of break-even analysis.

Exam Probability: **Medium**

48. *Answer choices:*

(see index for correct answer)

- a. Contribution margin
- b. Spend management
- c. Process costing
- d. Throughput accounting

Guidance: level 1

:: ::

The U.S. _____ is an independent agency of the United States federal government. The SEC holds primary responsibility for enforcing the federal securities laws, proposing securities rules, and regulating the securities industry, the nation's stock and options exchanges, and other activities and organizations, including the electronic securities markets in the United States.

Exam Probability: **Medium**

49. *Answer choices:*

(see index for correct answer)

- a. cultural
- b. corporate values
- c. imperative
- d. process perspective

Guidance: level 1

:: Generally Accepted Accounting Principles ::

A _____ is a reduction of the recognized value of something. In accounting, this is a recognition of the reduced or zero value of an asset. In income tax statements, this is a reduction of taxable income, as a recognition of certain expenses required to produce the income.

Exam Probability: **High**

50. *Answer choices:*

(see index for correct answer)

- a. Revenue recognition
- b. Fixed investment
- c. Write-off
- d. Insurance asset management

Guidance: level 1

:: ::

A _____ is an individual or institution that legally owns one or more shares of stock in a public or private corporation. _____ s may be referred to as members of a corporation. Legally, a person is not a _____ in a corporation until their name and other details are entered in the corporation's register of _____ s or members.

Exam Probability: **Medium**

51. *Answer choices:*

(see index for correct answer)

- a. open system
- b. Shareholder
- c. information systems assessment
- d. personal values

Guidance: level 1

:: ::

_____ is the income that is gained by governments through taxation. Taxation is the primary source of income for a state. Revenue may be extracted from sources such as individuals, public enterprises, trade, royalties on natural resources and/or foreign aid. An inefficient collection of taxes is greater in countries characterized by poverty, a large agricultural sector and large amounts of foreign aid.

Exam Probability: **Medium**

52. *Answer choices:*

(see index for correct answer)

- a. information systems assessment
- b. deep-level diversity
- c. Tax revenue
- d. imperative

Guidance: level 1

:: ::

A _____ is a fund into which a sum of money is added during an employee's employment years, and from which payments are drawn to support the person's retirement from work in the form of periodic payments. A _____ may be a "defined benefit plan" where a fixed sum is paid regularly to a person, or a "defined contribution plan" under which a fixed sum is invested and then becomes available at retirement age. _____s should not be confused with severance pay; the former is usually paid in regular installments for life after retirement, while the latter is typically paid as a fixed amount after involuntary termination of employment prior to retirement.

Exam Probability: **Low**

53. *Answer choices:*

(see index for correct answer)

- a. corporate values
- b. interpersonal communication
- c. process perspective
- d. surface-level diversity

Guidance: level 1

:: Financial accounting ::

_____ is a financial metric which represents operating liquidity available to a business, organisation or other entity, including governmental entities. Along with fixed assets such as plant and equipment, _____ is considered a part of operating capital. Gross _____ is equal to current assets. _____ is calculated as current assets minus current liabilities. If current assets are less than current liabilities, an entity has a _____ deficiency, also called a _____ deficit.

Exam Probability: **Low**

54. *Answer choices:*

(see index for correct answer)

- a. Associate company
- b. Finance charge
- c. Advance payment
- d. Money measurement concept

Guidance: level 1

:: Real estate ::

Amortisation is paying off an amount owed over time by making planned, incremental payments of principal and interest. To amortise a loan means "to kill it off". In accounting, amortisation refers to charging or writing off an intangible asset's cost as an operational expense over its estimated useful life to reduce a company's taxable income.

Exam Probability: **High**

55. *Answer choices:*

(see index for correct answer)

- a. Amortization
- b. Land trust
- c. Buying agent
- d. Short sale

Guidance: level 1

:: Accounting systems ::

In accounting, the controlling account is an account in the general ledger for which a corresponding subsidiary ledger has been created. The subsidiary ledger allows for tracking transactions within the controlling account in more detail. Individual transactions are posted both to the controlling account and the corresponding subsidiary ledger, and the totals for both are compared when preparing a trial balance to ensure accuracy.

Exam Probability: **Low**

56. *Answer choices:*

(see index for correct answer)

- a. Open-book accounting
- b. Invoice processing

- c. Control account
- d. Substance over form

Guidance: level 1

:: Accounting terminology ::

A _____ contains all the accounts for recording transactions relating to a company's assets, liabilities, owners' equity, revenue, and expenses. In modern accounting software or ERP, the _____ works as a central repository for accounting data transferred from all subledgers or modules like accounts payable, accounts receivable, cash management, fixed assets, purchasing and projects. The _____ is the backbone of any accounting system which holds financial and non-financial data for an organization. The collection of all accounts is known as the _____ . Each account is known as a ledger account. In a manual or non-computerized system this may be a large book. The statement of financial position and the statement of income and comprehensive income are both derived from the _____ . Each account in the _____ consists of one or more pages. The _____ is where posting to the accounts occurs. Posting is the process of recording amounts as credits , and amounts as debits , in the pages of the _____ . Additional columns to the right hold a running activity total .

Exam Probability: **Low**

57. *Answer choices:*

(see index for correct answer)

- a. revenue recognition principle
- b. General ledger

- c. Mark-to-market
- d. Cash flow management

Guidance: level 1

:: Pricing ::

_____ is the difference between a lower selling price and a higher purchase price, resulting in a financial loss for the seller.

Exam Probability: **Low**

58. *Answer choices:*

(see index for correct answer)

- a. Benchmark price
- b. Profit maximization
- c. Nonlinear pricing
- d. Capital loss

Guidance: level 1

:: Accounting ::

_____ are designed to facilitate the process of journalizing and posting transactions. They are used for the most frequent transactions in a business. For example, in merchandising businesses, companies acquire merchandise from vendors, and then in turn sell the merchandise to individuals or other businesses. Sales and purchases are the most common transactions for the merchandising businesses. A business such as a retail store will record the following transactions many times a day for sales on account and cash sales.

Exam Probability: **Low**

59. *Answer choices:*

(see index for correct answer)

- a. Pipeline planning
- b. European training programs
- c. Special journals
- d. AICPA Code of Professional Conduct

Guidance: level 1

INDEX: Correct Answers

Foundations of Business

1. b: Variable cost

2. : Productivity

3. a: Comparative advantage

4. d: Error

5. b: Board of directors

6. : Officer

7. b: Interest

8. : Expense

9. c: Arbitration

10. c: Asset

11. : Buyer

12. a: Regulation

13. d: Internal Revenue Service

14. c: Strategic alliance

15. d: Protection

16. a: Capital market

17. b: Financial services

18. a: Entrepreneur

19. d: Decision-making

20. b: Import

21. a: Strategic planning

22. d: Income statement

23. d: Market value

24. d: Efficiency

25. b: Business process

26. d: Balance sheet

27. : Franchising

28. b: Analysis

29. a: Quality management

30. a: Cash

31. : Good

32. c: Office

33. c: Energies

34. b: Initiative

35. c: Accounting

36. : Exercise

37. c: Creativity

38. b: Scheduling

39. c: Loan

40. : Stock exchange

41. : ITeM

42. c: Health

43. c: Opportunity cost

44. b: Marketing research

45. a: Revenue

46. b: Image

47. a: Best practice

48. b: Threat

49. c: Supply chain

50. c: Credit

51. c: Specification

52. : Manufacturing

53. c: Organizational culture

54. c: Cultural

55. : Technology

56. a: Sony

57. b: Need

58. c: Law

59. a: Explanation

Management

1. a: Organizational commitment

2. a: Board of directors

3. a: Economies of scale

4. d: Initiative

5. : Labor force

6. : Policy

7. d: Senior management

8. b: Assessment center

9. c: Revenue

10. a: Size

11. a: Environmental scanning

12. d: Organizational learning

13. c: Inventory

14. a: Layoff

15. b: Enron

16. c: Threat

17. a: Job rotation

18. d: Cost

19. d: Market research

20. b: Ambiguity

21. b: Problem

22. b: Job enlargement

23. c: Chief executive officer

24. a: Project management

25. : Coaching

26. a: Delegation

27. a: Meeting

28. d: Bounded rationality

29. d: SWOT analysis

30. d: Collaboration

31. c: Review

32. b: Sexual harassment

33. a: Strategy

34. d: Job satisfaction

35. a: Time management

36. b: Kaizen

37. a: Empowerment

38. d: Management by objectives

39. b: Business model

40. d: Product life cycle

41. : Myers-Briggs type

42. : Industry

43. : Profit sharing

44. : Variable cost

45. a: Vertical integration

46. d: Referent power

47. : Mediation

48. b: Balanced scorecard

49. b: Authority

50. c: Office

51. d: Supervisor

52. : Management

53. b: Outsourcing

54. c: Strategic planning

55. a: Cost leadership

56. a: E-commerce

57. b: Standard deviation

58. : Small business

59. b: Wage

Business law

1. c: Misrepresentation

2. c: Subrogation

3. a: Trial

4. : Argument

5. a: Presentment

6. : Trade

7. b: Economy

8. d: Rescind

9. : Petition

10. b: Duty

11. b: Authority

12. d: Forgery

13. b: Marketing

14. d: Relevant market

15. : Mediation

16. a: Constitution

17. a: Prima facie

18. c: Asset

19. c: Garnishment

20. b: Aid

21. c: Personnel

22. : Assumption of risk

23. a: Internal Revenue Service

24. c: Contributory negligence

25. : Apparent authority

26. c: White-collar crime

27. : Adoption

28. d: Merger

29. c: Statutory Law

30. d: Free trade

31. a: Consideration

32. c: Consumer credit

33. b: Fee simple

34. c: Consumer protection

35. c: General partnership

36. b: Money laundering

37. c: Exclusionary rule

38. d: Contract law

39. c: Acceleration clause

40. b: Securities and Exchange Commission

41. c: Private law

42. a: Federal government

43. a: Jury Trial

44. b: Mortgage

45. d: Health insurance

46. c: Commerce Clause

47. c: Management

48. c: Wire fraud

49. b: Adverse possession

50. d: Creditor

51. a: World Trade Organization

52. b: Output contract

53. : Intellectual property

54. c: Securities Act

55. b: Insolvency

56. b: Proximate cause

57. d: Writ

58. a: Broker

59. a: Testimony

Finance

1. a: Asset

2. b: Asset management

3. a: Financial management

4. b: Total cost

5. a: Fixed asset

6. a: Aging

7. : Initial public offering

8. b: Expense

9. c: Forecasting

10. c: Long-term liabilities

11. d: Manufacturing overhead

12. d: Public company

13. a: Cost allocation

14. a: Face

15. c: Financial risk

16. b: Managerial accounting

17. b: Cash equivalent

18. c: Bank of America

19. c: Bad debt

20. d: Finished good

21. d: Cost object

22. : Break-even

23. d: Gross margin

24. d: Cost

25. d: Opportunity cost

26. a: Hedge

27. : Future value

28. c: Rate of return

29. c: Certified Public Accountant

30. : Capital expenditure

31. c: Standard cost

32. b: Currency

33. b: Advertising

34. a: Commercial paper

35. : Mortgage

36. a: Citigroup

37. b: Source document

38. c: Balanced scorecard

39. c: Normal balance

40. : Cost accounting

41. : Monetary policy

42. a: Government bond

43. b: Budget

44. d: Expected return

45. b: Shares

46. c: Financial analysis

47. c: Trial balance

48. d: Sole proprietorship

49. b: Net income

50. a: Convertible bond

51. d: Securities and Exchange Commission

52. d: International Financial Reporting Standards

53. d: Public Company Accounting Oversight Board

54. c: Intangible asset

55. a: Board of directors

56. : Risk management

57. : Discounting

58. d: Journal entry

59. c: Schedule

Human resource management

1. c: Job performance

2. d: Best practice

3. d: Part-time

4. : Functional job analysis

5. b: Emotional intelligence

6. : Reinforcement

7. b: Graveyard shift

8. d: Mergers and acquisitions

9. d: Reasonable person

10. : Meritor Savings Bank v. Vinson

11. c: Age Discrimination in Employment Act

12. : Structured interview

13. : Career

14. : Intellectual capital

15. b: Performance improvement

16. a: Person Analysis

17. b: Self-actualization

18. c: Professional association

19. d: Cross-functional team

20. c: Job evaluation

21. d: Drug test

22. d: International Brotherhood of Teamsters

23. d: Efficiency wage

24. d: Bureau of Labor Statistics

25. d: Employee handbook

26. b: Lilly Ledbetter

27. c: Six Sigma

28. b: Human resources

29. c: Trade union

30. c: Substance abuse

31. d: Union shop

32. d: Expert power

33. d: Coaching

34. b: Resignation

35. b: Externship

36. c: Total Reward

37. a: Professional employer organization

38. a: E-HRM

39. d: Resource management

40. b: Executive search

41. b: Arbitration

42. : Strategic management

43. a: Management by objectives

44. a: Minnesota Multiphasic Personality Inventory

45. b: Cafeteria plan

46. : Free Trade

47. : Vesting

48. d: Balance sheet

49. : Succession planning

50. : UNITE HERE

51. d: Kelly Services

52. : Pregnancy discrimination

53. c: Learning organization

54. b: Training and development

55. c: Industrial relations

56. a: Minimum wage

57. a: Onboarding

58. : Task force

59. a: Skill

Information systems

1. : Enterprise systems

2. : BitTorrent

3. a: Web mining

4. a: Web page

5. a: QR code

6. : Social media

7. a: Authentication protocol

8. c: Fault tolerance

9. c: Computer fraud

10. : System

11. c: AdWords

12. b: Total cost

13. d: Computer security

14. d: Web content

15. d: Privacy

16. b: Change control

17. b: Help desk

18. a: Data mart

19. b: Network management

20. b: Data cleansing

21. b: Computer-aided manufacturing

22. d: Top-level domain

23. a: Carnivore

24. b: Business model

25. a: Data field

26. c: Debit card

27. c: Telnet

28. a: Consumer-to-business

29. d: Decision-making

30. : Magnetic tape

31. d: Information literacy

32. a: Reputation management

33. d: Strategic planning

34. b: Disintermediation

35. d: Competitive intelligence

36. c: Data aggregator

37. c: Master data

38. b: Virtual reality

39. d: Netflix

40. d: Groupware

41. a: Payment system

42. : Geocoding

43. a: Operating system

44. c: Decision support system

45. : YouTube

46. a: Information technology

47. b: Strategic information system

48. c: Monopoly

49. : Online advertising

50. c: Database model

51. a: Geographic information system

52. d: Search engine optimization

53. c: Data model

54. c: Unstructured data

55. d: Data

56. a: Commercial off-the-shelf

57. b: Information privacy

58. b: Byte

59. b: Network interface card

Marketing

1. b: INDEX

2. a: Evolution

3. b: Household

4. a: Feedback

5. b: Property

6. d: Telemarketing

7. d: Attention

8. a: Performance

9. b: Database

10. : Preference

11. d: Trade association

12. : Choice

13. b: Corporation

14. c: Total cost

15. a: Derived demand

16. d: Pricing

17. a: Merchandising

18. c: Regulation

19. b: Advertising

20. d: Price

21. d: Target market

22. a: Data analysis

23. : Problem Solving

24. d: Public relations

25. a: Auction

26. d: Audit

27. a: Code

28. c: Marketing strategy

29. c: Insurance

30. c: Focus group

31. d: Loyalty program

32. c: Relationship marketing

33. a: Sponsorship

34. d: Brainstorming

35. c: Direct marketing

36. b: Adoption

37. d: Ford

38. d: Early adopter

39. b: Cognitive dissonance

40. a: Exploratory research

41. d: Health

42. d: Market development

43. : Qualitative research

44. c: Good

45. c: Entrepreneur

46. b: Stock

47. a: Logistics

48. : Questionnaire

49. c: Complaint

50. d: Competitive intelligence

51. c: Technology

52. b: Consumer Protection

53. a: Data warehouse

54. b: Product line

55. : Testimonial

56. d: Argument

57. c: Concept testing

58. : Mobile marketing

59. b: New product development

Manufacturing

1. d: Dimension

2. c: Production schedule

3. a: Cash register

4. b: Supply chain risk management

5. c: American Society for Quality

6. a: Chemical industry

7. b: Chemical reaction

8. a: Statistical process control

9. c: Malcolm Baldrige National Quality Award

10. b: Strategic sourcing

11. c: Quality by Design

12. d: Opportunity cost

13. b: E-procurement

14. d: Thomas Register

15. c: Sales

16. b: Purchasing

17. c: Zero Defects

18. : Electronic data interchange

19. : Process capability

20. : Reflux

21. d: Quality management

22. b: Minitab

23. b: Average cost

24. b: Steering committee

25. a: Reboiler

26. d: Strategy

27. a: HEAT

28. b: Interaction

29. c: Inspection

30. c: Global sourcing

31. : Remanufacturing

32. b: Consortium

33. c: Procurement

34. b: DMAIC

35. b: Water

36. : Goal

37. : Bill of materials

38. c: Manufacturing

39. b: Virtual team

40. b: Process flow diagram

41. a: Milestone

42. d: Time management

43. : Control chart

44. c: Resource management

45. : Ball

46. d: Licensed production

47. d: Project

48. : Design of experiments

49. a: Poka-yoke

50. c: Check sheet

51. : New product development

52. d: Vendor relationship management

53. a: Kaizen

54. d: Volume

55. : Pattern

56. : Process capital

57. a: Six Sigma

58. : Pareto analysis

59. a: Supply chain management

Commerce

1. a: Amazon Payments

2. a: Electronic commerce

3. : Board of directors

4. c: Direct marketing

5. c: Uniform Commercial Code

6. c: Accounting

7. a: Charter

8. a: Commerce

9. b: Permission marketing

10. b: Issuing bank

11. a: Optimum

12. a: Broker

13. : Strategic plan

14. : Auction

15. c: Collaborative filtering

16. c: Tool

17. b: Authorize.Net

18. : Marketspace

19. b: Evaluation

20. : Regulation

21. c: Customs

22. d: Appeal

23. d: Aid

24. a: E-procurement

25. : Bankruptcy

26. d: Supervisor

27. c: Consumer-to-consumer

28. b: Good

29. b: Merchandising

30. : Electronic data interchange

31. b: Total revenue

32. b: Economic regulation

33. : Electronic funds transfer

34. b: York

35. d: Industrial Revolution

36. a: Common carrier

37. b: Fraud

38. : Tangible

39. c: Public relations

40. d: Purchasing manager

41. b: Revenue

42. d: Leadership

43. a: Minimum wage

44. : Business-to-business

45. b: Welfare

46. d: Merchant

47. c: Real estate

48. c: Revenue management

49. a: Raw material

50. b: Incentive

51. : Frequency

52. b: Consortium

53. b: Insurance

54. b: Performance

55. : British Airways

56. : Bill of lading

57. d: Economy

58. b: Economies of scale

59. : Invoice

Business ethics

1. : Stanford International Bank

2. : Perception

3. c: Pollution Prevention

4. b: Transformational leadership

5. a: Fannie Mae

6. b: Workplace politics

7. b: Social networking

8. b: Fair Trade Certified

9. d: Lawsuit

10. a: Corporate governance

11. : Employee Polygraph Protection Act

12. c: Affirmative action

13. d: Sherman Antitrust Act

14. : Toxic waste

15. d: Socialism

16. a: Transocean

17. c: Electronic waste

18. d: Pollution

19. : Siemens

20. c: Corporation

21. b: Corporate structure

22. : Planet

23. : Pyramid scheme

24. a: Ethical leadership

25. a: Sustainability

26. : Greenpeace

27. a: Natural gas

28. b: Criminal law

29. a: Trojan horse

30. b: Principal Financial

31. c: Tobacco

32. a: Sullivan principles

33. b: Statutory law

34. b: Lanham Act

35. c: New York Stock Exchange

36. c: Locus of control

37. a: Dress code

38. c: Public relations

39. c: East Germany

40. d: Interlocking directorate

41. a: Individualistic culture

42. b: Collusion

43. : Kyoto Protocol

44. c: Marketing ethics

45. c: Feedback

46. c: European Commission

47. b: Biofuel

48. d: Planned obsolescence

49. c: Patriot Act

50. a: Lead paint

51. : Aristotle

52. : Great Depression

53. d: Sexual harassment

54. c: Antitrust

55. a: Empowerment

56. a: Vigilance committee

57. c: Federal Trade Commission

58. a: Dual relationship

59. : Corporate social responsibility

Accounting

1. c: Benchmarking

2. b: Liquidation

3. c: Marital deduction

4. a: Cost basis

5. c: Fixed cost

6. a: Accounting management

7. a: Taxable income

8. a: Par value

9. a: Cost pool

10. c: Financial ratio

11. : Information systems

12. : Audit

13. c: Disability insurance

14. : Periodic inventory

15. d: Indirect costs

16. b: Securities Exchange Act

17. c: Accounting records

18. b: Fair Labor Standards Act

19. c: Target costing

20. c: Outsourcing

21. b: Parent company

22. b: Interest expense

23. : Debt ratio

24. d: Times interest earned

25. d: American Accounting Association

26. a: Finished good

27. c: Ledger

28. a: Worksheet

29. b: Asset

30. b: Financial Accounting Standards Board

31. a: Credit card

32. : Voucher

33. d: Electronic funds transfer

34. c: Return on investment

35. d: Revenue

36. b: Common stock

37. d: Intangible asset

38. b: QuickBooks

39. d: Income tax

40. c: Forecasting

41. a: Petty cash

42. d: Net present value

43. d: Zero-based budgeting

44. d: Beneficiary

45. c: Return on assets

46. d: Corporate governance

47. a: Limited liability partnership

48. a: Contribution margin

49. : Securities and Exchange Commission

50. c: Write-off

51. b: Shareholder

52. c: Tax revenue

53. : Pension

54. : Working capital

55. a: Amortization

56. c: Control account

57. b: General ledger

58. d: Capital loss

59. c: Special journals

CPSIA information can be obtained
at www.ICGtesting.com
Printed in the USA
LVHW031222301019
635717LV00006B/660/P

9 781538 857441